NESTWORK

RSA·STR

THE RSA SERIES IN TRANSDISCIPLINARY RHETORIC

Jennifer Clary-Lemon

NESTWORK

New Material Rhetorics for Precarious Species

THE PENNSYLVANIA STATE UNIVERSITY PRESS
UNIVERSITY PARK, PENNSYLVANIA

This book is freely available in an open access edition with
the generous support of The Pennsylvania State University
Libraries. Digital copies are available for download through
the Pennsylvania State University Press website.

Library of Congress Cataloging-in-Publication Data

Names: Clary-Lemon, Jennifer, author.
Title: Nestwork : new material rhetorics for precarious species
    / Jennifer Clary-Lemon.
Other titles: RSA series in transdisciplinary rhetoric.
Description: University Park, Pennsylvania : The Pennsylvania
    State University Press, [2023] | Series: The RSA series in
    transdisciplinary rhetoric | Includes bibliographical
    references and index.
Summary: "Examines how humans interact with small,
    uncharismatic species through three rhetorical case studies
    of human responses to bird species decline that challenge
    anthropocentric models of rhetoric"—Provided by publisher.
Identifiers: LCCN 2023005079 | ISBN 9780271095448
    (paperback)
Subjects: LCSH: Birds—Nests. | Human-animal relationships.
    | Bird declines. | Rhetoric. | Barn swallow. | Chimney swift. |
    Bobolink.
Classification: LCC QL675 .C53 2023 | DDC 598.156/4—
    dc23/eng/20230330
LC record available at https://lccn.loc.gov/2023005079

The Pennsylvania State University Press is a member
of the Association of University Presses.

It is the policy of The Pennsylvania State University Press to
use acid-free paper. Publications on uncoated stock satisfy the
minimum requirements of American National Standard for
Information Sciences—Permanence of Paper for Printed
Library Material, ANSI z39.48–1992.

For the birds, and those who love them

Contents

Illustrations

Acknowledgments

When you write a book during a pandemic, it seems like the writing of it belongs more to the people (and nonhuman kin) that helped you along the way than to you. And so first and foremost, this book belongs to the barn swallows, to the chimney swifts, and to the bobolinks whose bodies and absences kept me company and inspired so much of the thinking behind *Nestwork*. This book also belongs to the land on which I live and work, governed by the Haldimand Treaty of 1784, belonging to Six Nations of the Grand River, and those who work to care for the lands of Ontario that house and support all of the humans and nonhumans written about here. This landscape has thought through me.

Too, this book could not have been written without the institutional support of the University of Waterloo, inclusive of the UW/SSHRC Robert Harding/ Lois Claxton Humanities and Social Sciences Endowment, which supported the building of *Hirondelusia*, and the UW/SSHRC Explore Grant, which supported travel and research costs. I am appreciative of the research leave that enabled the writing of *Nestwork*. I am also grateful for the support and collaboration of the Contemporary Art Forum of Kitchener and Area (CAFKA), as well as the *rare* Charitable Research Reserve, Birds Canada, and Bird Ecology and Conservation Ontario for their support of this research. I also wish to acknowledge with gratitude the journal *enculturation*, which published a prior version of chapter 1 and gave me permission to reprint here.

I am indebted to all of those who helped guide me throughout my fieldwork and those who were generous with their time and expertise about the birds of Ontario: Mike Cadman, Megan Hiebert, Larry Sarris, Myles Falconer, Christopher Grooms, Kaelyn Bumelis, Zoé Lebrun-Southcott, Jenna Quinn, Tom Woodcock, Jeffrey Driscoll, David Gascoigne, Winifred Wake, and Brendon Samuels. I am especially thankful to those folks who let me onto their property and talked with me about their reasons for caring for the birds in their lives: Kathryn and Michael Boothby, Diane Hood and Bill Ferguson, Victoria Lamont, Dave Westfall, Sandy and Jamie Hill, and Ray Lammens. You all made this book a work of magic for me during a time that felt dusty and isolated.

I appreciate those who have acted as readers and champions for *Nestwork*: Penn State University Press and its excellent team of editors; Caroline Gottschalk Druschke and Thomas Rickert, for being such thoughtful reviewers; and Erin Rand, who has been my steadfast writing group partner for years of reading about tree planting and now, birds of all kinds. I am also thankful to my online group of BIMRs, whose shared stories of successes have helped keep me going during these strange times. I'm thankful to collaborators on other projects who took on more than a fair share of work so that I could finish this book, especially David Grant and Laurie Gries. For the chance to share some of this work as it emerged with a variety of generous audiences, I thank my graduate students in ENGL 788 and participants in the 2021 RSA Seminar on Ecological Feelings|Feeling Ecological (and I am especially grateful for the urging of my co-leader, Joshua Trey Barnett, who encouraged me to share it!). I would also like to thank my research assistant, Christopher Rogers, for his unwavering attention to this project, excellent web development skills, and handiness with a 2×4.

Finally, there are people who helped me write this book at a time when I believed the world—my world—to be falling to pieces. I thank my mother, Ramona Mattix, for always believing in my wacky ideas, and for stepping in to help with childcare in a pandemic whenever I needed time to write. I thank my daughter, Rapunzel, for listening to me talk about bird facts and recognizing when quiet and coffee were the things I needed most. Finally, I thank my collaborator and partner, Marcel O'Gorman, who steadfastness of belief in this project and in me was unparalleled. You've made me believe in crazy love.

Introduction | Turning Otherwise

It is midwinter in Ontario; the day is cold and clear. I have heard that there is a spot in Riverside Park on the Mill Run Trail where, if you hold out your hand with a little birdseed in it, a chickadee will perch there to feed. I'm not a fan of the cold weather, though the sun is bright, and I dress in layers to combat the chill that makes my eyes water. When I get to the park, I see that they have built an eight-hundred-foot wooden boardwalk that crosses over the Speed River and into the wetlands of the Whitney Trail. I don't quite know what I'm looking for, so I walk awhile, taking care to avoid the most slippery of the planks still in icy shade. I see a stump with some birdseed still on it, so I hold out my hand to the air, hopefully, but there is nothing, only silence and cold hands and the occasional curious squirrel. I walk further down the boardwalk, where I finally hear the frrp! he-he-he-he of what I assume are chicka-dees, a familiar backyard chirp that I wouldn't have otherwise noticed. I stop again near the railing, take off my glove, and hold out my sunflower-seed-filled hand to the air. To my surprise and delight, a black-capped chickadee alights on my fingertips to pick through the seed, mostly shaking off seeds too big for its beak in haste to find a seed just right for taking to a nearby bush and cracking against winter-hardened bark. While it perches on my fingers, I am aware of its tiny, scratchy feet, how they grip my fingertips like a perch. How delicate and light they are. How used to pass-ersby these birds have become, enough to pick and choose their way through leftover piles of birdseed frozen to the ledges in favor of these sunflower seeds from my autumn garden. We stay like this, me afraid to move, two or three curious chickadees who return, again and again, to rummage and eat from my hand. After a while, I feel myself getting colder, red-nosed with one gloved hand in my pocket and one bare hand of sunflower seeds in the freeze. One of the chickadees who has been particularly curi-ous returns again to my hand, picking through the assorted seeds. It mistakes the thin crescent of my pinkie nail for a seed and pecks once, twice, grabs hold with a small tug—enough to make my eyes open wider. I am so close.

I open with a story about proximity. About the ways, as Sara Ahmed suggests, as humans, we are "touched by what we are near" (2010, 30). About the ways that humans want to touch nonhuman animals through other objects. About the ways that humans try—and often fail—to get close to the nonhumans that they find themselves near. And about the implications of this failure in a time of biodiversity loss, what some scientists are now calling the sixth extinction. What you will read in these pages looks to the agency of those small species who, over the course of our lifetime, will disappear: the barn swallow, the chimney swift, and the bobolink. It also draws attention to the infrastructural efforts that humans build, make, and are attuned to—much like the boardwalk built for the chickadees—as part of the material arguments that humans, nonhumans, and things cocreate. Through site-based rhetorical fieldwork, this book urges us to think differently about the singular autonomy of human agency and the reliability of a human-centered rhetoric during an epoch marked by rapid species decline. This is a book about illogic, and about peculiarity. This is a book about how humans and nonhumans are affected by one another, how they are persuaded by one another—or not!—through the capacities of built objects. This is a book about getting *so close*, and also a book about loss. This book is a call for new material rhetorics of the nonhuman, of an acknowledgment of precarity that surrounds all who exist in the Anthropocene.

Nestwork: New Material Rhetorics for Precarious Species joins scholars working at the nexus between rhetorical ecologies (Edbauer 2005; Stormer and McGreavy 2017; McGreavy et al. 2018), ecological and environmental rhetorics (Killingsworth and Palmer 2012; Gottschalk Druschke and McGreavy 2016; Jensen 2019; Shivener and Edwards 2020), and posthumanism (Barad 2003; Braidotti 2016, 2019; Haraway 2016). It turns to the work of both rhetorical new material scholars (Rickert 2013; Propen 2018; Gottschalk Druschke 2019) and critical new material scholarship of Alison Ravenscroft (2018), Veronica Strang (2017), and Zoe Todd (2016) to imagine both rhetorical and ethical ways through the Anthropocene. It does this in two ways: theoretically and methodologically. *Nestwork* engages a theoretical framework that privileges an attunement to environs and decision-making beyond the rational or logocentric, assuming an "underivable rhetoricity" (Davis, 2014, 536) as a starting place for persuasive being in the world. Thus, a primary turn in ecological-rhetorical thinking here is acknowledging the affects that circulate among all bodies, human and nonhuman, when they are caught up in rhetorical being together—in the narrative above, me, the boardwalk, the birdsong, the birdseed, the weather, the chickadee, the desire for closeness. Elsewhere I have called this a new material environmental rhetoric (Clary-Lemon 2019b), a framework that provides a particular thread for interdisciplinary scholarship that draws together elements of the ecological, the rhetorical, and the posthuman. In this case, I extend such a framework to account for, as Booher and Jung (2018) note, what "posthumanist rhetorics bring to the conversation: frameworks for theorizing rhetoric in terms of interactions between meaning and matter wherein nonhuman elements actively participate alongside symbol-using animals to effect change" (29). For *Nestwork*, then, I ask that readers allow both built structural elements and bird-based persuasion as central actants in a particular ecological milieu.

Strange Birds: Thinking Rhetorically, Thinking Ecologically

In rhetorical studies, acknowledging posthuman models of thinking that attend concurrently to both the discursive and, as Diane Davis (2017) has it, the "biozoological" accomplishes the difficult work of, as she says, "respect[ing] the radical ruptures and infinite heterogeneities between and among human, animal, vegetal (and more) ways of thinking and being" (438). For Davis and many others, this means respecting the addressivity and affectability of beings participating in a rhetorical situation and the relations between and among them as constructing particular messages of suasion or meaning. A widening out from humanist assumptions of rhetoric that rest on human exceptionalism—that humans are the only symbol-using, persuading creatures—is a marked change from the way that rhetoric has historically thought of itself (see Kennedy 1992). Yet such a dependence on the Great Chain of Being to define rhetorical sensibility, as Davis suggests, is nearly resolved when confronted with current research about plants and animals' own rhetoricity: the ability to investigate, use tools, engage in goal-directed behavior, have memory, adapt to their environment, show intent, and communicate across generations and in various ways (2017, 436–38). It becomes impossible to think that plants and animals are not rhetorical, though perhaps in a different way from humans.

Some of these arguments are captured by the ecological turn in rhetorical studies, which, as Dan Ehrenfeld (2020, 307) notes, gathers together not only scholars working with rhetorical ecologies but also those in circulation studies, network and complexity theories, composition studies, and posthumanism more generally. Ecological thinking is dependent on expanding notions of agency in complex systems and noting their interdependency on one another. As McGreavy et al. (2018) argue, rhetorical-ecological approaches turn our attention to the articulation between rhetorical elements (as opposed to imagining them as separate and static) and to transhuman ways of meaning-making, often drawing from processual and systems-thinking stemming from contemporary movements in composition studies (5). It is also characterized by a turn beyond the linguistic and toward the material-discursive and affective that underscores the importance of bodies, objects, and matter in acts of suasion. This turn is reflected in, as McGreavy et al. note, "engaged rhetorical practice" (5) that uses fieldwork specifically as a site of rhetorical being-in-the-world. More than this, however, ecological rhetorical study underscores the notion of ecological care in turning focus to potentials for "change, ethics, and justice" (5), which I take up in this book's concluding chapter.

In turning attention to processes and articulation between rhetorical elements in service of ecological care, I have found Nathan Stormer and Bridie McGreavy's (2017, 2) ecological notion of rhetoric most generative for thinking about an expansive notion of a new material rhetoric that includes nonhuman others. Their work builds on Jenny Edbauer's (2005, 9) scholarship on rhetorical ecologies to reframe the rhetorical situation in terms of "affective ecologies that recontextualiz[e] rhetorics in their temporal, historical, and lived fluxes." Stormer and McGreavy build upon the work of both Edbauer and Rickert (2013) by moving out from traditional components of rhetor, audience, message, and context to a focus on rhetoric as an emergent phenomenon sensitive to its environs—what they term rhetoric's ontology. As such, Stormer and McGreavy work to shift the notion of rhetorical agency and its force or impact toward rhetorical *capacity*, "emphasizing the ecology of entanglements between entities over the abilities that are inherent to humans" (2018, 5).

Rather than a focus on rhetorical agency always via the specific participants involved, a focus on rhetorical capacity shifts focus. Relations, rather than agency, situate an attention to discourse as "the performance of addressivity rather than as signification" (McGreavy et al. 2018, 8). In any situation deemed rhetorical, then, an assessment of the rhetorical capacity of various actors in a fluctuating ecological system begins by examining addressivity rather than signification. This turns attention to the "aesthetic, creative, performative affordances of a rhetoric" in addition to the invariable focus on the meaning-maker, aligning a rhetorical-ecological ontology with both the affective and the distributed (7). Such a shift aligns with Davis's focus on the underivable rhetoricity of beings while making room for posthuman accounts of the rhetoric of nonhumans, and resonates with Rickert's call for an ambient rhetorical attunement to "memories, networks, technologies, intuitions, and environments" (2013, 67). It also makes available for nonhumans much of what has always been reserved exceptionally for humans, as well as making room for the "strange," as Stormer and McGreavy (borrowing from Morton 2011) have it (9).

Notably, for *Nestwork*, such a framework also asks that readers align themselves with accepting rhetoric not as a discursive thing in the world but instead as a "worldly capacity that all life and all cultures respond to and develop" (Rickert 2020, 415). As Rickert argues, this requires an attunement to survival and an acknowledgment of environs, and an attunement to such environs as open and changeable. But it also requires an acknowledgment of relationships that balance one's need to survive and one's practices of dwelling and world-building with others in ways that allow for mutual flourishing (417). In a time when "extinction obituaries" are written in newspapers to contend with an extinction rate up to ten thousand times the natural rate, both survival and flourishing may be at odds with living in the Anthropocene (Sullivan 2022; Ritchie and Roser 2021). Still, as Rickert asserts, "when one being is able to communicate to other beings in some fashion, or otherwise turn or transform the situation—then . . . we have rhetoric" (417). And as Vinciane Despret shows in *Living as A Bird* (2022), bird worlds themselves show us something of the kinds of birdy rhetoric humans must attune themselves to in order to dwell better with them in future; indeed, this book is about revealing the ways that we have not yet learned to think, act, respond, and dwell well with birds.

Although Despret is a philosopher and not a rhetorician, nonetheless she makes a clear case for the ways that paying attention to birds, specifically, allow for a concurrence of "acknowledging the way other beings are themselves attentive" (2022, 5). In Despret's analysis of over one hundred years of ornithological controversy about *who humans assume birds are*, specifically around the issue of territory and territorialization, she reveals that indeed, bird behavior across species is fundamentally rhetorical. An individual example of such rhetoricity is captured by the recent work of Cynthia Rosenfeld (2021), who notes in a detailed analysis of the bowerbird's use of visual rhetoric that individual species can engage in aesthetic object selection, use of perspective signifiers, and color composition (80–81). In examining the nuanced ways that birds respond to one another, to space and place, and to human intervention, Despret (2022) shows the varied ways that they communicate in fundamentally rhetorical ways: not only are they consistently acting, playacting, territorializing, expressing, and learning, but, as Despret argues in her detailed research on a variety of bird species' particularities, they often make choices so complex that humans don't understand them at all (148). *Nestwork* captures some of these misunderstandings and points to ways that we, as humans, might try harder and better to dwell with birds, given our current role as harbingers of their demise. It also allies itself with Despret's call for why we must pay different kinds of attention to small creatures: to "intensify other dimensions, create new relationships, demand that other things be heard (silences and chords), other things be experienced (emotions, rhythms, forces, the flow of life and moments of calm), other things be savored (things that are more intense, that carry the most importance, the differences that matter)" (148). *Nestwork* is a book about which differences matter, and how much, and for how long. It is about, as Stéphan Durand says in the afterword of Despret's book, what happens when differences "are invited to speak for themselves" (2022, 168). It is about making a different kind of attention.

For some, the allowance of a rhetorical sensibility for birds is perhaps an easier stretch of the imagination than allowing for a rhetorical sensibility of things. Scholarship that accompanies the place of things in our notion of the rhetorical is often seen as at odds with such capacity; if abiotic things (objects, minerals and metals, materials, weather) can be said to have any rhetorical capacity, it is that of the object-oriented withdrawal of the "strange stranger" (Morton 2011, 165). Yet some of the work done in the rhetoric of things seeks to make more porous the boundary between biota and abiota, in part by focusing on how "things depend on other things" (Hodder 2012, 40) and, I would add, other-than-human beings (see also Barnett and Boyle 2016). This blurring of the boundary between animate and inanimate and their respective capacities for addressivity is played out on the pages of *Nestwork*, particularly in examining the nonhuman worlds that exist between birds and human-made structures, as discussed in chapters 1 and 2 of this book. Such an approach, examining what rhetorical scholar Amy Propen, borrowing from Karen Barad (2007), terms "agential entanglements" (Propen 2018, 1) shows how far the posthuman turn has come into rhetorical studies.

A situated, affective view of space has similarly been taken up by scholars in geography, most notably by Nigel Thrift (2004), who draws on both a Deleuzian-Spinozan theory of affect and contemporary affect theorists Eve Sedgwick, Brian Massumi, and Martha Nussbaum to make the case that the affective realm is a "form of thinking" (60) arising from (among other things) the encounter and relations with built spaces. Urban communication scholars Greg Dickinson and Giorgia Aiello (2016) extend Thrift's work by pointing attention to the importance of bodies, materiality, and movement as key to understanding more fully the ways that urban spaces produce suasion (1294–96), noting that viewing photographic images or films of cityscapes and buildings is an entirely different experience of such structures than moving within and through those same structures. Both Thrift and Dickinson and Aiello rely on the central notion of *presence*—what Caroline Gottschalk Druschke (2019) notes as physicality in service of the ecologically situated, trophic rhetorician—to provide some degree of specific and affectual knowing both about place and about other-than-humans that is otherwise unrecoverable through textual or visual means. Here, the physicality of presence, both human and non, is another node of communicative output appearing throughout *Nestwork* that works to transform situations.

Before turning to what I see as a fundamental methodological intervention into rhetorical new material studies, what rhetoric can offer the posthuman deserves close attention. As the discussion so far has shown, the tie of rhetoric to the posthuman is a strong one. Yet as important, and what *Nestwork* offers to posthuman scholars, is an explication of what an ecological, new material environmental rhetoric can offer to posthuman accounts. Posthuman scholars habitually step around rhetorical studies in their haste to put their finger on a way in to posthuman analysis, often settling on narrative and literary reading as the most available. In part, this may be attributed to some posthuman scholars' already literary background; for others, perhaps in some degree to rhetoric's coupling with composition as the "poor cousin" of literary studies (Glenn and Carcasson 2008, 287), or perhaps rhetoric and composition's American roots in an increasingly globalized world (Phelps 2014). In any case, the rhetorical is not, as a field, as seemingly available as either literary reading or narrative storying in helping posthuman scholars articulate communicative potentials inherent in intra-actions. Examples are readily available. Serenella Iovino and Serpil Opperman insist on the term "narrative agencies" to describe the rhetorical capacity of nonhumans (2014, 21); environmental philosopher Thom van Dooren uses "lively stories" as a way in to the entanglements of extinction (2014, 7); Alison Ravenscroft (2018) provides a postcolonial and posthuman analytic through an examination of Waanyi writer Alexis Wright's novels; Rebekah Sheldon, a literary theorist, advocates "choratic reading" as a way to examine posthuman circulation (2015, 214). Sheldon's work perhaps gets at the crux of the rhetorical-literary tension in her assertion that it is a kind of reading that will help dissolve friction between object-oriented ontology and feminist new materialism by diversifying scholarly approaches to the posthuman: "Choratic reading, by contrast [to the object-oriented method of Harman], begins from the assertion that acts of literature—very much including scholarly readings—are performed in material composition with the affordances of their media, the sensorium of their audiences, and the deformations of dissemination as they transduce across and are deformed by the irruptions of the choratic plane" (2015, 216). Any rhetorician might read Sheldon's appeal as a call for a rhetorical sensibility rather than a hermeneutic one. Yet Sheldon adds this approach as one of a number of possibilities to diversify our research practices, placing such reading alongside Erin Manning's SenseLab and Katherine Hayles's (2012, 19) call for "practice-based research" for the posthumanities.

It is my hope that combining text, field, and making, and providing a rhetorical vocabulary with which to do so, will draw posthuman scholars' attention more closely to Donna Haraway's oft-cited claim that "it matters what stories we tell other stories with" (2016, 12). Such a claim suggests that it is not only narrative production or diffracted reading, per se, that calls for the attention of the posthuman, but rhetoric. *Nestwork* offers to posthuman scholars what a current emphasis on narrative is lacking—the critical *storying about* stories, or a turn to the rhetorical as another way to imagine posthuman analysis. As scholars in technical communications insist, ecological crises themselves do not persuade humans into action (see Ockwell, Whitmarsh, O'Neill 2009; Spoel et al. 2008). And as Val Plumwood (2002) suggests, we have reached the limits of the rational for having difficult conversations about biodiversity loss that engage bottom-up approaches to communication that might result in action to mitigate ecological crises. Thus, the movement away from pure narrative and toward examining the components of those stories we make stories with—about preconceptions about conservation, about persuasive nonhuman agency, about material-discursive structures on landscapes, about rationality itself—offers a rhetorical vocabulary that is clearly missing from contemporary posthumanism, even as posthuman theorists yearn for it.

New Material Rhetorics, Ethical Worlding, and Indigenous Knowledges

What must also be recognized as missing from many posthuman and new material accounts is the consideration that many of them rely heavily on white,

Eurocentric philosophies with which to make their cases to the exclusion of worldviews that have long held together a holistic cosmology of natureculture, a critique that many Indigenous scholars take up (see Hokuwhitu et al. 2021). In part, then, the role of an ecological approach to a new material environmental rhetoric is to acknowledge outright those thinkers and scholars who have pushed against the trend to cite Eurowestern philosophers to the exclusion of Indigenous ones. As I point out elsewhere (Clary-Lemon, 2019a), this move is being spearheaded by Indigenous scholars in social anthropology, geography, and sociology but is only recently being engaged explicitly in rhetorical studies (see Gries et al. 2022; Clary-Lemon and Grant 2022; Ruiz and Arellano 2019; Ruiz, 2021). To that end, it is not my intention to engage in "Columbusing knowledge" (Arola quoted in Sackey et al. 2019; Arola and Rickert 2022) by forwarding a collection of Eurowestern voices that emphasize the *new* in new materialism. Indeed, the theoretical framework articulated here is shaped as much by the critiques proffered by Indigenous and Black scholars of new materialisms than predominantly white scholars of new materialisms themselves. I take seriously the critiques of new materialism by scholars such as Kyla Wazana Tompkins (2016), Zakiyyah Iman Jackson (2015), and Alison Ravenscroft (2018), who point out that these theories not only ignore the ways that metaphysics are racialized but also risk "leaving the Western liberal human intact, making the 'human' in 'post-human' stand in for all of 'us'" (Ravenscroft 2018, 354), without an acknowledgment of the huge role that, for example, whiteness, privilege, and settler colonialism have in determining not only what is human, but which humans on earth cause the most damage in the Anthropocenic moment (see also Shomura 2017).

Thus, part of the goal of *Nestwork* is to engage both methodologically and practically with what scholars might think of as theoretical allyship between new materialist and posthuman thought, and Indigenous theories, cosmologies, traditional ecological knowledges, and practices. A "theoretical alliance" between Eurowestern theories and Indigenous knowledges, as Matthew Whitaker (2022, 151) reminds us, is not without difficulty, nor is it meant to brand this particular book as a decolonizing force. Instead, such a move sits to problematize how all of us think through species precarity by encouraging a close connection to the situated forces of where they take place and whom they most affect—and recognizing that these cannot be separated. It takes seriously Christina Cedillo's (2022) call that to center Indigenous knowledge-making at all requires a recognition of "stories as embodied epistemologies and temporality as material" (102). Threaded throughout *Nestwork* you will read about the variety of interventions, both historical and contemporary, that global Indigenous peoples from Cali-fornia to Ecuador to New Zealand have made into thinking and acting rela-tionally with nonhuman others. You will also read about the specific people and struggles for land rights happening where this book takes place, in south-ern Ontario—because land, thinking, and creatures are bound up in relation to one another.

To that end, *Nestwork* makes three main moves of theoretical allyship in ser-vice of what Eve Tuck and K. Wayne Yang term "settler harm reduction" (2012, 21), or what Andrea Riley Mukavetz and Malea Powell (2022) note as the action of echoing and affirming Indigenous knowledges as part of such harm reduction (209). The first lies in choosing theoretical vocabulary from both Eurowestern traditions and specific Indigenous traditions while considering the colonizing work that local and federal governments do in shaping contemporary environ-mental policy outcomes. Thus, I reflect on the role of similarity and difference in defining species precarity with the use of the Greek prefix *alloios* (chapter 1), I consider the role that colonial violence plays in shaping the baselines for human interaction with nonhuman species (chapter 2), and I consider ontologi-cal notions of temporality that acknowledge the Greek notion of *pheno* as fully immersed in global Indigenous conceptions of nonlinear time (chapter 3).

The second move of settler harm reduction is a close consideration in each chapter of specific field sites and the contemporary Indigenous peoples of southern Ontario whose lives and livelihoods are intimately connected to cur-rent frontline policy arguments about land use planning, treaty rights, and polit-ical movements—and thus environmental conservation. I am indebted to the Six Nations of the Grand River (the Mohawk, Seneca, Oneida, Cayuga, Onon-daga and Tuscarora nations), the Mississaugas of the Credit First Nation, and specifically, the Anishinaabe scholars of Ontario who have helped contextualize treaty rights, cultural sovereignty, and linguistic imperialism in regards to the local species in this book, especially Leanne Betasamosake Simpson (Michi Saagiig Nishnaabeg, Alderville First Nation), and Joseph Pitawanakwat (Ojib-way, Wiikwemikoong Unceded Territory on Manitoulin Island). In drawing in current fights for treaty rights happening on the lands and animals that sur-round field sites in *Nestwork*, I hope to draw readers' attention to the notion that both Indigeneity and Indigenous knowledge are not only local and specific (see also Gross 2021) but tied intimately to the land and creatures that inhabit that land. To consider land rights in tandem with negative environmental impact brought on by settlers makes real Cedillo's assertion about Indigenous peoples that allies itself with posthumanism, the new material, and better ecological consciousness: "nature is culture when one lives with the land rather than on it" (98). Finally, including treaty rights in case study considerations of species decline makes clear that much of the collective action taken on behalf of the nonhumans living on the land to decrease human impact, both local and global, is often spearheaded by the knowledge and practices of Indigenous people in fights over self-governance and land rights.

The third move of settler harm reduction in *Nestwork* is in methodologically affirming the importance of embodied stories, told through the consideration of nonhuman beings and things and the way we might consider difference to speak through them, and acknowledging the centrality of attunement to alternate models of time through which to view the stories that we privilege about conservation action. As Ravenscroft (2018) reminds us in bringing together non-Indigenous and Indigenous theories and practices, to do this work also means "to see Indigenous materialisms as part of the field through which new materialism has itself been materialized" (354). Thus, I urge my readers here to examine the new material, the stress on rhetorical ecologies and ecological models, and the examination of the posthuman as *settler* ways into conversations that Indigenous people have already reconciled as ways of being, and that often Indigenous and Black scholars reject such models as a powerful strategy of "decolonial refusal" (King 2017, 164). To that end, while I amplify in particular work done by Indigenous new material scholars here, noting the ways that they have shaped this project, I also acknowledge that for many scholars, new materialism's critiques outweigh its usefulness in providing an embodied, humane philosophy for all.

Nestwork: A Note on Methods

I turn once again here to my introductory narrative, which to a reader is a simple storied snapshot of a person's intentional encounter with a common North American songbird, *Poecile atricapillus*, the black-capped chickadee. Yet it may also be seen as a particular rhetorical situation, an act of persuasion on both sides of the glove, and the affordances and capacities that all agents in the situation bring to bear on the circumstances. We might examine the capacity of each element—human, bird, boardwalk, birdseed, weather—to meet, interrupt, or extend particular capacities or desires, whether the desire to be in close proximity (human), or the desire for a preferred meal (chickadee), or the desire to expand and contract (boardwalk). To extend such a lens further, when forwarded as a lively moment in rhetorical fieldwork, such a situation moves beyond a static sense of observation, instead becoming, as Candace Rai and Caroline Gottschalk Druschke (2018, 2) have it, an "ecological, emplaced, material, and new material" perspective. I would add to such a perspective that fieldwork that brings with it rhetorical sensibilities situate both "being there" (1) and "being through there" (Dickinson and Aiello 2016, 1294) as circumstances that privilege a profound physicality, and as Gottschalk Druschke notes (2019), urge us to take seriously "a physicality of relationality," or an affectability that nonhumans inspire in humans (see Gries 2020) that is central to conceptions of the new material. We each, the chickadee and I, have particular relations with, for example, the boardwalk structure, the kind of seed, the frigidity of winter elements that affect what is possible in the exchange. While conventional rhetorical study may be seen to tie itself traditionally to texts, more expansive, new material rhetoric that imagines rhetoric in vivo instead, as Rai and Gottschalk Druschke note (2018, 1), "enhances the capacity to understand and observe rhetoric as a three-dimensional, situated force." Such a force privileges bodies, haptics, sensuality, and affect as and where they take place (see, for example, Ramírez 2022). It gives rise to stories as gifts from birds, to be sung through human rhetors.

I have taken up both Gottschalk Druschke and Dickinson and Aiello's call to emplace rhetoric by choosing rhetorical fieldwork as a method here; however, the method is more than a simple pairing of an appropriate tool for a particular theoretical framework. What I call *nestwork* is a layered approach to method: it is a making and a traveling and a storying through both words and things in service of affirmative ethics, in Braidotti's (2011; 2017) terms, and in doing so, it begins to build knowledge-worlds more ethically, to align itself with more "response-able coexistence" (Gries 2020, 302). In privileging storying and making, nestwork also echoes A. I. Ramírez's (2022) assertions about stories and about making: through both, ideas are given light—*dar a luz* (122)—or birthed. Nestwork calls to mind, as Marilyn Cooper (2019) suggests, the connections between writing and making at the point at which technē (making) meets mētis (a knowing or intelligence borne in practical life) (77). While Cooper focuses specifically on writing as making, nestwork turns to the metaphor of the nest not only to embody writing made of practical and embodied knowledge but also to underscore the importance of technē, as Tim Ingold (2000; 2013) does when he turns to bird nest making as a model for human making and infuses it with ecological care.

Ingold, like Cooper, maintains that the movement together of disparate parts employed in making, whether a house, a watch, or a nest, at some point yield to a particular form created out of "attentive engagement" with those materials (2000, 354). What changes inanimate twigs and grass and mud and feathers to a nest is not simply the movement of an individual bird with an assortment of materials, just as this book is not a conglomeration of a kind of writing and a kind of fieldwork and a kind of theory giving rise to a couple kinds of things. As Ingold notes, "The key to successful nest building lies not so much in the movements themselves as in the bird's ability to adjust its movements with exquisite precision in relation to the evolving form of its construction" (359). This book of nestwork has not only relied on an ability to work through theory with my own body or bird bodies or structure bodies or textual bodies, or blending narrative with theoretical exposition, or acknowledging Western and Indigenous approaches, or waiting on bird time to grant me opportunities to observe nonhuman others or build structures or build stories, or gathering writing, observation, and being-through-places together to create public interventions into extinction events. Instead, it has relied on the intermingling of all of those with an ethic of care, a bird's rhetorical sensibility not only to find the right material and wait for what appears but to consider its placement in the whole as the whole emerges—and to be attuned to that whole as it may change or fail. Nestwork is a kind of crazy love and ecological care, a rhetorical technē in a strange present.

Such a framework must, if it seeks to explore a posthuman ethic of "zoe-egalitarianism" (Braidotti 2013, 103), pay attention to embodied and material movements of humans and nonhumans in its collection of data. It is one thing to call traveling to a particular place an environment or "field" within which a researcher does research. It is another thing altogether to recognize the land-based politics of that field: who has cared for it over time; who currently lives on or occupies it; who returns to it, year after year; who changes it, and by what means; who is responsible for it; who tells its stories through their bodies. When we practice this recognition, it is impossible to come to the "field" with anything less than knowing how colonial relationships work, whether in human access and ownership to land and water rights, or in human colonization of the nonhuman other. It changes the focus of a project from "things"—textual manuals, animals, buildings—to, as Cedillo (2022) has it, recognition and relationship (122). Such a position creates not only a yearning to get so close; it also helps construct a critical and ethical sensibility, particularly for settler scholars, to *do better*.

Yet to think critically about colonization and its effects requires backing up from those immediate-seeming outcomes of reintegration and reconciliation. It instead takes first steps toward truth-telling and accountability in our account of *the field* itself, or, as de Castro (Skafish 2016, 404) suggests, "It's a matter of who sees whom as what in which situation: who is human *here*, who is human *now?*" This is how researchers begin the ethical and potentially decolonizing work of the posthuman—to know that sometimes we are meant to get close, to turn toward; sometimes we are meant to be kept at a distance, to turn otherwise; and in every case, that we examine closely who "we" are.

Such a contradiction is arguably the work of any study that seeks a way through the Anthropocene among small, disappearing critters. Nestwork is done through both its discursive elements—emails and interviews with government employees, nonprofit environmentalists, engineers, planners, scientists, and citizens; maps and site plans; environmental impact assessments, reports, white papers, and legislation—and its structural/material and nonhuman elements.[1] It is done through traveling, listening, observing. It may seem small or rather obvious to some that to spend time with nonhuman species one must go to where they might be; yet in in the case of precarious species or species at risk, the emphasis is on *might*, on waiting, on time. While presence might be said to depend on the literal encounter of, say human and bird, in the case of species whose numbers are dwindling year after year, often presence takes forms that extend beyond the proximity of the bodies of humans and birds. *Nestwork* examines those other-than-human forms that speak: human-built structures, the latent nest, the waiting, the season, the space that absence takes up. It looks to those affects that stick and circulate among humans and nonhumans and the rhetorical capacity nonhumans have to move us, to attune us to time and season, to force us to cope with grief and with privilege—even if such capacity offers up "contradictory, complex, shifting, and recalcitrant conditions" (Rai and Gottschalk Druschke 2018, 2). Unlike a text or an image, there is no imagining a nest into being where there is none. There is no replay of dusk when waiting for swifts to roost. There is no way to recreate the feeling of the air moving against your face when a swallow gets close enough to touch, or the sting of one hundred mosquitos while you wait for something, anything to happen. And there is no way to construct out of nothing the feeling of despair that emerges out of each absence, or the way that absences pile up inside one another. I believe that these reminders of movement, time, materiality, and bodies all speak to the commonalities between seemingly disparate methodologies emerging from posthumanism, geography, Indigenous studies, and rhetorical study, but I also see them as attending to what is still possible.

As Stephanie Springgay and Sarah Truman (2017, 1) ask of this kind of methodological reflexivity, "If the intent of inquiry is to create a different world, to ask what kinds of futures are imaginable, then . . . [we] need attend to the immersion, friction, strain, and quivering unease of doing research differently." *This* is nestwork. I firmly believe that it was the being-through-there in the variety of sites and with other-than-humans that similarly gave rise to seemingly nonrhetorical conclusions to this book, which sit at the aesthetic, creative, and performative (Stormer and McGreavy 2017, 7) juncture between rhetoric, arts-based research, making, and care. It brings together method and methodology to create worlds in which "how we make things affects the things we make" (Sheldon 2015, 214).

Places of Persuasion, Places of Precarity

In figuring field sites as central to the work of posthuman accounting for "both kinship and ethical accountability" (Braidotti, 2013, 103) that characterizes a naturecultural approach, I turn here to a short discussion of some of the main actors in the chapters ahead that shape the nature and culture of these respective environments. I do this to attend closely to Rai and Gottschalk Druschke's argument that in such an ecological, emplaced, material, and new material perspective, "the places of persuasion become not only heuristics for locating and enacting the available means of persuasion, but also the tangible places in which rhetoric as capacity and constellation reveals itself" (Rai and Gottschalk Druschke 2018, 2). In other words, I seek here to provide background on bits of the constellation that affect all species in this book, in order to later elaborate on how and why human encounters and entanglements with them perhaps emerge as they do.

The first contextual item that bears a closer look is the notion of species precarity. In North America, precarity is humanly determined by two sets of legislation: in the United States, The Endangered Species Act (ESA, passed in 1973; see US Fish and Wildlife Service 1973), and in Canada, the Species at Risk Act (SARA, passed in 2002). Both acts supply criteria by which species might

be listed as endangered, list those species in danger of extinction, lay out definitions of levels of precarity or threat, offer directions for recovering habitat, spec-
ify guidelines for implementations of recovery plans for threatened species, and
legislate punishments for those not following the respective acts. In the United
States, species who are in decline may be listed as either "endangered" or "threatened"—either in danger of extinction, or likely to become endangered in the
foreseeable future (ESA 1973, 2–4). In Canada, species in decline are given one
of four designations, in levels of precarity: extirpated (species that no longer
exist in Canada but do exist elsewhere), endangered (species facing imminent
extinction or extirpation), threatened (species likely to become endangered if
nothing is done), or of special concern (species likely to become threatened or
endangered based on identified threats) (Environment Canada 2019).

It should be emphasized that despite the fact that many species in decline
either do not observe borders or migrate across them, they are not listed in tandem on both acts, and they can move between classifications as they are periodi-
cally assessed. Thus, even to consider the species in this book as precarious is an
act of rhetorical savvy: neither the barn swallow, chimney swift, or bobolink are
listed as threatened in the United States, despite their worldwide average decline
of over 50 percent in the last fifty years (Cornell University 2019). Unlike the
common chickadee, which opens this book, all three species have been listed as
threatened in Canada; the chimney swift since 2009, and the barn swallow and
bobolink since 2011 and 2010, respectively (Government of Canada 2020).[2] In
some respects this draws attention to the different processes by which species
are listed across borders; in the United States, a species must be listed through
a candidate assessment program of either the Fish and Wildlife Service or
National Marine Fisheries Service, or petitioned by an individual or organization. In Canada, species are adjudicated by the Committee on the Status of
Endangered Wildlife in Canada (COSEWIC), which writes an assessment
report that must then be evaluated by the minister of the environment before a
species is placed on the Species at Risk listing. It is possible that the recent claw-
back of environmental protections throughout the United States in recent years
has to some degree impacted the regulatory bodies that are charged with assess-
ing endangered species. In 2019, changes to the ESA maintained that the process
of assessment include a consideration of economic factors in determining precarity, as well as determining what precarity into the "foreseeable future" means
on a case-by-case basis (Aguilera 2019). Although these changes were repealed in
2022, they point to the very notion of species precarity as a bureaucratic problem

that sits between who gets to determine population decline and whether or not there are human economic gains and losses to be had in that determination. Here, precarity is rhetorical for humans, unlike their avian counterparts.

Because of these recent changes to the ESA, because population decline of species is not arguable, and because I live in one of the hearts of species decline of these three species (Nebel et al. 2010), I turn to the Species at Risk Act (SARA) as a powerful actor and moderator of species precarity in North America. As a social determinant of precarity, SARA gives rise to the actions that each province must mandate to its citizens about how to engage with precarious species. Once a species is listed on SARA, not only does it become illegal to harm the species, but its "critical habitat" must be protected on any occasion where human development or encroachment might affect it—on private land as well as public (Government of Canada 2021). Deemed "recovery strategies" or "action plans," such mitigative strategies take many forms and are legislated through provincial action until specific federal actions are listed on SARA. These mitigative strategies are commonly invoked and undertaken in cases of human development (construction and demolition projects, infrastructure design) and are applicable to all species in SARA (plant and animal).

Both the barn swallow and chimney swift may be said to be parallel species to human beings: the primary nesting habitat for both birds are human-built dwellings, and historically their numbers have increased with human development. Human development, in the case of these two birds, provide attractive options for nesting beyond the traditional. Instead of cliff faces and river edges, barn swallows prefer old barns, eaves, culverts, boathouses, garages, and bridges (COSEWIC 2011); rather than seek out an old-growth hollow log in the few remaining forest preserves, chimney swifts choose urban living inside brick chimneys, wells, silos, barns, and tobacco curing sheds (COSEWIC 2007). Given the burgeoning human populations, then, and the common tandem living these species do with humans, one might think that contemporary bird populations would reflect this similar growth. However, in the last thirty years, both species have seen large declines in numbers (for barn swallows, 38 percent in the United States and 67 percent in Canada; for chimney swifts, 67 percent in the United States and 95 percent in Canada), which matches the general decrease in the family of aerial insectivores of which both species are a part, which has declined approximately 73 percent since 1970 (Rosenberg et al. 2019; Spiller and Dettmers 2019; COSWEIC 2007; 2011; Brown and Brown 2019). To that end, these species are naturecultural ones: tied to human structures, for these species "critical habitat" means human buildings, not some pristine wilderness area. Thus, habitat destruction or decline means not only conserving wilderness areas but preserving historic buildings or bridges, in many cases.

It is when such preservation cannot be done that things get really interesting when it comes to mitigative action plans legislated by SARA. For all species on SARA, a disturbance of critical habitat by humans requires the conservation, protection, or provision of at least that much habitat in return. In the case of tearing down an old bridge or historic chimney, SARA requires the construction of human-built structures that mimic these habitats: for barn swallows (see chapter 1), the erection of artificial nesting structure buildings and nesting cups; for chimney swifts (see chapter 2), the erection of artificial chimneys (which may be attached or unattached to nearby buildings). The field sites in this book—visitations to artificial nesting structures, encounters and nonencounters in old barns and chimney stacks—are thus both places of persuasion and precarity. In the case of these artificial nesting sites, I have sought to examine such infrastructural mitigations as nonhuman arguments about the capacities of rhetoric to circulate among actors in these interspecies entanglements.

Although not an aerial insectivore but a grassland bird, the case of the bobolink (see chapter 3) shows many similarities to declines in barn swallows and chimney swifts, particularly in number—a loss of nearly 88 percent in Canada over the last forty years and 74 percent in North America (COSEWIC 2010; Rosenberg et al. 2019). Major contributors to declines in all migratory bird populations are listed as habitat loss, human development, insect decline due to pesticide use, and unpredictable weather attributed to climate change that effect breeding environments and nestling mortality (see COSEWIC 2007; 2010; 2011; Saino et al. 2011; Rosenberg et al. 2019; Cox 2018). The bobolink, too, has modified its breeding and nesting behavior to coincide with anthropogenic development: over time, its primary habitat has shifted from tall-grass prairie to "surrogate habitat" (COSEWIC 2010, 10) of primarily row-crop monocultures, in particular, hay. This puts bobolinks closely on the radar of farmers, who grow and harvest hay at precisely the time that bobolinks tend to nest, and who are increasingly harvesting crops more often because of the augmented use of fertilizers and pesticides (USDA [US Department of Agriculture] 2010, 1). The SARA-based mitigations of the bobolink come down to acceding to bird time: finding a solution between the forty-two-day nesting cycle of the bobolink with an extra ten days needed for fledglings to avoid harvesting machinery, and the thirty-five- to forty-two-day cycle of harvesting hay (5). The mitigation and story of precarity and entanglement in this case is the "hay delay": convincing farmers to delay haying by sixty-five days to let the bobolinks complete their breeding cycle. Such arguments take place in fields, in bird bodies, and in forage harvesting machines, and they represent the tensions emergent between humans and other-than-humans when precarity, through SARA, is an operative term that shapes decisions about both economic and physical livelihood.

Nestwork: New Material Rhetorics for Precarious Species

Each chapter of this book devotes its attention to one singular species. What each species, and each chapter, offers readers are small and pointed ways in to the problem of a biodiversity loss so big that it is unfathomable. As biologist Bruce Wilcox (1988) observes, "For every species listed as endangered or extinct at least a hundred more will probably disappear unrecorded" (ix), a sobering reflection when paired with the statistic that current biodiversity loss exceeds one thousand times the historic rate (Pimm et al. 1995; Diaz et al. 2019). What we might gain from an examination of the entanglements between human and nonhumans via a new material lens is not, to be clear, a solution to an ecological problem but a rhetorical understanding of nonhuman difference in a time of crisis. *Nestwork* offers a glimpse into the ways that humans and nonhumans work to create those small moments of possibility and of vulnerability in a time of endings, whether through mud, spruce two-by-fours, brick, or grass; beak or hammer or delay.

Chapter 1, "Barn Swallow," or "Infrastructural Mitigations and the Dull Edge of Extinction," introduces readers more closely to the habits and dwelling of *Hirundo rustica*. It examines a variety of sites in southern Ontario, one of the North American centers of barn swallow decline, and examines the infrastructural mitigation of the erection of "barn swallow gazebos" and artificial nests as a SARA-mandated recovery strategy for the barn swallow. Endangered species, with good reason, often remain invisible to scientists, engineers, and construction workers throughout development decision-making. Instead, often they make themselves known through governmental building plans, human-based discursive accounts, and site-based artificial (human-made) nesting structures. Thus, chapter 1 of this book makes Rosi Braidotti's (2019) notion of presence, and the *strange present*, central to determining rhetorical capacities of nonhuman encounter. In examining a variety of barn swallow structures and their affective

and rhetorical function on various landscapes, I observe the barn swallow mitigation structure as a particular kind of nestwork, a peculiar new material argument that determines how humans and nonhumans interface now, and will in
future, on a species-reduced landscape.

In chapter 2, "Chimney Swift," or "Building Precarity with Fake Chimneys," I
examine the rhetorical ecologies, agentive factors, and affective tensions at work
among chimney swifts, SARA, insects, climate, humans, and artificial chimneys, the legislated infrastructural action required in the case of chimneys
that are torn down or capped. These empty simulacral mitigations, refused by
the swifts, serve as monuments to both the absence and presence of species
extinction and to the difficulty of approaching alterity affectively—getting close
enough, for example, to mark either loss of species or desire for future reconciliation. Drawing on rhetorical scholarship that emphasizes the materiality and
movement of bodies in service of memory work (Blair 2001; Dickinson, Blair,
and Ott 2010; Dickinson and Aiello 2016), I examine field sites at the border of
naturecultural tensions and human loss, from public parks and family farms, to
failed artificial chimneys on the roofs of university buildings, to mass roosting
inside a decommissioned nuclear reactor chimney. The artificial structures, as
complex architectural superpositions of the *zoe* and *bios* (Braidotti 2006), provide sites for intervention and reflection on the Anthropocene.

Chapter 3, "Bobolink," or "Being on Bird Time," turns slightly away from the
focus of chapters 1 and 2 that home in specifically on physical infrastructure.
Chapter 3 turns toward time, invoking the concept of *pheno*, or an attunement
to what appears. Here I examine the case of the bobolink, or "rice bird," known
to feed primarily on grain, and the complex rhetorical entanglements represented by the bobolink's interaction with standard governmental mitigations of
the "hay delay" in monoculture crop farming. Recognizing the tensions between
the economic efficiency privileged by farmers and government and the bobolink's right to nest between May and July, I survey the potential for a different
kind of attunement when humans are forced to reckon with *bird time*. Taking
readers through three farm field sites in southern Ontario, I speculate on the
success of such mitigations that often equate compliance with financial incentive by closely examining field-based human-bird relations around decision-
making, property ownership, and generational time. To do so, I situate bird time
against notions of *chronos* and *kairos* (Peters 2015), placing it within Indigenous
phenological notions of time that frame it though nonhuman being (Reid and
Seiber 2016): *pheno*.

While the last chapter, "Conclusions for Irreconcilability," revisits the ways that nonhumans turn us otherwise toward and against their being-in-the-world through the examination of both infrastructure and time, it also extends potential interventions that offer a reworking of tensions between *zoe* and *bios*. Working from Isabelle Stengers's assertion that "we need researchers able to participate in the creation of the responses on which the possibility of a future that is not barbaric depends" (2015, 73), I conclude with practice-based possibilities for human response to the Anthropocene that move beyond governmentally mandated mitigations in consideration of species decline. The first is the creation of research/art objects, represented by my cocreated art installation of a barn swallow mitigation structure designed for human use and reflection. The second is an act of care, represented by the lengths an individual farmer goes through to peaceably cohabitate with barn swallows who share the spaces in which he works and lives. I close by advocating for the possibilities of honoring alterity and its agential capacity by the use of both creative and reconciliatory human measures.

It is my hope that if you are reading *Nestwork*, much like me and the chickadee, you are curious. Curious about your own rhetorical capacity, curious about your entanglements with more-than-human others, curious about your own vulnerability in the Anthropocene, curious about seeking alternative ways through dualistic thinking long privileged by Eurowestern philosophies (and even new materialism itself). It is my hope that *Nestwork* will help you stay with your curiosities, stay with our collective troubles, and help move you to act in ways that may, for the moment, seem peculiar—to turn otherwise for a complicated future.

Turning Otherwise

My argument in this book is that these entanglements of human and other-than-humans, mitigated by discursive legislative acts, shape human attunement to small and uncharismatic species at risk in weird ways and tell stories about human impacts on species decline. To entangle in these ways is risky on both sides, and these entanglements demonstrate mutual rhetorical vulnerabilities, what Stormer and McGreavy say "requir[e] being at risk in varying passive-active relations" (2017, 13). Of course, the risks inherent in these entanglements are far riskier for the animals involved than the humans. Yet I argue that through these mitigations' failures, they nonetheless have the capacity to help humans develop new attunements to time and space in service of conservation. This is characterized perhaps most materially by the failure of those immediate and large infrastructural relations represented by barn swallow structures and artificial chimneys, but also in being forced to reckon with the seasons of plants and animals that may only be reconciled with human action. Thus a main examination of these entanglements is to ask of them what rhetorical capacity is given rise to in each, how proximity, contiguity, and absence function, and to what end. Perhaps the best thing we have is the possibility for different and strange relations through these vocabularies, a "wish to make contact with the other" (Sutton and Mifsud 2012, 228) in whatever shapes that may take, with whatever misunderstandings such contact offers: a fake chimney, a bird gazebo, a late-cut hay patch refuge in the middle of a field, a story, a piece of art. Such relations allow for *turning otherwise*, in the end—not only toward, not only away, but headed for the peculiar, the nonlogical, the strange, the vulnerable, the eccentric.

To that end, what I hope readers of this book take with them is the capacity to do their own bit of nestwork: to examine the precarious species around them, to engage with the histories of the places they share with others, to honor the knowledge of their local areas gifted to them by Indigenous folks doing the difficult work of fighting for sovereignty, to build better worlds with theories and practices that acknowledge, holistically, lived knowledges that underscore the reality that "we do not only 'live as earth' or have it within us—we *are* earth" (Cedillo 2022, 97). I hope, as a reader, you will gift this work to others; to remember Ursula Le Guin's carrier bag, what Despret (2022) calls "that antidote to the epic poison of victorious man, creator of weapons" (111). Le Guin calls on all of us to write—to make—stories, "those precious and fragile objects which enable us to keep, transport, protect, carry something to someone. . . . The things which keep beings and objects safe" (Despret 111). Le Guin (1989, 166) gives us a list of such spaces, to be held in books and stories and words: "a leaf a gourd a shell a net a bag a sling a sack a bottle a pot a box a container. A holder. A recipient." I give you this one more, to hold close: a nest.

1

Barn Swallow | Infrastructural Mitigations and the Dull Edge of Extinction

Between April and June, I set out to three different mitigation sites to get closer to the strange structures that I had seen repeatedly on the sides of highways in Ontario: something like advertising kiosks, but not; something like tiny houses in progress, but not; something like small wooden bus shelters, but not. By reading the Species at Risk Act, I find out that these are structures built to persuade barn swallows to nest in them when humans destroy already-existing nesting habitat for the birds, such as tearing down a barn or rebuilding a bridge. Sleuthing around online led me to environmental assessment reports of barn swallow nests discovered in Dashwood on an old bridge slated to be rebuilt an hour away. A second "feel good" online engineering report about two swallow structures built on a farm field and monitored seasonally by Bird Studies Canada clued me in to structures on Townsend Road, within another hour's drive. After reading press about Townsend Road, I contacted one of the leading biologists in charge of monitoring those structures. He tells me he is no longer working with swallows, and that "most authorities are hesitant of providing any locations of species at risk." But in the case of the barn swallow, he says, "There are tens of thousands of nesting sites across the province and the presence of these nesting structures being built all over is no secret to the public." He gives me the coordinates of the Townsend structures and says there are two structures within a five-minute drive from my house, right next to Vista Hills, a subdivision that will soon boast over two thousand homes, each selling for between eight hundred thousand and one million dollars. It is early spring, and the province has closed schools, businesses, and universities because of a global viral pandemic. Armed with GPS, written permission from the university to travel for fieldwork-related purposes in case I am stopped by the police for leaving my home, steel-toed boots, and a reflective vest, I do the only thing permissible in this terrible spring: get in my car and drive.

This is nestwork, a mode of inquiry that hinges on the naturecultural. It depends on an attunement to time and to season and to hope. To view the barn swallow mitigation structures at the three sites I've located—Vista Hills subdivision, Townsend Road farm field, and Dashwood Bridge—requires imagining myself as somehow able to get close to the birds that may or may not be present to use them, and imagining the stories behind why they were built. Before attending to the structures or birds, I think and read about them both, what they are each trying to accomplish. I learn about the Migratory Birds Act and SARA, the specifications of each structure and how they are supposed to be built to attract barn swallows. I learn that despite government-mandated monitoring of structures, barn swallows will "prospect"—do a flyby, as it were—but will rarely nest in them (BECO [Bird Ecology and Conservation Ontario] 2015; Campomizzi, Lebrun-Southcott, and Richardson 2019). What I don't learn in my research is how it feels to walk next to these strange nonbarn, nonbridge spaces, looking for nests, looking for swallows. What I don't learn until later is how these structures work to defamiliarize landscapes and small flying creatures; how they promote confusion and curiosity across species; how this disidentification may help, as Rosi Braidotti suggests, unseat "anthropocentric thought" and "human arrogance" (2019, 388); how traveling among structures is synecdochic of a global pandemic already predicated on the unequal relation between humans and nonhumans (Morris 2020).

Hirundo Rustica, SARA, and Nonhuman Entanglements

Known to live on every continent but Antarctica, before European colonization barn swallows (in Latin, *hirundo*, "swallow" and *rustica*, "rural") nested in caves, holes, and crevices and have been recorded nesting on historic Native American and Canadian First Nations wooden structures (COSEWIC 2011, 9). A long-distance migratory bird and aerial insectivore, the barn swallow breeds and nests in northern locations before overwintering in southern, warmer climates. Barn swallows' longstanding ties to humans are discursively represented in human historical and contemporary record, as the small sampling of Indigenous names for *Hirundo rustica* suggest: in Anishinaabemowin, *zhaashaawanibiisi*; in Cree, *mīscaskosīs*; in Iñupiaq, *tulugagnasruǧruk*; in Yaqui *kutapapache'a* and in Tepehuán *pipídamuli*; in Wayampi *masuwili*; and in Sami *láhtospálfu*. Such naming is echoed in South America (where North American swallows overwinter); in Europe and Africa (where European subspecies overwinter), and in Asia and

India, Indonesia, and Australia (where Asian subspecies overwinter). When listed as threatened in Canada, the species was not yet listed in either the United States or the United Kingdom as threatened or endangered, which situates them, at present, in similar ways to the house sparrow, which currently appears on the IUCN "Red List"[1] but are not otherwise threatened globally (Whale and Ginn 2017). In their article "In the Absence of Sparrows," Helen Whale and Franklin Ginn (2017, 93) ask of this small declining species at home but not elsewhere, "If birds are evocative of place, what happens when birds disappear?" Further, what happens when the notion of precarity is argued across borders, but the decline of one subspecies of bird (the aerial insectivore) is globally in decline? The barn swallow, while still abundant in some places in the world, nevertheless acts as a kind of canary in a coal mine for aerial insectivores as a whole. Given their rhetorical perch in the conversations of precarity, they are also species that attune us specifically to place and landscape as they disappear.

Blue-bodied, red-throated, white-bellied, and easily cupped in the palm of a hand, barn swallows have been associated in myth and superstition with luck, protection, and healing and have been said to carry magical stones of red and black in their bodies that, when placed under the tongue, are "able to sway people with . . . eloquence" (Webster 2008, 247). From the Bible to Pliny to Shakespeare, swallows have been associated with the oncoming of spring, freedom, and the love of and fidelity to home (Columbo 2003). Because of their long-standing mythological status as a magical bird, barn swallows have often been treated with caution or otherwise protected by humans. Folklore had it that to destroy a swallow's nest on a farm would mean a decline in yield (Columbo 2003). Yet this is not the case in contemporary farming, in which swallows are often seen as pests because of the messiness and perceived unsanitary nature of their nests and guano. Thus, swallows and humans have been bound up with one another in complicated and contradictory ways over time that involve both human story and human development. Today, swallows prefer to build their nests on almost exclusively human-made structures and rough surfaces, like wood, because mud (their primary nesting material) does not stick well to smooth surfaces, such as steel. Like bobolinks, they are known to shadow large farm machinery for the insects such threshing evokes and thus often settle quite closely into domestic farming routines (Cocker and Mabey 2005, 316). Perhaps because of their size and ubiquity, the barn swallow, as a small nonhuman body, does not carry significant persuasive weight about species decline, whether it is absent or present. In Jamie Lorimer's words, species like the barn swallow lack *nonhuman charisma*, that quality of persuasive, affective being-in-the-world formed from both ecological proximity and corporeal—visual or textual—understanding (2007, 917–18). Compared to the iconic cuteness of the panda or the familiarity of the orangutan as endangered species, the barn swallow barely stands a chance.

The barn swallow might be said to have three notable embodied conditions, or what Jakob von Uexküll would term an *umwelt* (an understanding of both animals and their worlds as a complete and inseparable whole; see Buchanan 2008). They are: close ties to human structural development, susceptibility to temperature changes around breeding and migration times in the north (Saino et al. 2011), and dependence on insects as a food supply (particularly flies, beetles, moths, bees and wasps, and ants; this diet also affects nestling growth) (McCarty and Winkler 1999, 286). It is perhaps no surprise, then, that the Government of Canada notes the barn swallows' decline along these parallel lines in its SARA species profile (2011): "The main causes of the recent decline in Barn Swallow populations are thought to be: (1) loss of nesting and foraging habitats due to conversion from conventional to modern farming techniques; (2) large-scale declines (or other perturbations) in insect populations; and (3) direct and indirect mortality due to an increase in climate perturbations on the breeding grounds." In other words, the other persuasive bodies that interact with the barn swallows, contributing to their movement across landscapes and their decline, are *entanglements*: the small family farm (complete with barns) converting to the steel behemoths of industrial farm buildings, the decline in flying insect biomass reaching 75 percent in the last twenty-five years, in large part due to human poisons (Hallmann et al. 2017), and weather in any given year remaining unpredictable because of anthropogenic changes to global climate. A further discursive and material recorder of these entanglements, and thus a persuasive and agential body, is the Canadian government and their reach through SARA.

A legislative document since 2002, SARA governs the conservation of all endangered species in Canada. Although a bid was made to list the barn swallow on SARA as early as 2011, it was not until 2017 that *Hirundo rustica* was officially approved as a threatened species by Catherine McKenna, the minister of environment and climate change. Although the barn swallow, as a migratory bird, has some protections under the Migratory Birds Convention Act of 1994 (which protects the bird itself), its listing on SARA both extends to critical habitat conservation (beyond the bird to its habitat) and qualifies the barn swallow as an "individual" with a "residence." SARA describes such residences as a dwelling-place, such as a den, nest or other similar area or place, that is occupied or habitually occupied by one or more individuals during all or part of their life cycles, including breeding, rearing, staging, wintering, feeding or hibernating [s.2(1)].... A residence would be considered to be damaged or destroyed if an alteration to the residence and/or its topography, structure, geology, soil conditions, vegetation, chemical composition of air/water, surface or groundwater hydrology, micro-climate, or sound environment either temporarily or permanently impairs the function(s) of the residence of one or more individuals.... Under SARA, Barn Swallows have one type of residence: the nest. (Government of Canada, 2019, 1)

Under "damage and destruction of residence," SARA lists moving, damaging, disturbing, or blocking access of a nest regardless of occupation. With this language, SARA uses a metaphor of human similarity with its qualification of barn swallow nests as "residences," though it lamentably asserts a false individualism to the birds, who settle in breeding pairs and have historically been known to roost in groups up to one hundred thousand (Turner 2006, 48). Because barn swallows often commit to the labor-intensive build of over one thousand flight returns to gather mud for just one nest, they also often return to the same nesting area for many years, only abandoning a nest once faulty or parasitic (Langlois 2005). Because of this site fidelity, the destruction of a nest by human intervention often means the loss of nestlings in any given year.

SARA mitigations recognize that the main human threat to barn swallows lies with the overt destruction or tampering of habitat in the forms of residences/nests followed by similar anthropogenic destruction of insect species or an impact on climate that affects the swallows' *umwelt* and attendant species decline. This humanistic appeal to the conflation of nests with residences is a much easier action to practically legislate (to individuals and companies) than a wholesale attempt to stop or mitigate the rather mysterious conflation of decline—the additive or synergistic effects of changing human-modified habitat, prey availability and foraging habitat, and climate on a temperature-sensitive species.

The turn by SARA to nests-as-place, which builds on the body-only protections of the Migratory Birds Act, is an important one, and a key for human grappling with the disappearance of a species from a landscape. As Whale and Ginn note in their turn to the ways that humans sense place, "Place arises through presence" (2017, 94), a presence that is often dependent, for humans, on a place remaining unchanged, an "impossible demand" (95) on any landscape. Whale and Ginn turn to Nigel Thrift, who argues that "place, in this sense, is a slippery *becoming* that 'can never be completed'" (Thrift 1999, 317, quoted in Whale and Ginn 2017, 95). "For Thrift," Whale and Ginn suggest, "to get a grip on an 'ecology of place' is to recognize that 'places are "passings that haunt" us,' forever slipping out of reach" (ibid., 310). Whale and Ginn turn our attention specifically to the problematics of place in conservation by using the work of geographer Steve Hinchliffe, who studies the conservation efforts around the endangered black redstart bird as political ecology. He notes that conservation itself is concerned with resisting such becoming, instead hoping to "revea[l] presence and rende[r] the present eternal" (Hinchliffe 2008, 88; see also Bowker 2004). We expect species to always be with us, always waiting to revel themselves, just outside our gaze.

This attunement to the 'long now,' dependent on physical presence, represents a complex tension and problem-making for conservationists in particular, because "while nature 'has to be present' to be saved, many species resist the reductive binaries of absence and presence, defying the static spatialities of modes of recording, protecting, and sheltering" (Whale and Ginn 2017, 97). Perhaps there is no better case of this presence/nonpresence than the ivory-billed woodpecker, declared extinct in 2021 after being last seen in 1944, but whose ghost has been revived by reported sightings throughout the 1980s and 1990s and most notably, in 2022—enough for one news source to declare them "back from the dead," based on trail camera images (Milman 2022; see also Cokinos 2009). In other words, the presence of place depends on what humans can detect and assess, and often the "signs" of precarious species are subtle and shifting. In trying to preserve an eternal present, human ability to closely track nonhuman presence, to attune themselves to what appears, is compromised. In the case of human destruction of infrastructure in which nonhumans also dwell, this is a peculiar kind of slippage.

Coming into Becoming: The Strange Present and Posthuman Affects

On the one hand, the slow disappearance of any species posits a problem seemingly too complex to halt—it is not just the nest, or the swallow; it is the insect, the farm field, the change in climate, the resistance to invasive species. On the other, human conservation efforts depend on the *places* and *presence* of these precarious species with which to monitor and decide their fate, constructions that depend on an environment's seeming unchangeability over time. It seems, then, that contending with species precarity in part requires an ability by humans to sit with both mutability and absence while striving for invariability and presence. For the critical posthumanities, these tensions need not be constructed as incommensurabilities. As Braidotti (2019) suggests, the tenets of posthumanism argue that "man" is no longer the "allegedly universal measure of all things" and embrace a postanthropocentric being in which "species hierarchy and human exceptionalism" are myths (32). She argues for critical cartographies, maps-as-ways-through these new sensibilities, which articulate "what kind of knowing subjects are we in the process of becoming and what discourses underscore the process" (32). In constructing such cartographies, Braidotti turns to "in-between" states of assemblages that "displace the binaries" inherent in bifurcating, for example, "nature/technology," "local/global," and "present/past" (33). The move to examine knowing subjects through these middle states is worth quoting at length (2019, 33): "These in-between states defy the logic of the excluded middle and, although they allow an analytic function to the negative, they reject negativity and aim at the production of joyful or affirmative values and projects" (Lloyd 1996; Braidotti 2011). In other words, Braidotti (invoking Genevieve Lloyd's reading of Spinoza) recognizes that to split up the world this way gives many invested in dismantling unequal power differentials points of analysis and critique. However, Braidotti's cartographic framework asks that scholars move out from this critique, using the middle spaces offered between terms as a potential space for joy and/or affirmative ethics.

In the case of species decline in the Anthropocene, Braidotti's call can be a tall order. There is nothing joyful or affirmative about what van Dooren terms the "dull edge of extinction" (2014, 13). Indeed, Braidotti acknowledges that often the pendulum of examining the posthuman and postanthropocentric swings between mourning and celebrating, apocalypse and euphoria (2019, 36). Similar swings are notable in van Dooren's examination of the disappearance and conservation efforts behind the whooping crane, which he notes are beset with "violence and care, . . . coercion and hope" (2014, 13). Rather than situate an examination of species decline at either one of the anxiety-provoking poles of violence and mourning or hope and celebration, both of which, to some degree, depend on either backward- or forward-looking, I instead try here to situate a creation and analysis of the "knowing subjects" of these bird-structure-human-SARA assemblages as products of a particular present that only occasionally relies on presence.

Braidotti draws on Deleuze and Guattari (1994) to articulate the notion of the present time as process, which I find central to moving toward reading human and other-than-human entanglements of precarity with affirmative ethics in mind. However, it should be noted that an unseating of the present or a rethinking of linear time is not the provenance of Eurowestern philosophers; such conceptions of time are notably the domain of a variety of Indigenous people, who articulate time as seasonal, cyclical, unfixed, agentic, and nonlinear, as well as located both spatially and in artifacts (see Reid and Seiber 2016; see also chapter 3). Thus, while I draw upon Braidotti's framing of the present here, I also recognize complications of linear time in discussion of the bobolink in chapter 3, which draws specifically on Indigenous conceptions of time to describe *pheno*, attention to what appears, to offer temporal alternatives to linear time.

For Braidotti, who draws from vital materialism, the present is a complicated concept and force because, as she says, "it does not coincide completely with the here and now" (2019, 36). "Approaching the present," she argues, "produces a multi-faceted effect: on the one hand the sharp awareness of *what we are ceasing to be* (the end of the actual) and on the other the perception—in different degrees of clarity—of *what we are in the process of becoming* (the actualization of the virtual" (36–37). When we consider the case of a species in decline (which suggests a certain inescapable future), the present is indeed a complex force of ceasing to be and becoming something else, embedded in both past and future. In particular, as Kyle Powys Whyte (2017) points out, such an inescapable future has already come to pass for many Indigenous people, a current dystopia forecasted by their ancestors (2). For now, I'll call this the *strange present*, to distinguish it from other conceptions of space-time and to treat it as a container for holding precarious species who are both here and not-here. Such time holds a present that is both stopping and starting, a time that offers a particular present that holds the in-betweenness of Braidotti's critical cartographies and the present absences of human conservation efforts for uncharismatic species.

As Braidotti notes, holding on to a strange present allows us to embrace contradiction, hold both "growth and extinction" in our minds at the same time (2019, 38). This is not to say that such an enfolding is easy or without resistance. Indeed, for many scholars, guilt, grief, and environmental mourning are key parts of considering and engaging with anthropocenic time (see Barnett 2022).

The collection *Mourning Nature* (Cunsolo and Landman 2017), of which the Whale and Ginn piece is a part, is a strong example of the ways these affects shape our ways of being and thinking the Anthropocene. While many of the pieces in that collection come to terms, in various ways, with environmental mourning and grief (what Braidotti [2019, 36] might term an "apocalyptic variant" of scholarship of anthropocenic anxiety), still others use such affects as generative turning points. On the one hand, scholars like Catriona Sandilands carve out a particular place for the grief for nonhuman others that comes with ecological degradation. As she says, "We have few public rituals for the loss of places, species, or ecosystems; in the face of everything from suburban sprawl to the Alberta Tar Sands, Judith Butler might call such losses 'ungrievable'" (2004, quoted In Sandilands 2017, 151). Part of recognizing this loss, Sandilands asserts, is accepting of the idea of "crazy love" (Rose 2013, 164), emerging from "our capacity to respond generously to the Other." Such crazy love is a concept that I draw on to frame the care by which nestwork must take place in the conclusion to this book. While Sandilands concludes that coming to terms with such generosity, loss, and love means we all to some degree embrace a "shared precarity" (Butler 2004)—what Braidotti might say is a "euphoric variant" of Anthropocenic anxiety (2019, 36)—it is important to note, as Sandilands does, that often "loss connects us in ways that plenitude does not" (165), perhaps creating within us a capacity for a different kind of attention.

I do not wish to throw away completely those immediate human affects that come with the contemplation of species extinction—this is not what anyone might call a "happy" subject. Yet like Braidotti's suggestion of the generativity that may come out of the negative space of bifurcations of nature and culture, I wish to note the work that negative affective attention does for an analytic cartography of species decline. Many pieces in the *Mourning Nature* volume critique, in particular, Freudian concepts of environmental mourning that circulate around the human subject and ego even as they grieve objects of loss. One such piece by John Ryan offers an alternative posthumanist account to Freudian melancholia that attunes humans to loss beyond the subject-object dichotomy. He articulates a posthumanist framework of such affect as one that importantly makes space for mourning networks beyond subject or object— "interdependencies, connectivities, relationships—between living creatures and their living and non-living milieux" (2017, 121). Ryan articulates a posthuman theory of environmental mourning, drawing from Cary Wolfe (2010) and Karen Barad (2010), suggesting it is dependent on "bodily experience and sense of place while counterbalancing anthropocentrism through the decentering of human subjectivity" (2017, 125). Ryan (2017) notes that such a posthuman theory of environmental mourning is both specific—involving specific species—and "is not simply a turn from anthropocentrism to ecocentrism (from culture to nature), but rather a return to a sense of relationality between species as the essence of mourning" (127). The specificity of looking at individual flora or fauna (rather than general feeling of sadness over a nebulous term like *environment*), for Ryan, foregrounds completely "the emotional and material connections people develop" with those individuals and thus attunes us to the "relational quality of loss" rather than loss itself (130). It is this relational quality to loss that draws us closer to the disappearance of small nonhuman species like the barn swallow, the chimney swift, and the bobolink, precisely through the material interventions and propositions we cocreate with them, as I discuss in depth in chapter 2.

Ryan's articulation of shifting our affects not to loss of subjects or objects but to loss of relations is a significant one, for three reasons. The first is that it resonates with Indigenous calls to honor relations as the connection between humans and nonhumans, as represented by Cedillo's (2022) call for an attention to relationship and relations as "felt and lived" as the starting place for ethical worldmaking (100). The second, for the purposes of this project, is that a species in decline like the barn swallow is in the *process of being lost*. That is, the barn swallow is at the point both of dying in larger numbers year after year (and is a grievable loss of material bodies in the present) and is also not yet gone. It is both absent and present, gone and also sometimes not gone (or even in abundance). The third is that such a species captures the in-between moment of the strange present, both an end to the actual (a ceasing to be) and an actualization of the virtual (a process of becoming less; a process of imagination), in Braidotti's terms (2019, 36–37). In this strange present, the barn swallow, as precarious species, does not share in human precarity—we are not exactly euphorically "all in this together" in the same way. Instead, the barn swallow joins us in the strange present in a place where we can examine becoming-loss alongside already-lost, to think and feel and live alongside the swallow as a creature with whom human relations are changing. Thus, a species like the barn swallow, who is both here and not-here, is one specific creature—alongside the chimney swift and the bobolink—whom we might examine as an agent who provokes specific human responses to a strange present.

The mitigation structure sites that I examine here press on those human responses beyond the polarities of hope and hopelessness, present and past, nature and technology. They turn attention to the relations between human and more-than-human and attune human attention to possibilities for action that may to some degree still embrace an affirmative ethics—by a turn to specific practices over descriptions, by an acceptance of the strange and the contradictory, by an embrace of curiosity and distinction over the privileging of human control of our own melancholia.

Turning Otherwise: *Alloiostrophos*

As I have suggested, the strange present allows for the contemplation of embracing the contradiction of species decline, both the here and not-here. This is central to the contemporary human response to barn swallow decline by the government mandate that when humans threaten barn swallow habitat—tear down old barns, build new bridges or convert old bridges to culverts, or rebuild old wharfs—they must provide at least as much replacement habitat for the birds. Unlike other mitigations that may mandate, for example, the purchase and conservation of additional wetland when encroaching on a threatened species' habitat, "replacement habitat" in this case means constructing additional human-built mitigation structures. While specific best management practices (BMPs) for species recovery vary from province to province in Canada, most are similar in terms of critical stewardship, monitoring, research, communications, and management when it comes to specific species. Where species like the barn swallow differ from other threatened species are in BMPs that require the replacement of any barn swallow nest with an artificial (human-made) nesting cup, and the replacement of a nesting site with an artificial nesting structure (OMNRF [Ontario Ministry of Natural Resources and Forestry] 2016). Such mitigations are suggested by SARA, but until they are federally mandated, rest in the hands of provincial bodies to implement and monitor. In Ontario, where barn swallow populations are most at risk, the construction and monitoring of artificial structures for barn swallows is carried out through the Government of Ontario's Ministry of Natural Resources and Forestry (OMNRF), who mandate such BMPs through the Ontario Endangered Species Act (OESA). While much of the work to protect common species like the barn swallow is done by traditional conservation activities such as research, educational outreach, and stewardship—statistical analysis of the Breeding Bird survey, public workshops, stakeholder interviews to gauge landowner attitudes—the construction of new structures stands out as a different kind of conservation practice altogether.

Through OESA, Ontario provides specific how-to conservation manuals to build barn swallow nesting structures. A Nesting Structure Design model by the Ministry of Transportation shows that these structures must be built of specific swallow-approved materials (rough-cut hemlock, barn board, galvanized fasteners, cedar shake shingles), be of a specific height and dimension, and come with preinstalled nesting cups to lure barn swallows to this habitat. As material-discursive plans, such models hearken to the description of SARA's categorization of nests-as-residences with their inclusion of a "maximum privacy" option complete with vented gables and raccoon guards (OMNRF 2016, 13). As recovery strategies, contracted design plans such as these are specifically tailored to SARA-mandated government regulations: for every nest destroyed, a nesting cup must be installed; for as much nesting habitat destroyed, a greater amount must be created; and the provision of "suitable nesting conditions" must be accounted for in the form of appropriate horizontal or vertical ledges, accessible entry, exit, and spacing, and sound structure that minimizes predation (2). Yet the finished products that arise out of these parallels, as my field sites show, are not only less barn- or bridge-like (as any passerby would attest to) but also appear to the uninitiated to be a human-focused structural anomaly. For example, they cannot be climbed by children (as in other kinds of public equipment), they offer very little shelter (as in other kinds of gazebos), and they are not particularly aesthetically appealing (as in other kinds of "nonpurposive" public art). As barn swallow nesting structures emerge on the landscape, they exert a persuasive, illogical, and loud material agency, telling us something about the peculiar moment in which we are living and the creatures we are (or are not) living with. Rather than offer simple problem-solution format (*if you build it, they will come*), these structures, I argue, function *alloiostrophically* on the landscape, at once making strange and making curious.

Just as posthumanist cartography turns to the in-betweens as generative places of becoming, I argue that these mitigation structures act in a similar way to underscore human-nonhuman entanglements in a strange present. Scholars in rhetorical theory, communication studies, and geography are noting the creative shift that paying attention to material sites, places, and spaces lends to rhetorical thinking (see, for example, Marback 1998; Blair 1999; Dickinson et al.

2010). Concomitantly, nonrepresentational theory is gaining ground in geography, and with it, an attention to the "onflow of everyday life" of humans and their surrounds, made up of material schema, practices, the vibrancy of things and their dispositions (Bennett 2010), and the role of affect and sensation (Thrift 2008, 5–12). This has given rise to scholarship in critical infrastructural studies and elsewhere that examines the role of material bodies such as sidewalks, water pipes, and buildings in city spaces, and how such assemblages encourage human movement, awareness, and feeling (Dickinson and Aiello 2016, 1296; McFarlane 2011, 162; Star 1999; Liu 2022). However, such human-focused scholarship does not generally examine the role of other-than-human actors along with humans, nor does it account for rural or nonurban structures not built for human use. As neither barn nor bridge nor art nor gazebo, the mitigation structure is a physical, material intervention of the in-between of nonhuman difference in a rhetorical ecology: it is propagated by barn swallow decline, mandated through SARA and OMNRF, and mediated through both barn swallows and human beings. Together, these persuasive bodies build rhetorical capacities by performing a particular kind of addressivity—one that promotes an allowance of difference by inviting curiosity—the *alloiostrophic*.

As Jane Sutton and Marilee Mifsud (2012, 222) note, *alloiostrophos* does not appear as a classical rhetorical trope the way that metaphor or metonymy do in ancient texts but instead is found in adjectival form in Greek lexicon. The authors consider this absence an "invitation to theorize" about what is possible beyond the rhetorical tradition of making comparisons and drawing on similarity to make arguments (222). While Sutton and Mifsud acknowledge the centrality of metaphor to create human meaning in order to "render the unfamiliar familiar by asserting a similarity in a difference" (H. White 1978, 5), they also acknowledge that metaphor's domination of human tropology is a reduction of linguistic resources. Beyond arguing that increasing such resources is an enrichment of human argumentation, Sutton and Mifsud argue that "metaphor inserts all that is familiar into difference, thereby making it difficult to make contact with difference *as difference*. In metaphoric systems, difference enters the realm of understanding in the form of the self-same" (2012, 224). In other words, given human propensity to view everything around them as somehow similar to their own experience, the discursive resources we have for considering the different, the strange, or the unfamiliar is limited. Such limitation certainly resonates with Jackson (2015), Tompkins (2016), King (2017), and Braidotti's (2016, 381) critique of "the humanist vision of the subject," in which humanist norms "embody difference as pejoration, and . . . differences get organized on a hierarchical scale of decreasing social and symbolic worth." To imagine new possibilities for tropic difference, then, is to also offer discursive-material opportunity to rethink humanist subjectivity in which difference is always equated with depreciation and disparagement (or alternatively, as always inclining toward similarity). As both Tiffany Lethabo King (2017) and Armond Towns (2018) point out, this is particularly the case for Indigenous and Black lives, in which the difference of othered black and brown bodies via Western white supremacist ideologies is both castigated and nullified, as Chad Shomura (2017, 3) puts it. Turning otherwise, allowing difference to speak and listening to what it might say rather than rushing to metaphoric or metonymic calls for similarity or contiguity, is central to ethics in the posthuman project.

Alloiostrophos draws our attention to what it might mean to turn or bend (*strophos*, turning/twisting/bending) otherwise (*alloîo-*, otherwise/differently). The *alloîos*, as Sutton and Mifsud note, orient us both toward the strange and toward change or alteration, as the term *alloiôsis* (alteration/change) suggests. However, Sutton and Mifsud's (2012) main claim for *alloiostrophos*, a turning otherwise, is that it functions metonymically—"signifying relations through contiguity" (227)—rather than metaphorically. "We see this distinction readily through rhetorical effect," they argue, "with metaphor producing assimilation, for example, rendering two distinct phenomena the same; and with metonymy producing association, for example, juxtaposing two phenomena rendering them distinct" (2012, 227). Thus, rather than a mitigation structure existing on the landscape as, say a "birdhouse" (a metaphor), such an object may instead function on the basis of contiguity—a "structure" that allows for both peculiarity (a nonhouse and nonbarn) as well as bending toward *infra*structure, what Star notes as a "fundamentally relational concept" (1999, 380). As Star argues, "One person's infrastructure is another person's difficulty" (380), always seen in relation to existing practices. A mitigation structure nears infrastructure but requires something else in its interpretation, and that something else is an inclination toward difference *as* difference.

As Sutton and Mifsud (2012) argue, *alloiostrophos* sits outside the logic of the first, next, conclusion telos of the classical tropes of *strophos* and *anistrophos*. Instead, the telos of *alloiostrophos* is one of possibility, as it serves an aggregative metonymic function (as opposed to an assimilative, metaphoric one) (227). Yet unlike metaphoric argumentation, they suggest, which wishes to "secure assent" in contact with the Other, an *alloiostrophic* rhetoric "wishes for a contact that would recognize and attend to the complexity of other possibilities as well as diversity and difference" (228). Such a possibility for persuasion not only fits well with a rhetorical-ecological lens, which depends on the rhetorical capacity of a variety of humans and nonhumans, but again points us back to the usefulness of specificity for such a task: *alloiostrophic* rhetoric, they say, "is configured in the idiosyncratic and particular lived reality of alterity" (229). Thus, a focus on specific species like the barn swallow (or chimney swift, or bobolink) and their lived reality, and not just extinction in general, becomes a way to examine "emotional and material connections" between humans and nonhumans central to theories of posthuman mourning (Ryan 2017, 130; see also Barnett 2022). Such an attunement, with its focus on specific loss, may increasingly be a primary modality of relation in the Anthropocene.

While it is clear that Sutton and Mifsud (2012, 2019) are tracing the history of human communication, they also offer up *alloiostrophic* rhetoric as an invitation to think differently about discursive possibilities in general, which can be extended in rhetorical ecologies that involve both humans and other-than-humans.[2] Although their work, as they maintain, lies mainly in rhetorical theory (that is, their aim is to historicize and complicate *alloiostrophos* as opposed to finding extended examples of such rhetorical moves), I argue that the action plans promoted by SARA can be understood as material models of such argumentation. They help humans attend differently to nonhuman presence that conservation actions depend on. They force nonhumans to contend with new possibilities for dwelling. They also move both humans and nonhumans toward an opening, toward curiosity, rather than a closed telos of conclusion or finality. As Hinchliffe offers, such opportunities may help humans "engag[e] with potentials, including likely presence as well as differentiated presences" (2008, 94).

In bringing the potential for mitigation structures, artificial chimneys, and bird time to act suasively on humans and nonhumans to the fore in this book, it is to ask readers to sit with polaric tensions—being here and not-here—such ecologies bring to human thinking. In the next section, I turn specifically to field sites of barn swallow nesting structures that exemplify these tensions while examining the rhetorical capacity of humans and more-than-humans as they contend with presence, absence, and a striving for proximity. Turning to specific species who both have been and are in the process of being lost because of human destruction of ecosystems—while striving to mitigate such damage—suggests a complicated vision for environmental concern, one that is caught between self and other. Hinchliffe (2008) draws on Steven K. White's (1990) vision of a postmodern ethics to think through such tension. White relies on Heideigger and postmodern ethics as a way to frame, like *alloiostrophos*, "experiencing otherness such that it remains other" (White 1990, 93). "Attentive concern for otherness," contends White, "means that the gesture of nearing, bringing into one's presence, into one's "world," must always be complemented by a letting go, an allowance of distance, a letting be in absence, thereby bearing witness to our own limits" (94). Yet Hinchliffe (2008) does not simply rest with this tension, or use it as a reflection on human finitude, as White does with Heidegger's terminology. Instead, he turns to "a more careful political ecology,"—and, I would argue, an affirmative one—that questions conservation efforts as only those that exist to fix presence and create "shelter" (Hinchliffe 2008, 95). Shifting from sheltering as a paternalistic and "smothering" move between humans and nonhumans, instead Hinchliffe acknowledges that human conservation efforts often require "letting go as much as bringing together," mixed with a curiosity and openness that allows for "a gathering together that is not too tight" (95). Human mitigations for the specific species in this book, then, are parts of rhetorical ecologies that gather together in one place fragile and oftentimes failed efforts to allow difference as difference. Yet they also help us recognize limits to our understanding, helping us attune ourselves better to the loss of relations between self and very specific, small, nonhuman others. Such attunements gather together in physical, emplaced sites of haptic and embodied encounter, as I next detail.

Vista Hills: The "Prospect" of Suburban Sprawl

The Vista Hills subdivision is in the midst of being built on the western edge of Waterloo, Ontario. It is being built on a parcel of the German Company Tract, part of sixty thousand acres of land bought by a group of Mennonites from Richard Beasley, who purchased it in 1796 from Joseph Brant (Thayendanegea), a Mohawk leader of the Six Nations. As a negotiation for Six Nations people fighting on the side of Loyalists during the American Revolutionary War, Brant was gifted by the British Crown six miles of land on either side of the Grand River, in an agreement known as the Haldimand Treaty (Treaty 3).[3] Because the province of Ontario is governed by over forty land treaties with First Nations, because those treaties guide the development of land throughout the province, and because the histories of those treaties are those filled with fraught negotiations and outright trickery, a care for the colonial legacy of the landscape here is very much tied to the degeneration of species due to human development. It should be noted then, that "human development" here means settler development that is guided by the Canadian government and various bureaucratic offices, and those guidelines have carved out a particular version of the landscape and the creatures who live within it, as well as dictated how settlers, descendants of enslaved Africans, and Indigenous people can use or develop it. Subdivisions in particular in Canada have a long history of contributing to both spatial and racial separation and redlining of urban, suburban, and rural living (see Harris and Forrester 2003). As various posthuman scholars have pointed out, those responsible for the making of the Anthropocene are not a kind of "universal man," but a particular Eurowestern capitalist human (see also Yusoff 2019; Malm and Hornborg 2014). To understand the story of declining species, then, is also to grapple with colonial legacies that have shaped, and continue to shape, relations in these ecologies. It is about considering how and where "we" dwell.

Vista Hills is being built as a suburban oasis, equally close to the town Costco and the town landfill, and borders a hydroelectric corridor to the east before hitting agricultural land. It is a new build, close to both the center of town and large suburban corridor streets that are home to big-box stores and other low- to medium-density suburban developments. Follow traffic-calming roundabouts and you will find yourself entering the development, now with its own elementary school within its borders, along streets such as "Cinnamon Fern" and "Wild Calla." To the north, houses are still being built, and the sounds of backhoes and Caterpillars backing up and piling dirt in all directions is easily seen and heard. To the east is the main arterial street that, if you follow it for two miles, will land you at the city's universities. To the west, Vista Hills has most of its lot homes already constructed; those are the houses that back up against Columbia Forest and the largest open space trail system in the city; this open space houses wetlands and rare plant species and is home to a variety of migratory bird species. If you walk through the construction debris and layers of spring trash blown in from the landfill, through knee-high brush that will be someone's move-in-ready backyard very soon, you will see the area between the subdivision and the forest, a corridor that will eventually hold paved walking paths that allow residents of Vista Hills to access the forest trails. It is this line between development and forest that gave rise to the two mitigation structures in the Vista Hills subdivision. Prompted by the demolition of a historic apple

Fig. 1 | Barn swallow structure in Vista Hills subdivision. Photo: author.

cider farm and mill a little less than a mile away, the corridor between subdivision and forest was deemed the ideal site for the building of replacement habitat, as it was within one kilometer of the old mill and within two hundred meters of appropriate foraging habitat, as dictated by the OESA. To walk the narrow corridor that houses the structures is to walk the anthropogenic line between nature and culture; forest behind you, rows upon rows of identical housing in front of you (see fig. 1).

The two structures at Vista Hills are similar, but not identical, to each other: they each have dimensions of three feet by fourteen feet, containing sixteen nesting cups apiece; they each have their four posts covered in galvanized sheet metal to act as predator guards; they each are covered in metal roofing and have a four-by-eight inch "window" hole cut in their narrow ends. Yet there are small differences: small wood "perches" that jut out from one structure that are absent on the other; one structure has wire mesh between the soffit and rafters and the other doesn't; one is a home to a small wasps' nest; one has a landing platform near its metal feet that the other is lacking. When I visit the structures for the first time in April, I don't see any swallows (nor do I expect to, since it is still barely above freezing and the swallows have not returned to their northern breeding sites). But I do see that one structure has a total of five nests in various states of development, while the other structure has six with one nestled in cross-hatched beam supports. I am excited, as most of the research I have done up to this point has suggested that swallows do not use the structures that humans build for them.

It is not until I return in May, after I have visited the Dashwood and Townsend locations, that I realize that my excitement has been completely unfounded and my powers of observation not even in the budding bird-watcher tier. I realize that the nests I've taken to be swallows' nests are in fact what SARA has already noted as a habitat threat: the nests of other kinds of birds, or what COSEWIC calls "interspecific competition for nest sites from invasive species"—usually the house sparrow or the American robin (2011, 26). At first glance, I was convinced there were swallows using the structures—because the nesting cups had nests in them, I assumed they were swallows' nests (*if you build it for swallows, swallows will come*). With more exposure to swallow habitat, over time I came to realize these nests were made of grass and leaves and ribbons of Tyvek gathered from the construction lots, and not, indeed, mud. I feel foolish for getting excited over robins. While I was disappointed that my assumptions were proven to be incorrect, I was also reminded of how incomplete my own human knowledge is between the smallest of distinctions between mud and grass and wonder just how far such an incompleteness extends, not only for me but for other humans sharing their space with small creatures.

The thing I notice most when I visit these structures are their absolute stillness. While the construction noise echoes on one side and blackbirds, crows, geese, and small songbirds gather together their voices from the forest tree line, the structures themselves attract no movement or sound. While their presence juts out, unignorable on the landscape, the absence of activity around the structures is noticeable. There is nary a house sparrow in the vicinity, even as I sit for hours and watch these structures, even as I arrive during a prime time for nesting and breeding for a variety of birds, swallows or not.

The structures are not in any way labeled or accompanied with signage. While they are closely accessible by foot when the leaves have not yet branched out in early spring, by midspring I have to tromp through thorny bush with knee-high wellies on and pray that I'll come out tick-free on the other side of my observations; in other words, I spend time wondering what the neighbors on Ladyslipper Drive think of these structures, if they try to get close to them or leave them be or even wonder about them. While I often see pedestrians walk the yet-unpaved dirt trails-to-be in Vista Hills, none of them approach the structures. Instead, they sit, immobile, as everything around them moves.

As Carole Blair notes of public memorials, these structures echo her attribution of "recalcitrant presentness" (1999, 17). They cannot be stored after they are "read," or put away once one has finished looking at them. As she suggests, such material rhetoric must be examined for what it *does* as well as what it is supposed to do—posthuman scholars might encourage us to examine this doing from other-than-human perspectives, or as de Castro suggests, to consider in every case who is human *here*, who is human *now* (Skafish 2016, 404). While Blair's analysis of material rhetorical texts is specifically based on the human—how material texts act on people (1999, 30), the attention she pays to material-discursive texts' durability, preservation, and reproduction, and contiguity to other texts and sites (and I would add, nonhuman others) is a useful heuristic with which to read mitigation structures that appear in liminal natu-recultural spaces. Too, material objects tell us about social and cultural conditions that surround them as part of a particular rhetorical ecology of humans and nonhumans. They reveal particular interspecies encounters grounded in an ecology of materiality, bodies, and movement (or lack thereof) (Dickinson and Aiello 2016), inclusive of texts such as SARA, human builders, and construction materials. When applied to the Vista Hills site, it is easily noted that the structures are not functioning as they are "supposed" to—there are no swallows nesting within them. So what *do* they do? How do they engage a strange present?

Mitigation structures interrupt the landscape, both in terms of where they appear—in spaces proximal to both human development and natural flora and fauna that would otherwise attract specific species—and, through their durability, they promote a noticing of how they fail. Though the structures do not generally attract swallows, they both act on other species (robins, for example, or wasps) and remain durable and immobile over time, though they are changed by the animals that build within them. Thus, they act as both suasive agents to a variety of fauna as well as reminders to humans about what they are not doing: acting as substitute habitat for nesting barn swallows. Despite the fact that mitigation structures are built to specifications, barn swallows do not prefer them and rarely use them, to the extent that researchers are using swallow decoys and sound recordings to attract the birds (BECO 2015; Campomizzi, Lebrun-Southcott, and Richardson 2019). Thus, what appears to be a simple solution based in equivalency is made far more complex by the energy of the encounter, the assemblage of actors, and the refusal of the barn swallow body.

In the case of the Vista Hills structures, human activity circulates around the structures but does not directly engage them (in that hikers use the trail system nearby and construction workers are in motion around them). While the structures otherwise fail to attract swallows to the extent that they build nests, they still act on the landscape as an object of curiosity. For humans, they clearly stick out as not-houses and not-trees on the landscape. And as I sat watching a structure in May I heard the unmistakable *"veet-veet"* sound of barn swallows nearby. As I sat and held my breath hopefully, two barn swallows flew from the temporary construction fencing toward the structure in figure 1, skimming its rooftop and landing inside to perch on its cross-beams before disappearing. What I witnessed, in Campomizzi, Lebrun-Southcott, and Richardson's (2019) terms (beyond ecstatic personal feeling of finally seeing what I was "supposed" to be seeing) was swallows' "prospecting" behavior—swinging by mitigation structures to see what they're all about, but otherwise not choosing them to build nests within. The swallows, after prospecting, likely determined that the structure was not-barn, and ultimately, not-home. Nonetheless, to see the swallows engage with the structure, however briefly, changed the structure on the landscape. It changed in an instant its particular present, when it ceased momentarily to be a not-barn, and engaged, for the tiniest of seconds while the birds alighted within, in a process of becoming something else.

Prospecting is a kind of curiosity on the part of swallows. We might even allow such inquisitiveness or interestedness as allowing a similar "occasion for joy and humbleness" on the part of humans, as Rickert (2013, 244) says of the propensity to dwell in entanglements with the Other while still allowing them to withdraw. Curiosity and withdrawal on the part of both swallows and humans, as I next take up in the discussion of the Dashwood Bridge site, are central affects that circulate around swallow mitigation structures and are key to determining specific arguments that structures make on the landscape. That is, swallows' curiosity changed the Vista Hills structures from static monuments to enlivened objects of interest, awareness, and concern for humans, if only for a few minutes.

It seems, in the case of Vista Hills, the swallows, the structures' builders, the site's developers, and I were all engaged in prospecting behaviors to some degree, mitigated by SARA instructions for action. Each of us, in different and specific ways, were engaged in a kind of searching, some prompted by curiosity (the swallows, me), some by necessity (the swallows; the developers; the builders), but all of us were engaged in the process of surveying and scouting for something, whether obeying a government mandate, monitoring success or failure, or looking for a suitable place to raise young. All of this activity and movement, whether flying, prospecting, or territorializing (swallow), observing, reading, researching, building, reporting (human), or legislating, confronting, authorizing, memorializing (SARA), are taking place in and around these structures, as they stand part of this rhetorical ecology, enabling and performing this strange present. As Jane Bennett would say, the structures have their own "trajectories, tendencies, and potentialities" (2010, 9). They allow the humans and other-than-humans who closely gather with them, though not too tightly, to sit with difference: the not-house, not-trees, not-barns, not-homes. Yet this difference, too, allows for disengagement by the residents of Vista Hills subdivision. Perhaps the activity that the structures most promote and embody in Vista Hills among all actors is echoed in the call of both swallows and suburbanites alike: we search, looking hard to settle.

And settlement is the operative word here, the damning indicator of both colonial legacy and human development. As both rhetorical and geographical scholars note, the suburbs themselves, which "depend on, reinforce, and demand private consumption," emerged with a distinct tie to capitalism (Hayden, 2003, 18; see also Stewart and Dickinson, 2008). Thus, it matters that the structures are built on the narrow corridor between suburban backyards and forests, a wayward curiosity for those settlers seeking, as Robert Topinka has it, particular zones of use that "prop up the market as if on stage," "funnel[ing] almost all movement toward consumption" (2012, 72). Topinka, borrowing from Henri Lefebvre (1991), notes that the suburbs function as a kind of "abstract space," an "overdetermined spac[e] that attempt[s] to crush any agency" (Topinka 2012, 66). It's no wonder that the structures on this landscape prompt no engagement from human passersby. The force of the suburbs on the mitigation structures of Vista Hills is a strong one, despite the swallows' occasional inquisitiveness. These structures in particular, unused by swallows, overarchingly stand as particular monuments to development, to absence, and to a capitalistic worldview that asserts that somehow a three-by-fourteen-foot structure will easily trade for a barn, or for a wetland.

These structures also echo such strange and unfair "trades" this land has seen over time and is reminiscent of the unequal access to property rights, ownership, and justice that characterize both the birth of the Canadian nation and its current struggles over Indigenous and settler land ownership. The structures' iconic position between the Vista Hills subdivision and Columbia Forest sits a little over four miles from O:se Kenhionhata:tie, an "Indigenous queer and trans space" of encampment, also known as Land Back Camp, which has occupied land in the area's city parks for the last two years, demanding access to land for Indigenous ceremony as well as an urban hub for Indigenous gathering, among other calls to action (O:se Kenhionhata:tie 2022). The anachronism of the Vista Hills structures, unused in a subdivided landscape, paired with the requests of O:se Kenhionhata:tie, embody the disenfranchising worldview that artificially separates "'social' and 'environmental,'" or culture from nature, as articulated by Veronica Strang (2017, 2). Issues of engagement, refusal, and withdrawal that bind human and nonhuman here close the gap between meaning and matter, helping unseat the Eurocentric commonplaces of dualism that separate, for example, human from animal, culture from nature, subject from object, or mind from body. If we are to understand that the land and the body are inseparable, we get closer to a naturecultural understanding of precarity.

While all of the mitigation structures studied here have been purposefully built in naturecultural spaces very close to human development, those spaces, and the affordances and constraints they offer the humans and more-than-humans around them, do differ in kind. That is, other elements of rhetorical ecologies come into play at different mitigation sites: at varying times it is location; invasion or competition from other species; weather; bugs; time of year; proximity to water; preservation of prior years' nests; deterioration of structures; human design. These differentiations encourage rhetorical capacities beyond, for example, simple choices of either engaging with the prospect or bypassing curiosity. They urge different responses, from refusal to engagement.

Dashwood Bridge: Curiosity, Refusal, and Nonhuman Propositions

Off of Highway 83 on the way toward Grand Bend, Ontario, where the banks of Lake Huron lap at the feet of Torontonians out for a day's drive, sits a new bridge that was built over the Ausable River, which flows on Treaty 29 land of the Anishinaabe and empties into Lake Huron. Verdantly green in midspring with burdock, ragweed, wild garlic, lamb's quarters, and Joe-pye weed, the bridge is neighbored by a farm and is home to more than a few ranging cattle. Near the farm sit what look to be scum-covered ponds but are, I discover, the Hay Swamp

Provincially Significant Wetland. When I first visit the Dashwood Bridge, it is because I have read the Environmental Impact Assessment (EIA) that has said that over eight species at risk were predicted to be affected by the building of a new bridge, that thirty-six bird species were known to the area, and seventeen barn swallow nests were found on the underside of the old bridge (Archer, 2016, 5). The new bridge, nondescript but for side railings that indicate that the highway itself is passing over water, replaced a seventy-year-old T-beam bridge. The "T"s are made of horizontal flanges and vertical webs, perfect for making a ledge for mud nests. Despite the presence of seventeen nests on the old T-beam bridge, the EIA suggests that the proposed new bridge would provide suitable nesting habitat with its concrete undersides and thus does not propose any further mitigations.

Yet in the face of the advice of the EIA that suggests no new habitat need be provided, when I pull over on the side of the highway and don my bright yellow safety vest to cross the road, vibrations rippling from the pavement through my body with cars passing at 75 miles per hour, it is because I am curious that a five-by-three-foot barn swallow structure unexpectedly sits about eight hundred feet southwest from the bridge's underside (see fig. 2). As I flatten grasses to get to the bridge itself, I perhaps see why: despite the EIA claiming the new bridge will provide enough nesting habitat to replace what has been lost by the demolition of the old bridge, there are no barn swallow nests under the concrete Ls of the new bridge, though there looks to be the destroyed remains of one mud nest crumbled into the hardscaping fill of river rock underneath. Because SARA requires monitoring of development sites for up to five years, I deduce that the nearby structure was likely built a year or more after the new bridge was complete as a secondary mitigation, once it was found that swallows were not returning to nest under the new Dashwood Bridge.

The structure itself is much smaller than those I've familiarized myself with in Vista Hills; it sits on two six-by-six pressure-treated spruce posts with angled wood two-by-four braces acting as post supports on the shoulder embankment of the highway, which gives the whole structure the look of a lean-to. On the underside of the structure, there are no nesting cups, but four small two-by-fours act as nesting ledges to try to attract swallows. This structure has no metal predator guards surrounding its posts, though it shares other architectural features with the Vista Hills structures. However, as I observe in both April and late May, its design really doesn't matter: there are no swallow nests built inside, nor prospecting barn swallows in the vicinity throughout my spring visits, despite

Fig. 2 | Dashwood Bridge barn swallow mitigation structure. Photo: author.

what seems to my uninitiated eye to be prime habitat: water, bank mud, and thanks to being bitten by a black fly, I know there are also plenty of insects. There are a few small sparrow nests on the ground, having blown out of the structure at some point, and one sparrow nest tucked into the southwest corner of the structure itself. In short, despite engaging the house sparrows, the swallows have refused this particular mitigation, twice: once in the form of the new bridge, and a second time in refusing the mitigation structure.

While the swallows have refused this structure, their absence is nonetheless tied to its erection, and they are thereby implicated in how this structure has both emerged and functions on the landscape. So, too, are human beings. When I first encounter the structure in April, workers are hosing down the bridge, which slows traffic to a few miles per hour. As I sit and take notes at the base of the structure, a red truck stops and rolls its passenger window down, and a woman calls out to me. "Excuse me," she says. Pointing at the structure, she asks, "Do you know what that is?" I tell her it's a barn swallow structure, and she thanks me while repeating what I've said to the driver. While I feel like I've done my Good Samaritan duty for the day, this exchange also fortifies what I've felt from the beginning of the project: that despite human conservation's best efforts to appeal to birds, we continue to fail. And we also fail other members of the human public that might also have a stake and role in similar conservation efforts.

Now, there is no mandate from the OMNRF to label or otherwise translate what kind of ecological entanglement a mitigation structure has with humans on the often-Anthropocenic landscapes on which they appear—no requirement for signage or even a government logo. Of course, such indications would likely be moot, given that the large majority of barn swallow structures in the province appear alongside Highway 401, the busiest highway in the world. The stretch of 401 that runs from London to Windsor, where the majority of obvious structures stand, is known as "Carnage Alley" for the number of multicar crashes and fatalities that happen along that length of road. While the structures have made it into the news (CBC News 2016), they are otherwise publicly rather inaccessible. In short, under very few circumstances can humans—always, in these cases, as drivers—engage their curiosities about mitigation structures, since they emerge most often at the side of heavily used roadways.

For some species at risk who do not choose to nest around humans, this lack of human engagement might perhaps make a promising preservation of undisturbed "habitat"; yet for swallows, who are used to (and seemingly prefer) human buildings in use, this does not otherwise improve structures' uptake by birds. While the structures themselves stand as a kind of monument of pursuit via a human urge to control swallows' habitat, they are not generally successful, nor accessible to either humans or swallows, making them a strange Other—and failure—on most landscapes. In the case of unused structures, as the

Dashwood Bridge structure models, I'd like to examine swallows' refusal as a challenge to the proposition for use that the structures invite. Here, these structures exert an *alloiostrophic* force by, in Sutton and Mifsud's (2012) words, failing to "secure assent" from the Other (228). Such refusal both invites a different rhetorical capacity of the structure—as an object of swallow refusal and human curiosity—as well as challenges the anthropocentric move in rhetorical posthuman and new material thought that suggests that humans are the only species who get to respond to conservation action, while nonhumans' only option is to withdraw.

This argument is taken up by Daniel A. Cryer's (2018) "Withdrawal Without Retreat: Responsible Conservation in a Doomed Age," in which he tries to rectify the gap between rhetorical new material theory forwarded by Thomas Rickert (2013) and Nathaniel Rivers (2015) and responsible conservation action that determines the line "between responsible intervention and irresponsible overreach" of human control over nonhuman actors (Cryer, 2018, 464). Conceptually, Cryer critiques the notion of nonhuman withdrawal, used by both Rickert and Rivers. Rickert (2013) uses a Heideggerian notion of the fourfold with which to frame withdrawal, and Rivers (2015) draws on object-oriented ontological (OOO) and new material frameworks of Levi Bryant, Ian Bogost, Timothy Morton, Graham Harman, and Jane Bennett to note that whether inanimate or animate, all objects and things "withdraw from other things in the world" (Barnett quoted in Rivers 2015, 423). On the one hand, Cryer (2018) acknowledges the importance and value of the power of nonhuman withdrawal, as advocated by Rickert. On the other, he contends that the notion of withdrawal—"the idea that all objects and lives, human and nonhuman, recede from our full grasp no matter how deeply we try to know them"—is best used as a lens through which we might read environmental texts rather than a way of "critiquing mainstream environmental discourse" (460).

In part, Cryer holds this view as a result of Rivers's (2015) argument that acknowledging that nature is not separate from culture while at the same time valuing nature as a peculiar kind of other requires a degree of human ability to see nature both ways, or what Rivers terms "deep ambivalence." Without this ability, Rivers argues, humans exist in a reductive contradiction, whether as an exploiter of natural resources or an environmentalist. Both sides, Rivers suggests, cast human beings as overly controlling and hubristic when it comes to nature. Cryer, on the other hand, suggests that there is more nuance in between these actions, even if the forwarding of solutions by environmentalists give us "the best among a series of wrong choices" (2018, 465). He suggests listening more closely to nature in order to determine what messages the physicality of objects offer, drawing from Bruno Latour's idea that nonhumans are "propositions" to the collective in any assemblage of human and nonhuman actors (466). Here, Cryer pauses to make what I see as an arguable distinction between humans and nonhumans in any rhetorical ecological entanglement: he suggests that "ultimately it is humans, in all their incomplete knowledge who must listen and decide" to the propositions forwarded by nonhumans (466). While Cryer recognizes this anthropocentrism, he nonetheless suggests that the onus of the propositions of the Anthropocene is on humans to respond to them, for, he says "*response-ability can never be reciprocal. The obligation to respond will always be on humans and never on nonhumans*" (467, emphasis in original).

I'd like to pause for a moment here to examine the case of the Dashwood Bridge structure, both in terms of the proposition the structure makes to both humans and swallows in this rhetorical ecology, and the primary response of refusal that the swallows make to such a proposition. While it might be said, following in the footsteps of Rivers's use of OOO scholars, that each of these nonhuman others withdraw from human imaginations to truly know them, it is also true that although human-made, the structures themselves shift the "obligation to respond" from humans to nonhumans. Once the structures have been constructed, not only does the choice of response move outside the control of human intervention, but the engagement of barn swallows with the structures themselves constitutes a nonhuman decision that will lead to another kind of entanglement—the turning of the structure into, for example, a nesting place, or allowing the structure, by refusal, to remain an object of human curiosity. In this way, the absence of swallow bodies on both the underside of the new Dashwood Bridge and the mitigation structure nearby, brought about not necessarily by population decline but by refusal of human-made habitat substitutions, represent a challenge to Cryer's assertion that humans bear the sole obligation to respond in such a rhetorical situation, that the "one-way responsibility is the ineradicable 'bold line'" (467) between humans and nonhumans.

I would argue that the one-way conceptualization of the responsibility between humans and nonhumans is less a failure of human imagination than a failure of Eurowestern philosophy to guide an approach for human-nonhuman interaction. As Leanne Betasamosake Simpson (2021) articulates in *A Short History of the Blockade*, Michi Saagiig Nishnaabeg people, among others, are quite comfortable living in reciprocity with nonhumans, recognizing that obligation—and infrastructure—is a two-way street. Comparing the generative nature of both beaver dams and blockades in relaying Anishinaabe stories of the beaver (*amik*), Simpson relays Kagige / Forever-Bird (John) Pinesi's 1919 telling of the story of the woman who married a beaver.[4] The story conveys the reciprocal relationship between the Anishinaabe people and the beaver by acknowledging the role each plays in maintaining a balanced relationship: the beaver may choose to give itself to the people so that they may be warm and fed, and in exchange, the people must offer human gifts to the beaver, give thanks via ceremonies, and return its bones to the water.

As White (B. White 1999) notes, the beaver story is not just a story, and Pinesi's retelling to a white outsider may have had its own aims of informing a settler about the reciprocal relations that Anishinaabeg expected with all their relations, including settlers. White (1999) acknowledges the following about the story of the woman who married a beaver: "Without gifts and respect, animals would not be so helpful to humans. They would hold themselves back and not allow themselves to be used by people. Without gifts and respect, the system would cease to function" (111). The beaver story changes, to use Cryer's (2018) terms, the "propositions of the [A]nthropocene" (467). It suggests that should the beaver refuse to play along—withhold its body—that the results will be disastrous for humans. The beaver's very presence in the lives of the Anishinaabe is an acceptance of a kind of proposition, as is the Anishinaabe's promise to care for the beaver, not only through gift giving, but through the preservation of habitat.

In the beaver story, beavers have the agency to "listen and decide" (466). If we imagine, for a moment, extending that same kind of capacity to barn swallows, to imagine that they are listening, gauging, and, finding new human-made structures wanting, *deciding* to refuse human-based control, this at once changes the nature of human-nonhuman relation decried by Cryer as one-way. Swallows' absent bodies *are* a response, constitute a decision. And without swallow bodies, humans are faced with a different and ongoing set of challenges about living in a world without swallows, a different set of propositions altogether. Humans themselves become removed from relation as their own capacity to respond becomes limited to that of the curious bystander and observer of something beyond their control. In this way, each element in this rhetorical ecology—swallow, structure, human, bridge, watershed, flora, fauna, season—has a degree of response-ability that, depending on flows and processes of movement, affects the relations with others around it. Here, the decision is not between human intervention and human overreach. Instead, the capacities for decision-making are relational. An unused structure gives humans another proposition of failure while still, as the red truck drive-by suggests, encouraging us to engage with potentials from unlikely to likely.

Finally, we may read swallows refusal beyond withdrawal as something that preserves the strange affirmatively, to use Braidotti's (2019) suggestion. To allow for their refusal as a form of listening to us suggests, in turn, that we have to listen more closely to them, allow their bodies, like the beaver, to tell us the stories we have ignored. This kind of listening not only attends to the physicality of animal and thing bodies on landscapes, but it also sees them as bound together in a way that suggests that the human proposition is not *if you build it, they will come*. Instead, it is *the system has ceased to function*. It suggests a proposition of caring for the commonplaces underneath and around the infrastructure—the water, the air, the soil—that grounds the coming-to in a collective, reciprocal ethics. Listening differently, waiting for response, moves us beyond the box that withdrawal-as-default places around nonhuman others and perhaps points us to other, better ways of worldmaking that Eurowestern philosophy has long forgotten. It encourages us to turn otherwise, and, to invoke Simpson (2021), to give and receive different gifts. Until that proposition is accepted by humans, we will perhaps have only a limited capacity to creatively respond to species' absence.

Townsend Road: When Structures Shimmer

Driving to Townsend Road sounds much like the name implies: close to the junction between Highway 74 and Highway 3, neither of which are more than one lane in both directions, the road is little more than a connector between the small towns of Townsend and Jarvis. This, too, is Treaty 3 territory, land of the Mississauga, who ceded three million acres of their land to the British crown in the "between the lakes" treaty, land that runs from Lake Ontario to Lake Erie. The Townsend Road structures are a fifteen-minute drive to the shores of Lake Erie, a twenty-minute drive from the Six Nations Reserve, and thirty minutes away from the heart of one of Canada's most heated land disputes in Caledonia, Ontario. In Caledonia, Six Nations people dispute the confused claims of the Haldimand Treaty and protest, through blockades and occupation of a site they have addressed as 1492 Land Back Lane, the building of a new subdivision on McKenzie Road (APTN News 2020). By all accounts, McKenzie Road will look rather like Vista Hills when complete. Land Back Lane echoes the origin of O:se Kenhionhata:tie's English name, Land Back Camp. Their name choice gestures to the "Land Back" movement, one that is spreading across North America, everywhere from Seattle to Massachusetts in the United States, and from British Columbia to Nova Scotia in Canada, prompted by Indigenous-led resistance coalitions like Idle No More. As Ronald Gamblin, a coordinator for the 4Rs Youth movement explains of land back alliances for Indigenous people, "It's about fighting for the right to our relationship with the earth." (Gamblin n.d.) The occupation of 1492 Land Back Lane is yet another instance of what Naomi Klein has termed "Blockadia" (2014), a "new paradigm in mainstream North American environmentalism" (Chen 2021), in which the focus of interrupting extractive and exploitive development—often serving the fossil fuel industry—falls on humans' willingness to bodily occupy spaces while pursuing legal stoppage of industrial action. In effect, blockadian efforts, whether represented on access roads or highways (as the Wet'suwet'en road blockade or the blockage of highway 16A to Mount Rushmore), or farm fields (as Ponka corn planted in the way of the Keystone XL Pipeline) change the nature of the land on which they occupy, positioning attention differently, and focusing means of persuasion directly on bodies.

I'm thinking about this pivot in mainstream environmentalism as I pull over to the side of the two-lane road, having first driven through a parking lot of an elder-care facility, which is the only development around for miles. The two Townsend Road structures sit close to the road, surrounded on all sides by farm fields in various states of muddy spring disarray when I first visit them in April. These structures are the biggest I've seen at sixteen by four feet, easily twelve feet high, and each has sixteen nesting cups and ledges for potential swallows to nest (see fig. 3). The structures are not identical, though they have the same cone-shaped metal predator guards and shingled roofline. One has about a foot of wraparound plywood extending from the roofline, while the other has at least four-foot plywood "walls" extending from its roof, complete with a square "window" on the long side and a round hole similarly cut in the short side. I spend a few moments wondering why on earth someone would bother cutting these holes, as they have not appeared on any ministry-mandated plans I've seen. I find out later that the structures have been built as part of a mitigation plan surrounding the demolition of an old barn in the town nearby but twinned as part of a 2015–17 study by Bird Ecology and Conservation Ontario and Bird Studies Canada to find out whether or not playing swallow sound-cues and offering swallow decoys attract the birds to the structures—like the Vista Hills structures, one structure was rigged with sound and decoys, and one was used as a control (BECO 2015).

It's a cold, clear day on my first visit, and I try to imagine what might attract swallows to the area. I see that the tilled cropland would offer foraging opportunity, and nearby runs Nanticoke Creek, where swallows might find a source of

Fig. 3 | Townsend Road structures. Photo: author.

mud. As I walk under each structure, neck craned up to the ceilings, I see the first real evidence of swallows since the project began: mud nests, some half-built, some fully formed, in many of the nesting cups and ledges. A few nests hang on in the tiny cross-beams of the structures, and guano has collected on one of the metal cones. While April is still too cold for migrating swallows, I allow myself a moment of hope: maybe these swallows will return.

It is when I return in late May to observe these structures that it seems like the whole scene has shifted: the dun-colored field stubble has given way to knee-high grass; the air is thick with insect humming, and bird calls are so numerous I can only parse out a blackbird from the rest of a chirping cacophony. When I get out of the car, I know something has changed. Instead of the usual stock-still structures, there are over a dozen red-and-blue bodies flying around, into, and nearby the structures. The sounds that the swallows make are much more complex than the "*veet-veet*" I have come to recognize: there are trills, warbles, and chirrups that echo loudly from inside the structures as I watch from yards away. For the first time I note the electric lines and poles that run alongside the road that were simply a part of the background in April but are now a

Fig. 4 | Townsend Road structure (with swallows). Note one swallow flying into the round window and another silhouetted against the left front support post. Photo: author.

perch for a half-dozen swallows as they intermittently rest before flying off again (see fig. 4).

As I wander underneath the structures and look up, this time I see nests-in-progress being built, a variegated line between yesterday's (or last year's) dried mud and today's wet mud, added flight return by flight return from Nanticoke

Creek. I think about this nestwork, all the swallows I see, between nine and fifteen at any given moment, and how swallow pairs work collaboratively, sometimes even with junior fledglings, to build their nests so quickly in spring. I think about how in a few weeks, there will be eggs; in a month, fully fledged young. By the end of July, these nests will be empty again. Bird time here is quick, attentive, and fleeting. I think about swallow spaces, swallow time: how different these structures seem now that they are teeming with fork-tailed birds; how elementary, watching them flit in and out of the window holes cut into the walls, such a design is, as it so closely mimics derelict barn windows, long devoid of glass. I think about how swallow bodies have defamiliarized these structures that have become so familiar to me over time. While I know that the success of these structures is an anomaly, my being here during this time as a human witness on these nonhuman affairs makes me think of this entanglement as also an encounter, characterized by its motion, its liveliness, its time and season, its place, and its new propositions.

As I sit, captivated by swallows, two children who I assume are brothers, one around ten and the other around sixteen, ride by on their bikes. Amid the loud clicks and chatter and zooming of the swallows, the younger says aloud to the older of the cacophony, pointing at the structures. "See those?" he says. "They are for birds." The older gives a nod and a minimal response—"Oh?"—and the younger continues. "Yes. See? But only those kinds of birds." I realize then that the swallows' use of the structures and their teeming, careening presence does something else, something to captivate human attention that isn't just my own. To listen to a boy explain these structures to his brother hints at how they function to move from confusion to a curiosity momentarily beyond the human. It temporarily moves all of us beyond "anthropocentric thought" and perhaps beyond our own arrogance about our relations to these species (Braidotti 2019, 388). The swallows' *presence* offers everyone who may witness them an awareness situated in being, a kind of lesson. A lesson about habitat, about the differentiation of swallows from others, about what counts as home, about what kind of relationship we have with the earth.

To frame the Townsend Road structures, I turn to Deborah Bird Rose's (2017) notion of "shimmer," which she borrows from Howard Murphy's anthropological work with the Yolngu people in North Australia. The Yolngu term, *bir'yun*, which translates as "brilliance" or "shimmer," denotes an aesthetic shift in art between what is roughly sketched and what is brought into brilliance by detail that adds a sense of motion, "much in the way that the eye is captured by sun glinting on water" (Rose 2017, G53). To experience shimmer, then, is not just to notice an aesthetic shift but also to be "enraptured" by an ephemeral moment, to be lured into beauty in a surprising but utterly captivating way (G53). As Rose notes of *bir'yun*, to be caught up in shimmer, for the Yolngu (and for Rose, who was adopted by the Flying Fox people) is also to tune into ancestral power through tuning into "ecological pulses" emergent through perceptions of both dull and brilliant (G54). Given that my own ancestors lie somewhere between Butte, Montana, and Wales, I wouldn't assume to try to locate or import Bird's notion of ancestral power into this experience; however, the notion of shimmer is one that helps characterize the part that extinction and absence—or differentiated presence—play in one's capacity to encounter it. As Bird notes, humans must be aware of the transition from dull to shimmer and back in order to attune themselves to the cyclical relations of the earth and our nonhuman kin. "For shimmer to capture the eye," she argues, "there must be an absence of shimmer. To understand how absence brings forth, it must be understood not as lack but as potential" (G54–55).

The Townsend Road structures were transformed in latter site visits by the addition of the swallows' movement, purpose, and flight as they met with and changed the structures' physical being—in short, the structures began to shimmer. My early visits, and indeed, my experiences with the Vista Hills and Dashwood Bridge structures, gave me much to contemplate about the role these structures play on the landscape, with birds, and with humans. My field notes are filled with the usual rote notes of weather, temperature, nesting cup count, building description, and remarks on other flora and fauna. Yet compared to watching a dozen birds fly and build around the two Townsend structures, the structures I encountered without them now seemed dull. I am reminded of the jump in my belly at the prospecting swallows in Vista Hills, how the absence of nests but the presence of curious swallows casted this absence as potential, rather than lack. Yet to see swallows' presence doesn't enliven only the structures; I am caught seeing everything around me newly. The nondescript flying bugs that I've been swatting at, I realize, are the source of the swallows' erratic flight patterns as they grab a beakful of insects; the electric lines near the road have shifted into perches; the nearby creek and its mud banks are invoked as building materials, even though I cannot see them. The occupation of swallow bodies in this structure has changed the landscape. The scene has shifted through the swallows, and with it, my attention.

Even as I know that the Townsend structures' "success" in attracting swallows is a nonexistent blip in the larger scheme of insect decline, habitat loss, and climate change, I cannot help but feel a shift in my own awareness, my own feeling, for swallows—*only those kinds of birds.* The discourses underscoring the kinds of knowing subjects on the scene suddenly shift from planning and mitigation, success and failure, to shimmer, rapture, captivation—maybe even crazy love. As my rational mind recognized the miniscule impact these strange structures were having on barn swallow populations, my affectual one still changed, from curiosity to something else, a different kind of attunement to this particular rhetorical ecology. In returning to Townsend Road, I was aware of the structures as both dull and brilliant; I glimpsed their shimmer on the landscape as they engaged with swallows—they became at once more functional and also more strange. The structures, with this shimmer, became something else, turned otherwise toward possibility, the possibility that proximity to nonhuman others offers to human attentions. As Jan Zwicky reminds us in *Learning to Die: Wisdom in the Age of Climate Crisis* (2018), "Awareness reforms desire; or rather, it allows other desires—for the well-being of others, nonhuman and human—to become immediate and powerful. . . . We actively desire the health of the ecological community to which we belong. We want to do what it takes to be at home" (56).

Swallow bodies in the Townsend structures mark both futility and hope. They change desire and focus attention differently, toward an opening, toward curiosity. They allow a holding of both "growth and extinction" in our minds at the same time (Braidotti 2019, 38). Whether for me, for a ten-year-old child, or for scientists who study the "success" of these particular structures, the swallows engaging with them marks a gesture of nearing, of proximity, even as it reminds us all that the reason that this display exists at all is because of intentional human destruction of ecosystems, every Vista Hills or McKenzie Road. It is a push-pull to be invited into the swallow-structure proposition, a bringing together while letting go. Seeing the birds is an invocation of human desire, a desire to be closer, to consider human roles in stewardship, to gather lessons from the land, to imagine both swallows and structures as *interlocutors* in a rhetorical ecology (Cryer 2018, 476). It is a reminder that to *do what it takes to be at home* requires a completely different set of skills in thinking through conservation that must begin with both human and nonhuman equality: who is human *here*, who is human *now*? To answer those questions as part of an affirmative, posthuman project is to answer, learning from those who protect the water and the land, to hold the strange present gently, "holding open without reconciling" (Minche-de Leon 2020, 207). Who is concerned enough for this land to move beyond occupation and toward care? The swallows and their structures, with

their differentiated presence across the landscape, tell the stories of broken treaties, unchecked development, and capitalism through their bodies. Swallows'
choices of selection or refusal, nestwork or seeking, abandonment or return,
charge the Anthropocene. We might listen to what is being said by shifting our
own rhetorical capacity: allowing ourselves to be moved by what appears, allowing ourselves to turn otherwise, seeking better relations. We might follow their
cues by attending to the notion of precarity, which is both theirs and our own.

2

Chimney Swift | Building Precarity with Fake Chimneys

It is dusk in late September in London, Ontario, and I am sitting on the sidewalk at the corner of Grey and Richmond Streets. After spending the summer traveling to find seven of nineteen empty artificial chimneys and swift towers in the southern part of the province, I am hoping for a last glimpse of roosting chimney swifts that have been reported to settle in the Labatt Brewery chimney from the spring to late fall. While the brewery has stood since 1828, the neighborhood is a bit forgotten, and the ambient urban sounds of night falling are all around: sirens, traffic, music from pedestrians' pocket devices, phlegmy coughs of neighbors out on their apartment balconies enjoying the best of a balmy autumn evening. As the sun sets, some young people come out to have a cigarette on their porch and we strike up a conversation, as their backyard has a clear view of the three-story, round brick chimney beyond the twelve-foot fencing that surrounds the brewery's industrial complex. I ask them if they've ever seen birds fly into the chimney in the evening, around sunset. They say that in midsummer they saw and heard bats go into the chimney around dusk, and I realize by the way that they are describing the behavior of flying creatures that they've seen chimney swifts. I thank them for the conversation and continue to wait as the night grows darker and cooler, my anticipation upon arrival settling into the disappointing realization that I am too late in the season. The swifts are gone, if they were ever there.

In trying to spot chimney swifts, I tell here a particular story of desire and attunement. Over the course of writing this book, I have gone from a person who would not know a chimney swift from a song sparrow or blackbird to a researcher of their habits, habitat, and natural history. In collecting textual evidence of both their presence and disappearance on landscapes, I have realized that the real story of chimney swifts is a complicated one, predicated on their shadowy, secretive existence emerging commensally with urban development. Their Latin name speaks to both their looks and mystery, *Chaetura* for "bristly" or "spiny tail," and *pelagica*, which translates to "of the sea" but is thought to refer instead to the nomadic Pelasgi Greeks, underscoring chimney swifts' enigmatic and dynamic behavior. Unlike barn swallows, which still seem for most living in North America to be "common," flying around by day and into still-available rural areas to nest in barns and other structures, chimney swifts by their very design are elusive. Although also an aerial insectivore, swifts are in the *Apodidae*—or "feetless"—family of birds, with legs so short that they cannot perch or walk on horizontal surfaces like other birds. Instead, swifts spend their entire lives in flight, stopping only to rest vertically on the dark hidden insides of columnar structures with appropriately rough surfaces for traction. In Anishinaabemowin, the chimney swift is known as *memitigoningwegaaneshiinh* (literally, "feathered tree wren") or *mizaatigoningwiisii*. *Mizaatigoningwiisii* ("sewing wing/feather" bird) in particular, is a descriptor of chimney swifts' unique biology. Biologist and coordinator for Nature London Brendon Samuels notes that the etymology of *mizaatigoningwiisii* is likely "attributable to the shape of the chimney swift's tail feathers. The tips of the rectrices (tail feathers) are rather spinose; part of the shaft of the contour feather is prolonged distally without barbs. This gives the feathers the appearance of having needle points at the end—hence the relation to sewing" (personal communication). I would venture to guess that for most of us, reading this book will be as close to a chimney swift as we will likely ever get. In other words, swifts, more than swallows, suffer from a kind of absenting presence, given their chosen habitat of the inside of tall, dark human-made columns when they are not in constant flight.

From the very first sightings of swifts, humans have thought they were something else—swallows, martins, bats. Even today, the Vaux's swift (*Chaetura vauxi*), a western aerial insectivore that is not currently listed as endangered by any international body, is often mistaken for the chimney swift, who migrates in the east and is listed as near threatened on the International Union for Conservation of Nature's (IUCN's) Red List and threatened on SARA. Such confusion has so surrounded exactly what kind of bird chimney swifts are that until 1886, when an account of the swift was published in *The Code of Nomenclature and Check-List of North American Birds*, it was known by a variety of other names and given two separate Latin names. At first thought to be another kind of swallow, the chimney swift was known interchangeably as a house swallow, chimney swallow, aculeated swallow, chimney-bird, diveling, American spine tail, and American swift (Graves 2004, 303–4). Those first records of experiences emerge steeped in the fact that, via the decimation and clear-cutting of millions of acres of forests by European settlers to the Americas, chimney swifts became visible through their adaptation to urban sites by being forced from their originary habitat. As one of the earliest ornithological accounts of swifts naively states in its observations in 1776, "It is a natural question to ask: where did the swallows build their nests before the Europeans came and made houses with chimneys? It is probably that they formerly made them in great hollow trees" (Graves 2004, 303). While this account is correct, it also overlooks that what made chimney swifts visible to Eurowestern humans was their synonymous "emergence" with colonization. It was European colonization of North America that led to a nearly 100 percent overhaul in swifts' breeding ecology. As Graves (2004, 300) observes, between 1672 and the late eighteenth century—in fewer than 150 years—chimney swifts, forced out of forest habitats, opted to nest exclusively in human-built structures, preferring instead historic columns built of roughly textured substrates, whether chimneys, silos, air shafts, tobacco sheds, wells, or concrete sewer pipes (COSEWIC 2018, 11). Today, there are fewer than two dozen known cases of chimney swifts roosting in trees in North America, to the point that when such behavior is noted, it is a cause for observation and scholarship (Graves 2004; see Hines, Bader, and Graves 2013). In other words, chimney swifts' commensality with humans uniquely coincides with colonization. Or to think about it another way, *Chaetura pelagica*, the "spiny tails of the sea" or "bristly tailed nomad" or "sewing wing/feather" bird *became* chimney swifts, became real to Eurowestern humans, during the act of colonization. Now, as they face imminent decline—over 90 percent in Canada since 1970 and 53 percent in the United States—humans are forced to contend with a different kind of absenting that colonization without consent makes present.

While we may consider acts of conservation and built mitigations specific kinds of hopeful activities, much as my waiting on a London sidewalk for swifts to appear might be, we also must contend with the creation of precarious subjectivity that such mitigations construct. As Kathryn Yusoff argues, "Subjectivity declared through precarity prepares an ontological field for the subject in which dependence is already inscripted in the material conditions of emergence; the orangutan declared in the midst of deforestation is already an abandoned being. Its presence, its proximity, is a preparation for death" (2012, 586). Thus, it is the precarious nonhuman subject, the *chimney swift*, who gets constructed as rare through human action. This happens in acts of deforestation, the building of urban environments, and the subsequent construction of fake chimney towers. Humans are then forced to reckon with not only our own hopefulness, or curiosity, or desire for proximity, or *alloiostrophic* relations with difference but also the complexities of human violence on nonhuman coopted subjects. In constructing swifts' precarity as dependent on human relations, we are forced to reckon with even their fleeting presence as loss. This chapter examines a number of field sites of both chimney swift mitigation measures and already-existing chimneys as particular material arguments about constructing hope and holding species loss close, making loss and grief visible in particular ways. It also examines the ways that in this strange present, chimney swifts attune us to time, storying the Anthropocene and its violence through their bodies.

Failure and Ambivalence: Material Arguments of Swift Towers

As an aerial insectivore, the reasons for decline in chimney swift populations are much the same as that of the barn swallow: human development, pollution, severe weather and climate change, and declines in insect biomass (COSEWIC 2018). What stands out in the case of chimney swift decline is its close connection to human urban development; unlike primarily rural-dwelling barn swallows, chimney swifts are even pickier about which structures they might choose to either nest or roost within. There is a difference between nesting and roosting; the black-bodied cigar-shaped birds arrive to North America en masse in late April and gather together to roost in large groups (usually in large chimneys) to stay warm and find mates. They later break off into breeding pairs to nest throughout the summer, at which point each nesting pair will claim its own, independent chimney. Roosting sites are different from nesting sites, and both are significant habitat for the birds. Because chimney swifts settle so closely to urban humans, habitat disturbance and intrusion are listed as primary reasons for their decline (COSEWIC 2018, v). This might take the form of, in some cases, development and demolition of historic buildings. In others, it might take the form of capping chimneys to keep birds and other critters out of them. In still others such disturbance is the common fault of property owners or chimney sweeps—although the birds nest in summers when chimneys are not usually in use, they may be disturbed either by the occasional off-season fire or seen as a fire risk and nuisance and destroyed if caught nesting in warmer months by chimney sweeps. Too, the changeover from fireplace to electric heat in the last century means there are far fewer chimneys that exist for swifts to nest in, and those that do often have been upgraded with interior metal liners that dissuade the birds, are too small (smaller than twelve inches when the birds prefer at least twenty inches), or have been capped.

Because of their primary choices of chimneys in which to roost and nest, chimney swifts are also far more likely to be exposed to contaminants and pollutants than other birds. Similarly, temperature fluctuations inside chimneys represent a threat to the success of their nesting behaviors; below 55 degrees Fahrenheit, the birds will abandon nests, and above 108 degrees, nestlings will perish. As such, chimney swifts most prefer chimneys that are connected to an internal source of warmth, like a basement, to modulate the internal temperature of the stack itself (11). Like barn swallows, chimney swifts show extreme site fidelity and return to nest in the same places year after year. In other words, chimney swifts are demanding about where they roost and nest: they prefer tall stacks that extend upwards of nine feet above a roofline and have an internal area of about three square feet, making nonresidential chimneys their pick beyond smaller residential chimneys. They also want to return to the same chimney each year. Thus, the place one might find the contemporary chimney swift tends to be in large, older (usually nineteenth century) chimneys attached to factories, schools, and churches, like the Labatt Brewery chimney that opens this chapter. Other well-known roosting sites in Ontario are located in urban centers, such as Toronto's Moss Park Armoury, and Pembroke's Memorial Centre Arena.

Despite the fact that chimney swifts are so choosy about their roosting and nesting habitat (that is, a chimney does not guarantee a chimney swift), nonetheless such structures are what SARA targets as critical habitat regarding the swifts. To that end, Birds Canada suggests that the preferred methods for habitat preservation are first, to retain original habitat; that is, not to demolish historic buildings and chimneys at all, or to allow for the demolition of buildings but leave chimneys to stand alone. The second option is to leave habitat unmodified by not capping existing chimneys or removing existing caps and instead installing a rain cap (which lets birds access openings in the stack). In the case of modifying or upgrading heating systems, they also suggest leaving old chimneys attached to original structures while building a second metal chimney to serve as a heat-venting source (Hiebert 2020). It is only when those options are not feasible that the suggestion of artificial habitat and infrastructural mitigation is raised: either building an artificial chimney onto a building that has had its chimney demolished or otherwise modified, or building a freestanding artificial swift tower not attached to a building.

Both artificial chimneys and freestanding towers in Ontario have been mod-
eled after successful American versions put forward by Paul and Georgean Kyle,
self-taught swift conservationists who donated ten acres of property to become
the Travis Audubon Chaetura Canyon Bird Sanctuary. The couple literally wrote
the book on how to construct swift towers (Kyle and Kyle 2005), building seventy towers in the Austin area where they live, which have had remarkable success in attracting nesting swifts. Their designs have spurred the building of over
179 towers in the United States and Canada (Graham 2011). However, the simple
act of exporting a tower design has not traveled well across country borders; in
Canada they are generally failures. Across Canada, both artificial chimneys and
freestanding towers have been built to try to attract chimney swifts; however,
only ten known structures have attracted swifts across the country (two roosts in
New Brunswick and Quebec, and eight nesting sites: one in Manitoba, one in
Ontario, and six in Quebec) (Bumelis 2021, personal communication). Experts
infer that it is the colder weather and the fluctuations in internal tower temperatures that result in so much more success in the United States than in Canadian
towers. Nonetheless, both artificial chimneys and freestanding towers continue
to be built as mitigations for the destruction of habitat.

Some of these mitigations have educational functions, as a stand-alone
wooden tower in the Willow Park Ecology Centre in Norval, Ontario, does,
which has signage attached to the tower that informs visitors about swifts and
their life cycles. Another recently built masonry tower was created as a $125,000
addition to a planned elementary school rebuild in Toronto (Bell and Rynard
2021). Despite humans' best intentions in these two cases, neither artificial structure has been occupied by roosting or nesting swifts, though often when new
towers are built they are given quite a bit of hopeful press (Sheikh 2019). This
offers quite the conundrum: where mitigations are the most successful (in the
southern United States), chimney swifts are not listed as a threatened species
and are generally more abundant. Where the mitigations are needed (in the birds'
northern migration routes where they are listed as threatened), they are not used
and are generally considered failures (Finity and Nocera 2012). Yet structures
continue to act as mitigations in the case of habitat destruction. It seems that in
Canada, the propositions that these unused structures are making only ever
result in one answer by chimney swifts, despite their varied approaches in man-
ufacture and location by humans.

It's difficult to say exactly what unused structures signify on these primarily
urban landscapes. Like barn swallow structures, they stand out as a strange

other on a landscape—either a double chimney on a building or a stand-alone stack in the middle of an urban cityscape. Occasionally, like swallow structures, they invite some prospecting behaviors from swifts (Finity and Nocera 2012); however, swifts are far less likely than barn swallows to use the structures built for them. Because the failure of swift towers exists on a much grander scale, the proposition of their emergence on landscapes moves beyond the agentive right-to-refusal of the barn swallow. These structures have far more symbolic potential for humans than true utility for chimney swifts. They function instead as a kind of desire-object that organizes behavior and feeling—as Lauren Berlant would say, such towers offer "a cluster of promises we want someone or something to make to us and make possible for us" (2011, 23).

In *Cruel Optimism*, Berlant (2011) suggests that optimism becomes cruel when objects of attachment promote ways of being that are unsustainable and damaging, but nonetheless artificially promising and affirming. Artificial swift towers are such objects because they sit somewhere between memorial and monument, somewhere between hope and despair. Given the 90 percent decline of chimney swifts in Canada over the last fifty years, each artificial chimney or stand-alone tower might symbolically stand in as a collective grave marker, or at least a place for "material solemnizing" for chimney swifts (Blair 2001, 279). Yet unlike true memorials, they resist what is necessary for mourning such loss because they avoid what public memorials do: give space and names for those deemed lost, missing, or unrecoverable (Blair 2001). The artificial swift constructions also resist a transparent semiotic monumentalizing; as Krzyżanowska (2016) notes, monuments exist as a "traditional carrier of collective memory in the material space of the city" (467). Without swifts to fill them, such towers have no referring subject to value, turn to, or commemorate—yet they are still objects representing this desire. Most monuments, reflecting "cultural, historical, and artistic values," provide a public opportunity to justify those values through the "conservation and maintenance" of such objects (467). Artificial chimney swift structures may occasionally garner public celebration when they are first built. However, they are often not only oddly nondescript, but they also fall into disrepair after the three- to five-year monitoring period passes without swift inhabitants and are often torn down or left to disintegrate. They may give lip service to conservation, but ornithological research suggests otherwise. They instead sit as structures of ambivalent attunement. In some cases, they continue the fantasy of the environmental "fix"; in others they allow humans to bear the disappointment of biodiversity loss; in still others they invite us to closely listen to bird bodies in their complete absence. As you will read in this chapter, in some cases, swift structures can hold steady a middle capacity to rearticulate human-nonhuman relations embodied in Braidotti's (2019) notion of knowing subjects—between nature and technology, present and past.

I'd like to frame the mitigative approach to chimney swifts' precarity—the building of artificial structures—as an ambivalent way of attuning humans to loss even while swifts' bodies provide another narrative. In the three cases of artificial structures that follow, I argue that these mitigations are complex sites of competing public narratives about loss and the present, as well as loss in the future. In their ineffectuality, they juggle the tensions of visibility and invisibility. Through their durability, preservation, reproduction, and proximity to other texts and landscapes, they constitute a peculiar addition to rhetorical ecologies of humans, nonhumans, and things. They offer paths to monumentalize loss, to embody and make visible human grief through hope-practices, and to story nonhuman narratives about species disappearance. I close with a final discussion of a currently occupied roost chimney on the site of a nuclear reactor as an object of cruel optimism, an anthropogenic site of attunement to both absence and presence that turns to Yusoff's question of biodiversity loss, violence, and colonization: "How do understandings of presence and making present those that are dead or soon to be dead mark the possibilities of both mourning and relating?" (2012, 579).

The Mississauga Tower: A Quasi-Monument

Mississauga, Ontario, is a city that rests on the outskirts of Toronto proper. Unless you are paying very close attention, there is very little indication of the marker between the suburbs of Mississauga and the sprawl that spreads out from the Toronto airport along Highway 401. Mississauga is bordered by the Credit River on Treaty 14 territory, the "Head of the Lakes" purchase in which the Mississaugas of the Credit First Nation (or MCFN, one of six Mississauga nations) ceded over seventy thousand acres of land to the British crown in exchange for roughly £1,000 in trade goods. The Mississauga, or in Anishinaabemowin *Missisakis* ("many river mouths"), were seasonal travelers on their lands and were historically known to settle at the mouths of rivers (Geernaert 2019; see also Praxis Research Associates 2018). This has made the Mississauga the focus of many colonial treaties that sought to claim water rights alongside land and has given rise to the MCFN's 2016 Aboriginal Title Claim to Water within their traditional lands that is still ongoing (Holmes 2015). This focus on the rights of the MCFN to the waterways on their land is also a focus on advocacy "for a healthy environment for the people and wildlife that live within [their] treaty lands and territory" (MCFN "Title Claim") and highlights the Credit River (*Missinnihe*, "trusting creek"), which the Timothy Street Park Chimney Swift Tower sits alongside. Because chimney swifts often stay close to water to feed on the insects it attracts, it is no surprise that the bank of the Credit was chosen for a stand-alone swift tower in Streetsville, a small neighborhood in northwestern Mississauga.

I travel to find the Timothy Street Park Tower because it is one of the seven towers that Birds Canada has given me GPS coordinates for. However, this tower was not built because a nearby chimney was destroyed. Timothy Street Park is a lot-sized residential greenspace located between a small multiunit housing development and some power lines, on the one side, and the Credit River, on the other. It was a donation to the city of Streetsville by a longtime resident, Chester Rundle, who lived across the street. Alongside the eighteen-foot-tall freestanding masonry chimney are other collectibles of Rundle's: a decommissioned windmill and water pump with a memorial plaque about him; a set of wagon wheels, a small birdhouse on a pole, and seven boulders carted from Niagara, two of which have glued-in marbles for eyes. Upon first glance, the park reads rather as a mish-mash of a yard extension of the housing next to it, less a park than where someone has dumped their nice historic detritus. In many ways, the greenspace is a memorial to a local resident who passed away in 1996. The chimney tower itself, however, has nothing at all to do with Chester Rundle.

As a plaque on the chimney tells me, it is a testament to a local conservationist who noticed swifts inhabiting the nearby Streetsville United Church and lobbied the city to build an independent masonry swift tower (Stewart, 2015). It reads, "Dedicated to Bill Evans and the Chimney Swift Action Team in recognition of their efforts to protect and conserve the chimney swift species" (see fig. 5). I have to admit that when I come upon the Timothy Street Swift Tower, I am utterly confused. It takes me some time and research to parse out the park's existence and the reason behind the erection of the tower itself, as I had previously assumed when I received the coordinates of the tower that they were only built as specific mitigations rather than citizen projects. Nonetheless, as I observe the well-built structure and put my ear up to the

Fig. 5 | Timothy Street Park chimney swift tower. Photo: author.

iron cleanout (which has "Bill Evans 2012" stamped into it) in early June, it is absent of any interior scufflings that might indicate the presence of chimney swifts. Like the thirty-foot windmill to its right, the masonry tower is just one more item in the park's strange collection, neither a home for swifts nor a working chimney.

The Mississauga swift tower is a strange structure indeed. As the short write-up in a neighborhood paper asserts, it is a tribute to "one man's struggle to save the chimney swifts," storied by a lifetime resident of the city of Streetsville and a self-taught naturalist Bill Evans, who worked with a local conservation group, a former OMNRF conservation officer, a local councilor, and local apprentices at a masonry training center to erect the tower. As the local interest piece says of the tower, "There are not too many projects that you can say are 100 per cent one guy's idea. But this one certainly was" (Stewart 2015). To encounter this particular swift tower is not so much about encountering a structure built for birds; it is instead a monument to men.

I say this not to denigrate the work of committed individuals in conservation or the attention such a citizen-driven initiative might bring to the plight of a threatened species like the chimney swift—after all, swifts are "named" on this masonry chimney. Yet actions such as the Timothy Street Park tower embody current public narratives about species loss, in which focusing on problems of extinction are often future-oriented and terrifyingly dystopic, but reflections on current solutions are optimistic (Randall, 2009). In a turn toward the optimism of conservation in erecting a stand-alone tower, the recognition of the loss of chimney swifts as a species—the "efforts to protect and conserve"—are overshadowed by the celebration of the "dedication" of the humans that prompted the structure's construction. Yet chimney swifts themselves, as absent from the structure, are propagated as both rare and mysterious in such absence. To return to Yusoff's (2012) assertion, the precarity of the chimney swift invoked by the tower's construction already inscribes the birds' dependence on humans in the material argument made by the structure itself. This particular structure redraws the capacity for swift agency in the ecology of this particular situation. In part, it does so because of its emergence on the landscape when it is otherwise uncalled for as a mitigation. It directs attention not toward the loss of chimney swifts, where it might have had an educational or memorial impact. Instead, the Timothy Street Park tower acts as a material object of epideictic rhetoric, a column of praise for human individuals doing the work of conservation, even as that work has very little known success. Such a celebratory object not only constructs nonhuman precarity—here the swift is already an abandoned being in favor of overdetermined human hubris and confidence in its preservation—but it also prevents real human acknowledgment of species loss in progress.

In Rosemary Randall's (2009) work with citizen action groups that focus on climate change, she suggests that solution-focused narratives of baby steps or green consumerism often are optimistically vague. Such positivity not only makes the present feel safe but also ignores loss as something to be projected into the future (119). The outcome, for Randall, are parallel narratives in which loss is split. Loss gets moved from the present into a version of a horrific future, while current, real, and lived losses become impossible to both recognize and mourn. What we are left with, as in the case of the Timothy Street Park tower, are ineffectual monuments to optimism that do not allow us to do the work of grief effectually, or as Randall claims (using the work of J. William Worden), will not provide us with mourning "tasks that can be embraced or refused, tackled, or abandoned" (121). The Timothy Street Park tower, as an optimistic solution, suffers from the kind of self-referentiality noted by Carole Blair (2001) of structures like the Gateway Arch in St. Louis: the tower refers only back to itself via the work of human volunteers and its own construction, doing little to truly recognize the nonhumans implicated by its presence or offer up cultural values that might intervene in their decline. Blair turns to the questions of such structures by invoking James Young, who asks "whether an abstract, self-referential monument can ever commemorate events outside of itself. Or must it motion endlessly to its own gesture to the past, a commemoration of its essence as dislocated sign, forever trying to remember events it never actually knew?" (Young 1992, 54–55).

When a passerby first comes across the Timothy Street Park tower, there is absolutely no way that they would otherwise know its purpose or intent, stuck as it is among the park's other peculiar debris. It is in this way abstracted even further from its already abstracted purpose, given the abysmal success rate of independent swift towers in Canada, and dislocated from the real series of events that have led to biodiversity loss on a mass scale. As a self-referential abstraction, in Young's words, the tower simply celebrates itself. The tower sits as a commemoration of human ingenuity without fully allowing engagement and recognition of a strange present, precisely because it withholds the truth of what is *ceasing to be*, in Braidotti's (2019, 36) terms. Although the tower is strange on the landscape and whispers, perhaps, at *alloiostrophos* by virtue of its brick almost-chimneyness, in this case it still functions to underscore a metaphoric system: the chimney is at once *like* other useless structures on this landscape— the windmill, the wagon wheel. Unlike barn swallow mitigation structures, the tower does not even accidentally attract other nonhuman species. It fails to secure the assent of contact with the nonhuman other, itself a metaphoric proposition, as Sutton and Mifsud (2012) remind us. Instead of opening up possibilities, this tower closes them down, its nonhuman subjects already abandoned. Instead, it sits as an object of cruel optimism, urging passersby to maintain an attachment to it that is no doubt problematic. The Timothy Street Park tower, as quasi-monument, completely excises nonhuman loss even as it appears to be a conservation object.

Neither an impossible future in which building a swift tower successfully attracts the birds (despite research suggesting otherwise) nor a present that simply erects freestanding masonry towers in the middle of a neighborhood greenspace allow for an acknowledgment of real loss. Without the ability to move beyond an intellectual acceptance of species extinction and instead toward a lived, emotional experience of the reality, humans are stuck in a kind of optimistic waiting-place about our own, and others', demise—one littered with cheerily "eccentric" items (Stewart 2015). As such, the Timothy Street Park Swift Tower's proposition on the landscape is not oriented toward swifts, who have already refused it. The tower, by virtue of its focus, doesn't really even function as a memorial to biodiversity loss or the loss of the what-was-once-common encounter of humans watching swifts entering and exiting urban chimneys. Such a recognition would perhaps better represent the network of loss that Ryan (2017) notes as the "emotional and material connections" (130) that people develop to a variety of species. Instead, the tower's existence is a simple monument to a man in a huddle of other monuments to another man, divorced from meaningful engagement with other humans and nonhumans, and devoid of acknowledgment of historic settlement and contemporary claims to Indigenous water rights.

At best, the Timothy Street Park tower is an ambivalent quasi-monument to nonhuman loss, reading more to the uninformed as an obelisk dedicated to a human individual than a meaningful object of relation. Given its location on the banks of the Credit River, its construction and dedication read like a missed opportunity. What might have emerged as a counter-monument (Krzyżanowska 2016) to the Eurowestern commitment to denigrate both species and nonwhite peoples—a moment, perhaps, to resist a simplified commemoration of individuals and even critique the causes of biodiversity loss or reflect on the role of the Credit River, its protectors, and Indigenous-settler-nonhuman relations—was itself lost. Instead, the tower is left on the landscape as another symbol of the rise of humanism and celebration of individual autonomy, as likely to be forgotten or ignored as the windmill or wagon wheel. Or even chimney swift.

Not all examples of swift towers are as reflective of monumentalizing human hubris as Timothy Street Park. As I next take up, some towers, even in their failure, represent hope-practices that encourage humans to turn otherwise, embodied devotions that recognize that the pain of species loss can also emerge as generative affective openings that grasp both disappointment and potential at the same time.

Fairnorth Farm: Practicing Hope

When I get into the car to make the one hour, fifteen-minute drive to Tillsonburg, Ontario, I have no idea where I'm going. The GPS coordinates I've been given by Bird Studies Canada are just that—an Excel worksheet of coordinates in one column with the name of the nearest town in another—in this case, Langton, in Norfolk County, twenty minutes from the north shore of Lake Erie. In the middle of Mississauga land ceded by the Between the Lakes treaty, Tillsonburg sits between Lakes Erie and Ontario. When I mention the name of the town to my collaborator, a longtime Ontario resident, they play me Stompin' Tom Connors's song "Tillsonburg." The lyrics highlight the noteworthy history of the area: "A way down southern Ontario / I never had a nickel or a dime to show. / A fella beeped up in an automobile. / He said, 'You'll want to work in the tobacco fields of Tillsonburg.' / Tillsonburg (Tillsonburg). / My back still aches when I hear that word!" (Connors 1989).

Stompin' Tom wrote of his work in the fields during the heyday of the Ontario tobacco belt from 1950 to 1960. Once producing over 90 percent of Canada's tobacco (over one hundred million pounds a year), Tillsonburg was one of Canada's epicenters of seasonal farm labor. Such land-based labor tells the story not only of the replacement of the plant *Nicotiana rustica* with a cultivated *Nicotania tabacum* over its 1,500-year history but also of the rise and fall of a crop first known for its cultivation, trade, and ceremonial value for Indigenous people for over one thousand years. Today, these fields tell a different story, one of the boom-and-bust of the "green gold rush" (Dunsworth 2019, 48) and its commercialization, and its downfall as a "sin crop." Such fluctuation is inclusive of a racialized labor history that kept most of the wealth from the commoditized tobacco industry white, while disincentivizing Indigenous workers by requiring registry to the National Selective Service, of which they actively resisted (see Dunsworth 2019; Stevenson 2001).

Today, most Norfolk County tobacco farms have been monetarily encouraged to grow other crops—primarily soy and corn—after the government offered a three hundred million buyout incentive to switch to other cash crops (Johnson 2017). This means that the roads to fifty-one-acre Fairnorth Farm, where a small stand-alone chimney swift tower sits, are littered with empty and dilapidated red-roofed and green-sided tobacco curing sheds (or "kilns"). As I've begun to note as customary during these field visits, I'm again confused as to why anyone living near acres of farmland would erect a swift tower when they are known so prominently as urban chimney dwellers. It isn't until I reread the COSEWIC details of chimney swifts' preferred habitat that I realize that these tobacco sheds are prime habitat for the birds, even though they are otherwise commonly sighted in cities.

It is mid-July when I pull up to Fairnorth Farm, and the first thing I notice among the buzzing of deerflies and the heat of the day are the oddly shaped birdhouses that sit on telescoping posts eighteen feet into the air, each with a series of sixteen to twenty of what look like plastic gourds affixed to them. The gourd "apartments" are filled with the busy shimmer of at least thirty small birds that I later come to realize are purple martins, another relatively common aerial insectivore that is not yet listed on SARA, but which researchers often study for insight into the migration habits of all aerial insectivores. Like chimney swifts, purple martins are entirely dependent on human-built birdhouses for their nesting habitats, as their preference for old-growth hollow trees is no longer a feasible choice.

I'm captivated by the martins, and they seem like a good omen for a structure built for swifts. I keep my eye peeled for the stand-alone tower, and I see it on the opposite side of the farm property from the martin colony, a tall, cream-yellow board-and-batten structure attached to the corner of an old concrete foundation that must once have been either an original farmhouse or barn but now houses a large pumpkin patch (see fig. 6). At the very top of the wood tower is a small rectangular chimney cap, but that is the only part of the tower that hints at its likeness to an actual chimney.

After knocking on the farmhouse door to get permission to examine the swift tower, I meet Kathryn Boothby and her partner Michael, owners of Fairnorth Farm. Kathryn tells me about the martins in her yard, and I notice the signage nearby Fairnorth Farm designating it as a member of ALUS Canada

Fig. 6 | Chimney swift tower at Fairnorth Farm. Photo: Marcel O'Gorman.

(Alternative Land Use Services), an organization dedicated to farmer-delivered conservation of "agriculture, wildlife and natural spaces" (ALUS 2021). I ask about the swift tower, and she tells me that she was inspired to erect it after the success of putting up the martin nests, which currently house thirty-nine breeding pairs. Despite the success of the martins and the use of the Kyles's Texas-based tower plans, I learn that the Boothby's swift tower, erected in 2017, has never housed chimney swifts. Like the Timothy Street Park tower, it too is a failure. However, unlike the Timothy Street Park tower, the swift tower that sits on the Boothby property is less a quasi-monument and more a hope-practice, opening up possibilities rather than closing them down.

In *Hope and Grief in the Anthropocene*, Leslie Head (2016) interviews climate scientists about the untenability of living "in the spectre of catastrophe" (1) while continuing to do the work in which they have been trained, and in many cases, love. Head argues that the modern subject living in the Anthropocene must move beyond a kind of "fix" mentality in order to both name and sit with the grief of real loss, to "experience the distress of not making a difference" (32). She sees a kind of productive potential in the work of mourning and situates hope not as an emotional antidote to loss but rather, borrowing from Ben Anderson (2006), as a practice and process that carries with it melancholy, grief, uncertainty, and the risk of disappointment. Rather than a personal feeling associated with optimism, then, Head (2016) rethinks hope as "something to be practised rather than felt" (75), aligning well with Braidotti's (2019) call for affirmative and joyful ethics in posthuman projects. Hope-practices, as I see them, are those undertakings that emerge from what she calls "moments of rupture"—"contexts of change and uncertainty" (Head 2016, 77) that then prompt generative possibilities. Hope here is not an affective site of optimism but a working-through of grief, a way to "bear" our anxieties about biodiversity loss (see Weintrobe 2013). But to do so, as Head maintains, "in the mode of child-bearing . . . holding, articulating, bearing witness and rendering visible" (32).

The failure of the tower at Fairnorth Farm is a hope-practice not because it seeks to fix a problem or performs metaphorically only to secure nonhuman assent of use, nor is it a hope-practice because it will be monitored and tended to as the materials begin to deteriorate. The Fairnorth Farm tower is a hope-practice because of the other conservation practices that the Boothbys have surrounded it with that prompt possibility and opening—a way to bear witness to the decline of the chimney swift while recognizing that its otherness and capacity for agency are supported by many other nodes in a rhetorical—and literal—ecology. Rather than seeking to reveal nonhuman presence to render the present eternal, in Hinchliffe's (2008) terms, the Fairnorth Farm tower instead makes peace with the ambivalence of swift presence. Making peace with, in Berlant's (2011) words, the possibility of the "change that's *not* going to come" (2) allows for a letting go and allowing for the distance between swift and human. A combination of the tower with other conservation initiatives allows for attendant uncertainty and disappointment. Tower building as a hope-practice might sustain the fantasy of a cure-all object, but when combined with other conservation efforts, together these practices offer multiple ways to make space for the potential of species abundance while allowing for species absence.

I realize only after researching Fairnorth Farm upon my return home that the erection of their chimney swift tower is more than a nod toward individual citizen conservation action. The Boothbys are well known in Norfolk County for the range of restoration activities they've undertaken since purchasing the property in 2005. I'm astonished to learn that not only have they supported researchers as they've radio-monitored their colony of purple martins (Dubinski

2019), but they have an extensive list of restoration activities documented by a range of local conservation authorities: the Carolinian Canada, Long Point Basin Land Trust, Otter Valley Naturalists, Ontario Power Generation, Norfolk Stewardship Council, and the Ontario Soil and Crop Improvement Association. Partnering with a range of these organizations, in sixteen years the Boothbys have removed 3.5 tons of garbage on their property, planted a prairie grass buffer between a ravine and stream on their property to address erosion, created a dug-out wetland habitat now inhabited by a variety of reptile and amphibian species, expanded eight acres of their woodlot with ten thousand plantings of native tree species, closed a drainage pipe on their property while maintaining amphibian habitat, created a forty-by-one-hundred-foot roadside buffer along one of their fields by planting native trees and growing a pollinator corridor of native plants, created a prairie demonstration garden, installed two dozen nesting boxes for Eastern bluebirds and tree swallows, and installed a snake nesting structure that is currently being used by Eastern hog-nosed snakes (another threatened SARA species) (Bishop 2018; *Carolinian Canada* 2012). The Fairnorth Farm tower is not built for a public gaze and thus elides possibilities for monumentalizing or memorializing. Instead, its presence produces metonymic association: with the martin houses, with the prairie demonstration garden, with new wetlands, with snake nests, with a range of nonhuman others.

In other words, the failure of the Fairnorth Farm tower does not stand alone as an isolated yes-no proposition for nonhumans on the landscape, a singular object of cruel optimism. It is instead, like many other doings on Fairnorth Farm, a recognition that any hope-practice risks disappointment and refusal among the tasks of building and restoring habitat. The tower does not stand alone, isolated from its environment. Instead, it is one among a host of practices that recognize that the soil, the climate, the flora, the water work together as a proposition *with* human-built habitats. The Fairnorth Farm tower is just as idiosyncratic on the landscape as the Timothy Street Park tower, but as part of a larger ecology of bearing witness to failures of conservation action while standing among a variety of other hope-practices, it stands as a desiring human wish for contact with the nonhuman other while acknowledging that such others may have completely other wishes, wishes that might be borne better by other practices, whether by promoting insect abundance, water health, or native trees. Either way, this tower, set among other everyday care practices, stands as an opening proposition to the swifts that allows a range of responses.

As a mark on the landscape, it is a kind of witnessing. It also, as a failure, offers an opportunity for reflecting on loss—the encounter with the tower holds at once both disappointment (they are not here) and potential (they might come someday) without resolution.

In part, what cemented the difference between Fairnorth Farm and Timothy Street Park towers so firmly in my mind was a culminating experience of my visits to Norfolk County. As I was leaving the Boothby farm, Kathryn suggested I drive down the road to a neighboring asparagus farm where, she said, her neighbor Ray Lammens had nestling chimney swifts in his barn. Unsure of what I had heard—chimney swifts in a barn?—I went from farm to farmhouse to farm again, where Ray, the owner of Spearit Farms, generously opened up his ancient barn door for me, moving aside a stack of propane tanks blocking a raccoon-chewed opening in the door ("Keeps out the cats," he explained). Up the rickety wood steps in the dust and half-light I went with a complete stranger, my nose catching the scent of long-gone animals. And there, against the west wall of a dilapidated barn, the dim punctuated by streaming sunlight from a long since shattered window, was a tiny, crescent-shaped nest of sticks, glued to the wall, with four chimney swift nestlings awaiting feeding. Bald and sightless, as they heard me approach, they let out a terrible screeching racket, thinking that perhaps I was the mama or papa bird come to relieve them of their hunger, or a predator ready to do the exact opposite (see fig. 7). As I watched, a swift parent flew to the open window and watched me carefully before flying away. Ray explained he noticed the swifts five or six years ago, that usually there are a few nests, but that this year, there is just one.

Seeing the baby swifts in an unexpected yet completely expected place, close to tobacco sheds and so near the Fairnorth farm that Kathryn Boothby joked about hoping her tower would "poach" Ray's swifts, I was changed by this encounter. To experience these endangered birds for myself and watch *their* nestwork, knowing that even had they been common, to see them inside a dark human-made tower was already nearly impossible, felt like a small bit of magic. To be present to these birds was also to be in a moment of the strange present, to know that I was witnessing both what is ceasing to be—a small moment of *thereness* for a disappearing species—and what is in the process of becoming—a time when swifts will not return. The loss of swifts was, in that moment, not an intellectual one, but a real, lived one. I stayed to talk with Ray for some time and received quite an education about the difference between SARA-mandated

Fig. 7 | Chimney swift nestlings on Spearit Farms. Photo: author.

mitigations and the extraordinary everyday alternative acts of conservation that he committed to, which I discuss in the last chapter of this book. When I left his generous company, he urged me to take one nest from his small collection of swift nests with me, to remember.

Queen's University Chimneys: A Swift Story

Of course, as scholars of hope note, "the conditions that make it possible to hope are strictly the same that make it possible to despair" (Marcel 1965, 101), as my timing failure to view the Labatt Brewery swifts in the introduction to this chapter demonstrates. It is the threatened nature of chimney swifts that makes mitigation actions hopeful and possible in the first place, an "indeterminate, *not-yet-become*" (Anderson 2006, 733) state of complete extinction. As Anderson notes, and what guides analysis of my final swift chimney site, "Some types of hope can also feed back to *continue* relations that diminish even as we are attached to them" (743). The four artificial chimneys on two university buildings at Queen's University in Kingston, Ontario, substantiate such a claim. They are complex examples of what happens when we listen to the disappointment inherent in hope by allowing nonhuman bodies to story their own demise at the hands of humans. They are objects that invite us to think about what now seems impossible about the relationships invoked by the term *commensality*: that in living together, we harm none.

Kingston (originally named Ka'tarohkwi by the Wendat/Huron people) is a small city of 140,000 people about a five-hour drive from me, on land with a complex history of being "purchased" from the Mississauga people without treaty documentation or transfer deed. The most specific descriptor of the size of the tract of land ceded is only recoverable in a handful of letters, described as "all the lands from Toniata or Onagara River to the River in the Bay of Quinté within eight leagues of the bottom of the said Bay, including all the Islands, extending from the Lake back as far as a man can travel in a day" (Shanahan 2018). Ka'tarohkwi was a traditional meeting place for the people of Six Nations; yet as McLeod (2019) documents of the transaction for present-day Kingston, "No reserves were set aside for the tribes, and the First Nations were eventually squeezed out of their beloved traditional territory." Because there is so little documentation of the transfer, the record of what is known as Crawford's Purchase is one that has been near forgotten and hard to recover discursively (Rupnik 2019). It is the nondiscursive nature of the same kinds of treaty stories that I've encountered closer to home—large swaths of land traded for a few goods like cloth and gunpowder—that stays with me as I make the long drive to Kingston, forcing me to think of the other ways humans collectively tell the story of cultural eclipse through their bodies and disappearance. Perhaps it is this thinking that colors my expectations as I arrive at Queen's University, the site of all four artificial chimneys in the downtown core of Kingston.

The four artificial chimneys are on the roofs of two separate buildings on Queens's nearly one hundred campus acres, two chimneys located on the roof of Fleming Hall (home of administrative offices, campus security, IT, human resources, and marketing and communications), and two on Craine Hall (which houses the campus physical plant). The Queen's chimneys are the only artificial chimneys on urban buildings—as opposed to stand-alone towers—of all of the coordinates I've been given by Bird Studies Canada. I know in advance from Chris Grooms, head of the Kingston Field Naturalists' Chimney Swift Project, that like the towers I have already visited, the artificial chimneys at Queen's are unoccupied and have never been used, so I have no qualms about waiting until early October to go observe them. When I arrive, Chris greets me on campus to act as my guide. I am grateful, as the huge campus and grand limestone and brick buildings of varying heights that compete with the smooth lines of new glass-encased high-rises makes it quite difficult to spot chimneys—artificial or not—among a host of rooflines. I am struck powerfully by both the inaccessibility of the chimneys and the urban nature of the chimney swift for the first time, as my main mode of observation becomes craning my neck to the sky and trying to decipher one chimney from another. The reminder of swifts' secretive existence—and my own distance from them—has never felt plainer as I strain and squint skyward.

All four of the chimneys built on Queen's buildings emerged from historic sightings of chimney swifts in a variety of campus chimneys since 1928 (Bowman 1952). The large populations of swifts were so noteworthy that the university was a location of a large-scale swift banding initiative lasting over fifteen years and banding anywhere between two hundred and four thousand chimney swifts in a given year (Greer 2010). As of a 2012 Ontario Swiftwatch report, only one nesting/roosting chimney has been identified as active in Kingston (Bird Studies Canada 2012). These statistics suggest just how ambivalent an attunement the Queen's chimneys urge in humans: at once a site of both mass bird bodies and a functioning heating system, they now sit empty on both counts. While various campus chimneys have been capped and then uncapped in response to preserving swift habitat over the years as the species has declined, Chris tells me that this has resulted in only a few swifts nesting on campus in any given year—an average decline of 6 percent a year. Despite the fact that all four campus chimneys were part of a large research survey that monitored the success of artificial chimneys in Canada (complete with twenty-four-hour video cameras wired through ethernet cables), in the five years of the study, no swifts were known to nest or roost in them. Now, Chris says, the artificial chimneys are falling into disrepair and will likely be removed as the campus responds to building maintenance.

The Crane Hall chimneys are only observable from the fourth- to sixth-floor stairwells from another campus building, but even then they are tiny rectangles from afar as I squint to get a good look. Because of campus suicides, Chris explains to me, the physical plant has changed all the locks to rooftop access routes, and so we cannot get any closer. The Fleming Hall artificial chimneys are a bit more observable, in part because at four stories the building is not as tall, and in part because Fleming Hall houses a huge original gray Kingston limestone chimney, clear on the roofline, that once was responsible for coal-powering not only the Queen's campus, but much of Kingston's downtown and hospitals. While the large main stack has since been decommissioned, the building contains a large amount of boiler infrastructure in the basement, which steam powers many nearby campus buildings. It is the slender, rectangular artificial chimneys that sit on either side of the large, cylindrical brick stack that contribute to a comparative sense of scale for swift habitat while showcasing the tension between visible structure and invisible appeals to swifts (see fig. 8).

Built in 1904, Fleming Hall burned down in a fire and was rebuilt in 1933. From 1933 to 1993, the main chimney in the building was open to roosting and nesting swifts, and the chimney was capped in 1993. Based on the advocacy of biologists and naturalists, in 2009 the chimney was uncapped, and a few swifts began to roost in it the next year (PEARL, n.d.), though they have not regularly returned. When the Fleming Hall chimney was uncapped, workers found sixty years' worth—over six feet—of chimney swift guano inside. Researchers working in paleoecological environmental assessment, usually reserved for sediment core sampling of soil and rock, were quick to see the guano deposit inside Fleming Hall chimney as one with a story to tell. Each layer of guano showed a chronostratified change—a marking of time based on diet. Grooms was one of the researchers on the project, and as he tours me around the bowels of Fleming Hall, warm from the boiler still encased in the basement, he shows me the tight spaces those researchers working in the basement had to squeeze into to try to gain access to the guano in the chimney.

What the researchers found in the sixty-year evidence of chimney swifts who returned, again and again, to this chimney, was not what I would have expected

Fig. 8 | Fleming Hall artificial chimneys (left and right). Note original chimney in building's center. Photo: author.

(not that I would be trained to know what to expect from a historic pile of bird poop). The story that those droppings contained was a ghost story. It is an archive of the historic diet of chimney swifts, a story of insect remains. The researchers examined the guano for the remains of insects, pesticides, and carbon and nitrogen, and what they found was yet another story. Based on the concentrations of pesticides found in the guano and the amount of bug remains and beetle remains (beetles being one of the main sources of food for chimney swifts), the scientists found a major shift in the diet of the swifts between 1940 and 1950, from beetles to bugs. The increase of bugs from beetles, as well as DDT and DDE measurements in the guano samples, coincided with large-scale DDT use in the late 1940s. DDT was known to have a disastrous effect on Coleoptera (beetles), yet beetles remain one of the chimney swifts' primary high-calorie-value foods. While acknowledging that habitat loss and environmental stressors no doubt are in part responsible for chimney swifts' decline, the research team concluded that "their population declines are probably a product of the general decrease in relative abundance of Coleoptera from the early 1970s to 1992" (Nocera et al. 2012, 5).

This conclusion runs counter to a COSEWIC (2018) report on chimney swift nesting and roosting habitat, which stresses a decline in manufactured chimneys as a primary source of swifts' drop in numbers. Yet this conclusion has been supported by other researchers of chimney swifts' decline, particularly those who have inventoried the use of urban chimneys, artificial structures and relative populations of swifts. What has been found that runs counter to the building of the mitigations I observed is the fact that even suitable chimneys in urban areas lack swifts—there is a low occupancy rate (about 25 percent) even in the most suitable of original chimney sites (Fitzgerald 2014). Other factors, such as prey decline and climate change, seem so much more at issue that it led a separate research team to "contend that the effort and expense of construction of artificial towers in southern Ontario may be better directed elsewhere" (511). In other words, those who study swift decline and artificial chimneys have declared the mitigation an epic failure.

The artificial chimneys and towers I've spent time with, I realize, are the perfect renditions of Anderson's claim about hope, that "some types of hope can also feed back to *continue* relations that diminish even as we are attached to them (2006, 743). Conservationists and governments are enamored of the artificial chimney as the hopeful "fix" of species decline, and their monumental appearance can often do the feel-good work of attachment to resolution-as-species-return. Yet the relation itself—between human and swift—continues to diminish. *The swifts are gone, if they were ever there.* Such a relation suggests another kind of hope, one that Berlant frames from the work of Anna Potamianou: "as a stuckness within a relation to futurity that constitutes a problematic defense against the contingencies of the present" (Berlant 2011, 13). This is a kind of hope that we cannot bear creatively or hold uncertainty within; instead, it is a fantasy, a "set of dissolving assurances" (3) about the change that is not going to come.

The Fleming Hall chimney, thus, is not just a story of chimney swift decline, though it clearly offers a powerful reflection on nonhuman withdrawal from human infrastructural propositions. In close proximity to the fake chimneys built on either side that tell of the swifts' refusal, the Fleming Hall stack, through bird and insect bodies, shows us conditions of both hope and despair. The memory of up to four thousand birds returning yearly to this one place with the hope that they will again, filled with centimeter-by-centimeter fecal narratives of the use of human-made poison, sits side by side with empty wooden boxes still hooked up to abandoned ethernet cables. Here, at Queen's, chimney swifts have given us an archive of their own demise, of the role of pesticides on their bodies and the bodies of their prey. These three chimneys, side by side, are less openings to possibility than they are a showcase of the "difficult relations of loss and violence," as Yusoff (2012, 578) puts it. Here we are given an unfathomable scale of loss—up to 240,000 birds, millions more beetles, in a span of sixty years—seen both visibly (in the guano deposits in the large stack) and invisibly (in the absence cultivated by the swifts' nonreturn to any of the chimneys available when they used to return en masse).

Yet as Yusoff reminds us, *thinking with* such violence—colonial violence perpetrated by humans with the use of DDT on a range of creatures—might allow us possibilities for "more nourishing ties" (580) with the Other. We cannot story the decline of the chimney swift as simply a matter of the destruction of historic urban buildings or the nebulous remembrance of long-gone old-growth forests. We must instead, as the Fleming Hall chimneys tell us, come to terms with the fact that humans' main mode of relating to the swift and its decline has been through "invisible ties that bind us to violence as a primary mode of relating" (582). Swifts are declining not because they don't have a place to roost, not because of climate change, not because their main food source has been decimated. Chimney swifts—as barn swallows and bobolinks—are declining because humans' main mode of relating to them has been, is, and continues to be, a violent one. While the Fairnorth Farm towers may show a degree of hope alongside other practices, the Fleming Hall chimneys are their Janus-faced counterparts. They serve as a powerful reminder of precarity, of cruel optimism, of the once-present and now absent, and point to the complexities inherent in the failure of trying to make nonhumans visible. As Yusoff contends, a human-focused struggle for nonhuman visibility emerges "as a kind of haunting configured around a profoundly human sensibility" (585). In pointing to the possibilities for thinking with the violence inherent in such hauntings, Yusoff points again to turning our attention to "violence as part of the scene of our relations (so that we might work towards it being a less visible part of that relation)" (585). This scene of ghost birds is a violent one, but the violence is quiet and invisible and told through bones and sediment and isotopes and chemicals, another nondiscursive path of being squeezed out of beloved territory.

Ghost Time: Thinking-With Violence, Thinking-With Hope, Turning Otherwise

I close this chapter with a final anecdote about a current chimney known to be a large roosting site for nesting swifts that I traveled to, another five hours from home, with the hope of seeing the kinds of swifts known to have once roosted in Kingston. I chose the site for two reasons: the first, I think, was because a site-in-use was a way to help me cope with my own sense of the scale of species loss. It was, itself, a site of cruel optimism, a "sustaining inclination to return to the scene of fantasy that enables you to expect that this time, nearness to this thing will help you or a world to become different in just the right way" (Berlant 2011, 2). A chimney-in-use by swifts perhaps sustained, for me, this cruelest of fantasies. The second was because of the site itself; this particular chimney was in a decommissioned nuclear stack on the Chalk River. In part, the site appealed to me because I cannot imagine a clearer symbol of the naturecultural tensions of the Anthropocene: an abandoned nuclear reactor, left for birds. In part, it also appealed to me because this is the only place I have visited in this project that also occupies an in-process land claim, the Algonquins of Ontario Settlement Area, Ontario's first "modern-day land treaty" that will assert Algonquin rights to twenty-two thousand square miles of their land (Government of Ontario 2021). Driving the five hours through Algonquin Park to get to Rolphton, Ontario, an isolated, now-abandoned "ghost town" that once housed hydroelectric dam and nuclear plant workers before both industries shut down (much like the contemporary tobacco industry), I'm thinking a lot about hauntings of people and animals, of living with ghosts in towns and in fields, of who counts as human *now*. I realize that my searches for swifts through encountering structures built for them in many ways have been a rendering of their precarity and their absence. Yet my interactions and conversations with the humans who have tried to monumentalize them, invoke them, or care for them—Kathryn Boothby, Ray Lammens, Chris Grooms—have been nonetheless facilitated by swifts. In that way, perhaps, the birds demonstrate a far-reaching rhetorical capacity, an agency that extends past their bodies, into their shadows and ghosts and stories.

My thoughts are muddled as I try to account for this particular trip—why am I going to an abandoned chimney in the middle of nowhere, to see what may or may not be there? Why am I researching a project about death, about disappearance? Why do I think it's important for word-workers to attend to extinction, as Gan et al. (2017) say, to examine "the violence of settler colonialism and capitalist expansion [and the ways that they] give rise to the ghosts of bad death, death out of time" (G7)? Perhaps I am thinking about death out of time and temporal frames of the other-than-human because this is nestwork, too. It is what forces me to reconcile the stories that our stories tell—through structures, through simulacra, through the occupation of land, through the shells of sixty-year-old beetle carapaces, through allying myself with new kinds of time that move with days and weeks and seasons rather than terminology and definitions and semesters. Through nestwork, our other-than-human relations tell their stories, but not always through words, not always the ones we want to hear, and they tell them often on their own time. Here on these pages I have been persuaded to wait, to listen, and to tell them again, differently.

When I traveled with my partner to find the Rolphton chimney, we were on a quick human clock. Most years, chimney swift counts sponsored by nonprofit agencies would have opened up this property for monitoring birds, as it contains a large chimney as part of a deactivated nuclear reactor. The year of a pandemic, however, everything was closed down—no counts in a pandemic year. Still, perhaps stupidly, I looked at the calendar and looked at the last year's swift counts in the area. May 16: 252 birds. May 22: 1,024 birds. May 30: 734 birds. June 3: 4 birds. In a span of two weeks of bird time, they disappear, go from there to not-there. It was May 29 in the middle of this two-year-long project, only a few days before the chance to see hundreds of birds shrunk to the chance to see a few. If I missed them, I would have to wait another year.

Such an urgent press for time in the immediate term in Rolphton came right up against the long tail of Anthropocenic time at the smallest scale possible: that of splitting an atom. The Rolphton reactor, or Nuclear Power Demonstration (NPD), was constructed in 1955 and was Canada's first nuclear power station, tasked with producing radioisotopes—that is to say, uranium—and producing heat and electricity (McConnell 2002). Today, the site houses industrial buildings and a decommissioned reactor, the chimney stack of the nuclear power plant now being used not to ventilate the buildings but instead to provide roosting habitat to thousands of spring migrating chimneys swifts. Underneath the chimney stack in a space of "deep geological disposal" (World Nuclear Association 2020) lies the nuclear waste generated in the twenty-five years the plant was in operation, handling naturally occurring uranium in the Elliot Lake mines, four hours north of the reactor site. These underground radioactive isotopes, uranium-235 and uranium-238, sit underneath the 150-foot chimney where thousands of swifts are known to gather and have a half-life of between 704 million and 4.46 billion years (IEER 2012).

As Michelle Bastian suggests, "this time of extinctions" marks a strange present that plays with units of measure of linear time, when "our hours are muddled, our dates disoriented, our counting confused" (2017, 159). My time in Rolphton was perhaps my strangest yet—a mad dash off the side of the highway as the sun descended in the rainy sky, knowing I had less than five minutes after sunset to try to find the chimney; depending on an aerial view of the location to guide us (as addresses of nuclear sites are never specifically given); the drizzle kicking up thousands of mosquitos at dusk; scrambling down a grass-slicked power-line corridor to try to catch a glimpse of a chimney alongside dense Ontario bush; the beating of adrenaline-fueled hope and despair if this one chance didn't work out until this time again next year. As I rounded down a curve in the path, panting from exertion, I stop when I'm greeted with the sight of five hundred birds chittering and careening their way into the round top of a tall chimney stack (see fig. 9). As I get closer to the bottom of the stack, which is attached to an abandoned trailer but still blinking with aerial antennae, my eyes and neck are trained on the black cyclonic mass of swifts circling the chimney. I take frantic notes in the rain, my ink mixing with water on the page. I note how the chittering of hundreds of swifts completely blocks out the sound of the Chalk River, immediately behind them; how each time the swifts circle the chimney, ten to twenty disappear inside; how watching them roost is like watching the reversal of smoke going inside of a chimney. The entire spectacle, resistant to any good camera angle because of the changing dusk and the movement of the birds, takes only thirty-five minutes, and then it is quiet and I am left feeling like I have just experienced a dazzling fireworks display but am not quite sure I've watched the end.

The Rolphton chimney jumbles up the spaces that are occupied by bird bodies, human bodies, brick columnar bodies, isotopic bodies. It drives home to me, once I am left empty by the last of the swifts disappearing into the stack but still thinking about radioactive waste deep underneath my feet, that each of the tiny black boomerangs I watched head into the stack were not on my time at all but on generational time, or, as environmental humanist Michelle Bastian suggests, "created year after year, [as] synchronies become a sequence" (2017, 162). These birds, who will leave this place in a few days to make the long journey south, are adapting as best they can to this strange present, finding the places left, the abandoned-by-humans places, the warm places, "seeking out gaps and openings

Fig. 9 | Chimney swifts roosting at the Chalk River Nuclear Reactor chimney. Photo: author.

that might remake the rhythms that support their lives" (162). These chimney swifts, on their own time and deep in the Algonquin nation, have no use for artificial structures, no time for city life, no care for being seen or for commensal living with humans. Their curiosity, habitation, withdrawal are joyful practices of their own nestwork, not mine. They have turned otherwise.

Of course, as Bastian reminds us, it is "easier to negotiate with the time of the living, perhaps, than with the time of ghosts" (12). It is easier to reflect on swifts' agencies and capacities when I see them for myself. Yet this is a kind of cruel optimism, an attachment to a desire-object growing out of impossible conditions. It's no wonder that those who have grown attached to swifts are also attached to the structures that fail to house them—such structures invite the promises of a world made whole. Naturecultural entanglements such as those represented by the kind of spaces chimney swifts do and *don't* inhabit—artificial chimneys, stand-alone towers, barn walls and decommissioned brick stacks—force us to try to reconcile, in our one-hundred-year human-scaled time, the irreconcilable: "not only the entanglements of phenomena across scales," as Barad (2017) says, "but the very iterative (re)constituting and sedimenting of specific configurations of space, time, and matter, or rather . . . the (iterative re)making of scale itself" (G109). It forces us to reckon with precarity, with death out of time, with the quickness of extinction and the slowness of radioactive decay. It shifts temporal orientations, reminding us again of Whyte's (2017, 2) indictment of settler colonialism that has forced many Indigenous people to live their ancestors' dystopian future now. The baselines of the Anthropocene—a time to look back on—are rapidly changing.

To find this strange present between these massively different timescales—a four-year bird's life, or sixty years of birds' lives, or one hundred years of a human's life, or two hundred years of a derelict building's life, or billions of years of the memory of the earth—is another kind of nestwork altogether. Instead of temporal reference points, we are left with monuments, hope-practices, legacies of violence, each defining precarity, each with the capacity to turn humans otherwise, to perhaps allow for a letting go that will be much sooner than we'd like. Humans are faced with the proposition of the extinction of a species parallel with ourselves. Such a proposition shows clearly a particular linear Anthropocenic future predicated on a present yoked to "commitments to modernity, that complex of symbolic and material projects for separating 'nature' and 'culture'" (Gan et al. 2017, G7).

It is possible, as Whyte (2017) contends, to be a different kind of human in the strange present, to model futures from Indigenous paradigms: "Our [Indigenous] conservation and restoration projects are not only about whether to conserve or let go of certain species. Rather, they are about what relationships between humans and certain plants and animals we should focus on in response to the challenges we face, given that we have already lost so many plants and animals that matter to our societies" (2). Such futures and projects would require humans—most of all, settler humans—to do differently. Instead, we accept these premises: We are humans. They are birds. We build chimneys, we abandon them. We build precarity. They adapt. They stay with the trouble. We are running out of time. Is it possible to allow for these differences, to let the Other be as other, as a mode of *resistance to* or *survivance of* the modern project of the Anthropocene? Can humans listen, attune, and respond better to our own curiosity, melancholy, and failure by reconceptualizing our objects of desire toward changed and better *relationships*, a different cluster of promises, different practices of hope, different attunement to loss in the present and in the future? Perhaps, in time.

3

Bobolink | Being on Bird Time

It is April in the second spring of the pandemic, and the province has declared another stay-at-home order, this time for six weeks. I look at the calendar and see that in six weeks, it will be the end of May, a time when many migrating bird species return to breed in southern Ontario. While my fieldwork on barn swallows and chimney swifts wrapped up the fall before, I am depending on this spring to travel to bobolink habitat: patches of tall-grass prairie, or out-of-the-way hayfields. Each of these possibilities is dependent on friendly farmers and generous opportunities to shadow bobolink monitors out on spring breeding bird counts. The province, however, is adamant: do not leave your residence except to get groceries. With everyone working from home, monitoring programs skip years. Chances to meet specialists through naturalist and conservation group meetings have ground to a complete halt, though I continue to email strangers and talk to them on the phone. My field notebook is filled with potential leads, crossed off one by one as I hear the same refrain: "We can't do that this year." Yet looking at the calendar, I know that by late May, bobolink nests will be built; maybe they will already have eggs. I see that the earliest fledging date for bobolinks is June 11; the latest, July 28. If the province lifts the ban, I will have twenty-two days to find bobolinks, maybe more if I'm lucky. Although the semester is over, I have never felt more stressed for time in my life. Whether I have a chance to look for or find them, by August the chance to encounter bobolinks will be lost. The calendar might as well be abstract art. I am on bird time.

This chapter is one that builds on the kinds of turning otherwise captured by barn swallow structures and human-swift hope-practices to examine another small, uncharismatic species at risk, the bobolink (*Dolichonyx oryzivorus*), and the agentic entanglements of time. Rather than engage human-built structures as mitigative practices that engage species loss, I turn here to the ways that bird bodies themselves act as persuasive time-based arguments on violent human practices, mitigated by both solar time and the growing of grass. The massive decline in populations of aerial insectivores like the barn swallow and chimney swift and grassland birds like the bobolink tell us with their disappearances that they are messengers who compress time in the Anthropocene. This has been evidenced most clearly so far by my encounters with decades of bird bones at Queen's, and chimney swifts who haunt abandoned nuclear power plants. Being in the presence of loss-in-process attunes us to new timescales of decline and forces us to reckon with present, past, and future, as I suggested in the last chapter. While increasingly humans are called on to reckon with the ghosts of such losses—in part, by building and coming to terms with a variety of mitigative failures discussed in this book—too, we are called to consider time and its capacity in new ways as we recognize the ways that Western temporalities are failing us. Current notions of linear and unitized time shape human conceptions of present and future in the face of extinction, as Randall (2009) suggests, creating a dystopic future but a hopeful now. Attuning ourselves to different, demanding, nonhuman temporalities—*being on bird time*—I argue, is one such way that we might move away from the arguments of the epochal, time-marking Anthropocene, one way to think ecologically, one way for humans to turn otherwise.

As Rose et al. suggest in the introduction to *Extinction Studies: Stories of Time, Death, and Generations* (2017), "The ways in which particular species make their lives depend on distinctive and often fragile synchronies and patterns, speeds, and slownesses, interwoven temporalities increasingly interrupted by the disturbances of a species "out of time," pursuing short-term profits or producing near-immortal products" (9–10). Humans, of course, are the species out-of-time here. Rose et al. suggest that we can't ignore the ways that human perceptions of Eurowestern clock or atomic time—what we might call *chronos*—privilege efficiency, production, and profit. And we also can't ignore that such conception of time rubs up against—disturbs, interrupts, extirpates— alternate nonhuman temporalities that do not concern themselves with those things. Yet as John Durham Peters (2015) points out, *chronos* (Χρόνος) traditionally dealt with astronomy and timing of the planets, giving rise to "cyclical and linear sky media such as clocks [and] calendars" (167). Peters contrasts *chronos* with its partner, *kairos* (καιρός). Taken contemporarily to mean a kind of "right timing," *kairos* is associated in ancient Greek with probabilistic, rather than predictive, variables in the sky: "weather, rain, hail, thunder and lightning, temperature, and clouds" (166).

We might interpret that both common cyclical temporalities (*chronos*) and probabilistic ones (*kairos*) unite human and nonhuman perceptions of time—the rising of the sun in the sky, for instance. Yet because astronomy became so coupled with *knowing*—documenting patterns, timings, cycles, orientations—*chronos*-media associated with scientific prediction and linearity, like calendars and clocks, have become the primary Eurowestern way of perceiving time, as a way to measure human activity (and its efficiency, production, and profit). There is an almost complete separation in Eurowestern notions of clock time with, for example, the synchronies and slownesses and fragilities of nonhuman animals, ripe with attunement to *kairos* and embodied temporalities. Such a separation, it is easy to suggest, similarly bifurcates knowing from a knowing subject. It is not a difficult stretch of the imagination to see the ways that the speed of modern time—Virilio's (2007) *dromosphere* of "Everything! Right! Now! hypercentre of temporal compression" (100)—in every way works against *zeitgebers* or "time givers" (Pittendrigh 1981) of the body clocks so needed differentially by all species on earth, such as "light, temperature, eating, and socializing" (Bastian 2017, 151). Within this push-pull of *chronos-kairos*, we might ask, as Bastian does, "How long does it take to learn how to tell time differently?" (166).

While I cannot answer Bastian's question definitively, I can substantiate Deborah Bird Rose's (2012) claim that "embodied time is always a multispecies project" (131), and each of these projects tell a particular story—of hope, violence, and the times we are in. Every species on earth is already forced to contend with human notions of clock time, "managing the timing of encounters, meetings, tasks and activities, . . . seen through the wide array of calendars, schedules, timetables, and so on, that arise from social institutions, logistical systems, personal life, and communications systems" (Bastian 2012, 24). Yet as Bastian eloquently counters, despite humans' slavish attunement to clock time, "far from being able to coordinate our actions with the significant changes our world is currently undergoing, we are increasingly out of synch" (24). This is a strange present. Clock time, and its attendant inclinations to humanism and efficiency, has been responsible for a speeding-up of environmental degradation with every cleared forest or belch of industrial machinery. Yet human response has been too slow. Bastian suggests that linear clock time "only affords certain relations, while obscuring others," existing "as a powerful social tool for producing, managing, and/or undermining various understandings of who or what is in relation with other things or beings" (25). It is also worth acknowledging that human time has not always meant the same thing to every human—its value and human belief in its control varies across cultures (see Levine 1997). Yet Bastian, among others, argues for other ways of time telling that perhaps do less damage than clock time, a time that often totalizes toward, as Rose (2006) says, a "will-to-destruction" (77). Alternate times offer possibilities of constructing middles between *chronos-kairos*, suggesting opportunities for different kinds of knowing subjects, in Braidotti's (2019) terms.

Bastian (2012) forwards the possibility of "turtle clocks" (42), noting that human attunement to leatherback turtles, in particular, "tell[s] us about the unstable time of an active Earth" while "tell[ing of] the frustratingly slow time of human efforts to respond to recognized environmental threats" (44). In telling of the turtle clock, which is dependent on both fishing activity and government policy, Bastian offers that it "tracks the changes in turtle populations alongside the lack of change in human shrimping techniques, enabl[ing] us to maintain an awareness of the intermeshing relations of turtles, governments, conservationists, and shrimpers. In doing so, it foregrounds the inherent difficulties of coordination in a complex multispecies world, rather than hiding such work under the cover of a "universal" time" (44–45). Alternative models of time, like the turtle clock, point to a way of understanding rhetorical ecologies in a way that is attuned to complex times that push against the *chronos-kairos* tension while involving nonhuman agency, human-based policy, and environmental activity. Like the turtle clock, an attunement to bird time, I argue, is another way that we might tell time differently in the service of turning otherwise.

Other Times: Indigenous Knowledge, *Pheno*, and Turning Toward What Shines

To enable thinking about time differently today requires an attunement to alternate temporal models, which are and have been abundant, by both human and nonhuman standards. While dominant thinking about temporality has been steeped in Eurowesten philosophies, scholars in feminist science studies, anthropology, Indigenous studies, queer studies, disabilities studies, biology, and botany offer up possibilities that extend beyond clock time, many of which I detail here. Deborah Bird Rose attends to alternate temporal models by her call for "multispecies knots of ethical time," noting that ecofeminists such as Ariel Salleh argue that "complex time concepts are necessary to understanding ecological processes" (2012, 128). This complexity has always been available and possible; as Peters suggests, human conceptions of time might look very different if they had been led by the different attunements of metallurgists, musicians, or mariners

(2015, 168)—or, I might add, the Anishinaabe, Māori, or Eastern Cree, or turtles, salmon, or birds. Attunements to other times are attunements to other rhetorical ecologies: the paces by which life unfolds.

As Julia Kristeva suggests in "Women's Time" (Kristeva et al. 1981, 71), the nature of clock time is one that comes with its own particular masculinist logics, a progression of linear order that suggests one kind of time and thus excludes others (like cyclical or monumental time). Temporalities that exist outside of these linear, productive, and progress-based logics, in which time, as a commodity, equals productivity or reproductivity, also tend to marginalize embodied alternatives, made abundant by feminist, queer, and disability studies scholars.

Notions of "queer time" resist heteronormative reproductive and family-based timelines by forwarding their own "logics of location, movement, and identification" (Halberstam 2005, 1). As Freeman (2010) suggests, queerness itself emerges out of "a set of possibilities produced out of temporal and historical difference" (35), and such difference emerges out of the constant reminder of "do[ing] too much of the wrong thing at the wrong time" (Kafer 2013, 35). Similarly, disability studies scholars push against normative notions of time, suggesting its forward momentum depends on embracing notions of "crip time" (Samuels 2017). "Crip time," according to Ellen Samuels, can lag and defy narratives of progress and also change direction, locating a subject in "wormhole[s] of backward and forward acceleration" as the recalcitrant young body acts like that of an elderly one, or a full-grown adult is treated like a child (Samuels, 2017). As Kafer (2013) elaborates in a joining of queer and crip time, such embodied temporalities recognize time "not just expanded but exploded; it requires reimagining our notions of what can and should happen in time, or recognizing how expectations of "how long things take" are based on very particular minds and bodies" (27). Feminist, queer, and disability studies scholars together offer up alternatives to clock time by basing them in disruptive embodied, physical phenomenon and focusing on the generative disturbance such phenomenon offer to social and cultural norms. Such embodied time speaks clearly to multispecies sensibilities and resists, to an extent, the logic of clock time. It also reinforces Judith Butler's (1993) observations of the problematics of clock time. She says, "The notion of temporality ought not to be considered as simple succession of distinct 'moments,' all of which are equally distant from one another. Such a spatialized mapping of time substitutes a certain mathematical model for the kind of duration which resists such spatializing metaphors" (244). Butler notes that Eurowestern philosophers such as Heidegger and Bergson, in trying to undertake such mapping, do so primarily in terms of these spatial metaphors. This is borne out in the work of feminist philosopher Elizabeth Grosz (2004), who tracks Eurowestern philosophers Darwin, Nietzsche, and Bergson and their philosophies of time. Grosz notes that "philosophy, like other forms of knowledge, directs its focus to the movement of time, to duration, only extremely rarely and often under the influence of either scientific-mathematical or phenomenological-experiential models" (5). If we accept Grosz's argument, then, we are left with temporal models that either, as Butler suggests, divide time up into mathematical chunks on clocks and calendars and timesheets— what Reid, Sieber, and Blackned (2020, 2337) call the logic of widely accepted "spatio-temporal ontologies"—or models that divide time up by bodily experience and phenomenon (as queer and disability studies might have it).

Grosz also notes that when philosophy turns its attention to duration—the passing and movement of time—it tends "to spatialize and visualize temporal movement in terms of the transformation of objects or subjects" (7). We might imagine such transformation in terms of decay and glitch or fertility and aging, often situated at the object/subject line. Such representations of time are also well documented by, for example, contemporary theory in mapping and geographical information systems in which material objects are perceived to have some kind of "temporal fixity" (Reid, Sieber, and Blackned 2020, 2349)—the idea of a mountain as an object fixed in time, or "endurant" is a common example that tends to stand in opposition to "perdurant," or processual and event-based objects that "unfold" over time (2337). Whether philosophically or geospatially, however, often the study of time via transmutation of objects is bound by its presentist focus and its bifurcated subject/object, human/nonhuman differentiation. Such a focus, emerging out of the privileging of Euclidian geometry and Newtonian physics and their attendant emphasis on observation in the moment, according to Reid, Sieber, and Blackned, thus "ignores nuances about the past and future . . . [and] might explain why time is de-emphasized in geospatial ontologies and why temporality is often reduced to change" (2349–50).

Scholars who study time both philosophically and geospatially have arrived at the conclusion that this presentist, change-based focus of current spatiotemporalities and their attendant linear logics faces real challenges. A mountain, after all, is both fixed/endurant and also a process and event/perdurant: it erodes and/or may erupt. A mountain, as in the case of Mount Taranaki in New Zealand, may also be a person (Roy 2017). Still, philosophers and geographers alike acknowledge that conceptions of bodies and space are far easier to define and understand than conceptions of time and temporality (Reid, Sieber, and Blackned 2020, 2338). A potential middle way has long been forwarded by Indigenous spatio-temporalities, which not only reject notions of linear time but represent temporality neither entirely mathematically nor entirely phenomenologically but relationally. Such attuned time, largely ignored by Eurowestern philosophies of temporality, is nonetheless aligned with its contemporary call, as articulated by Grosz (2004): "We will not be able to understand its [time's] experiential nature unless we link subjectivity and the body more directly to temporal immersion, to the coexistence of life with other forms of life, and of life with things, that is, until we consider time as an ontological element" (5). What Grosz calls for is a breaking with the traditions of the subject-object and human-nonhuman divisions when considering time ontologically. Yet these traditions have already been broken, as scholars in Indigenous studies, linguistics, biology, environmental science, and cognitive science that I discuss here note. In part, such oversight might be a product of Eurowestern philosophies of time also being, as Mark Rifkind (2017) suggests, *settler time*. Settler time forces us all to conform to colonial measures of a particular clock—unitized measures, a capitalist orientation, anachronistic thinking of Indigenous people, and a willful ignorance of longstanding Indigenous opposition to these frames. Rifkind argues for what he terms *temporal sovereignty* (179), which examines the force, trajectory, and harm of settler timescale and periodization on Indigenous people and imagines an Indigenous, sovereign futurity that honors Indigenous temporalities. His work is echoed by that of Juno Salazar Parreñas's work in *Decolonizing Extinction* (2018), who notes that the temporalities involved in extinction stories are fourfold: over "seconds and microseconds," "years and decades," the "*longue durée*" of human history telling "that entails a consideration of multiple centuries of trade, mobility, and colonialism," and "epochal time of thousands and millions of years" (8). Thus, to understand both infrastructures and rhetorical capacities that undergird human and nonhuman relations in periods of species decline, as Parreñas notes, "a single timescale alone is insufficient" (8).

Part of a move toward temporal sovereignty and embracing multiple timescales, I would argue, is offering up alternatives to spatio-temporal ontologies that honor Indigenous timeframes as alternatives to those called for by contemporary Eurowestern philosophy: not to engage in "taking" this knowledge out of context or from Indigenous peoples but as a reminder and an appeal to the ethical component of Rose's call for "multispecies knots of ethical time." To consider a temporal scale beyond the mathematical-experiential, human-nonhuman, subject-object, animal-thing binaries requires an attunement beyond clock or body, beyond the linear past-present-future that marks consideration of the Anthropocene as a geological epoch. In part, I make such an argument in service of acknowledging what unequal impacts such a time-based designation has on earthly peoples in both the Global North and South—a stark reflection of Whyte's (2017) reminder that, for many Indigenous people now across the globe, a dystopic and apocalyptic future has already come to pass. To this end, scholars such as Rangi Matamura (2021) point to Indigenous ways of decolonizing time, toward polychronic temporal systems that privilege "seasonal cycles, environmental relationships and traditions" (65) as one potential deviation from settler time. Arguably, such deviation is one that nonhuman bodies are already closely attuned to.

Matamura situates local and specific tribal Māori traditions of combining environmental, ecological, and celestial phenomenon to define both time and season, acknowledging the creation of an "environmental calendar" (69). Such a calendar is perhaps best exemplified by the interrelationships between Māori planting of sweet potato (*kūmara*) with the appearance of long-tailed and shining cuckoos, and its harvest with both the birds' departure and the appearance of the constellation Vega in the morning sky (70). Such notions of time are neither cyclical nor linear, as each element in the temporal consideration—star, bird, plant, person—exists on its own time, which changes from season to season, year to year. As Reid and Sieber (2016) point out, these layered notions of time are complex because of their interwoven nature; none of the activities of emergence of Māori time, for example, act independently. Reid and Sieber point not only to the interweavings of temporalities to acknowledge the value of Indigenous conceptualizations of time, but also to the interruptions such conceptions make to contemporary Eurowestern ideas of linear, nonagential time: for the Eastern Cree, time is seen as a cycle and the relationship between past, present, and future triangulated; for the Māori, such temporality appears as a double spiral (249). Reid and Sieber note that for the Cree Nation of Wemindji, the past is seen to be living in the present. They complement this disruption of linear time with the Runa of Ecuador, for whom the future is similarly alive and exerting agency (250; see also Kohn 2013). They point to the ways that time intervals for some Indigenous people such as the Amondawa of the Amazon (who do not have equivalent terms for *time* and *year* as does English) are "not based on countable units but based upon the interplay between ecological facts in the natural environment and social structures" (250; see also Sinha et al. 2011). These conceptions of time sit in the speculative middle, neither entirely mathematical nor entirely phenomenological.

Such interplay, or a relational concept of time, is what interested me as I began the process of trying to "find" an endangered bird that I could not recognize on a landscape I was unfamiliar with, trying to create relational partnerships with those who most know the land—primarily private property owners—and to do so on a compressed timescale that had migratory bird bodies and growing grass as its primary clocks. Of course, I wouldn't be the first to tune in to what European scholars of astronomy and botany have called "phenology"—"the study of natural phenomena in relation to climate and plant and animal life cycles' events" (Reid, Sieber and Blackned 2020, 2352; see also Demarée and Rutishauser 2011). However, neither strain of Eurowestern phenology, one climate-oriented and one plant-oriented, do justice to the complex interweaving of environmental time cycles represented by what Trevor Lantz and Nancy Turner (2003) call "Traditional Phenological Knowledge," or TPK. Thus, TPK differs considerably from the Eurowestern coinage of phenology. Lantz and Turner note that "TPK encompasses all knowledge of biological seasonality, including the observation of life cycle changes in specific plant or animal species to indicate the timing of the onset of growth stages in other species, linguistic references to phenological events, traditional conceptions of time as they relate to seasonal change, and spiritual beliefs about cause-and-effect relationships of seasonal change" (265). Lantz and Turner acknowledge that environmental indicators have long been symbolic of time, and that such phenological knowledge is widely accepted today in a variety of places (perhaps the most common for readers might be *The Farmers' Almanac*). However, Lantz and Turner provide more than a sense of overlapping environmental indicators in their close analysis of Indigenous British Columbia peoples in their example of the relationship between the Swainson's Thrush (*Catharus ustulatus*) and the ripening of salmonberries.

For the Haida, Squamish, Nuu-chah-nulth, Haisla, Oweekeno, Straits Salish, Tlingit, and Ditidaht people, the singing of the Swainson's Thrush is thought to bring on the ripening of salmonberries (266). In the Ditidaht, Haida, Oweekeno, and Squamish languages, the name of the Swainson's Thrush directly discursively corresponds to this relationship: in all four languages, the thrush is known as the "salmonberry bird" (268). While contemporary botany and zoology might time the arrival of the thrush with the ripening of the salmonberry, the correlation is more than scientific phenology or ethnobotany. Instead, in this one example, we see overlapping ways of being-in-the-world that give rise to a vibrant, moving ecology not beholden to one clock or one object lesson but to many (as Matamura [2021] would say, a polychronic temporality): a hungry people knowing when to collect fruit, a birdsong that ripens berries, a linguistic connection between the overlapping life and seasonal cycles of bird, plant, and human.

Too, these times are embedded in nonhuman "people" and their relationship with humans, storied through bird-human narratives in which the salmonberry bird interacts with Raven to sing each color of the berry into being so that they may eat (Turner and Bhattacharyya 2016, 737). As Turner and Bhattacharyya note, these stories also dictate human protocol (in which the relationship between Raven and salmonberry bird is a telltale "bungling host" [737] story) and lessons about human-nonhuman interaction and kinship. In the case of the W̱SÁNEC Straits Salish people, the name of the salmonberry bird's song not only mimics its call ("W̱EW̱ELEW̱ELEW̱ELEW̱E´S"), but it is this sound that calls the berries into ripening, color by color:

NENELK´ XELIK´ . . . ("the little black / dark red–headed ones")

NENELPKIK´ . . . ("the little light-headed ones")

NENELC/EMIK´ . . . ("the little red/ruby-headed ones")

NENELPWIK´ . . . ("the little blond/golden-headed ones")

W̱EW̱ELEW̱ELEW̱ELEW̱E´S! . . . ("Ripen, ripen, ripen, ripen!") (736)

The salmonberry bird example, to return to Grosz, represents time as an onto-logical element, a way of being in the world for bird, berry, and human that captures the relation between plant, animal, human, sound, ecosystem, climate, and ripening in which each part cannot be separated from the whole; where mind, body, and ecology unite. The salmonberry bird sits beyond Western sim-plicities of a turtle clock.

Similarly, in "Why We Fish: Decolonizing Salmon Rhetorics," Cutcha Ris-ling Baldy (2021), reflecting on the way the Hupa people live with the salmon of northwest California, notes that these human-nonhuman relationships are complex, "generative, and iterative" (171). Beyond simple naming of genus or spe-cies classification, life cycles of salmon are tied to story, season, and other ani-mals through the Hupa language. As Baldy documents, "Aside from denoting xulo:q'e' [silverside salmon] as the "first part of the spring run of king salmon," their word for mockingbird or nightingale, ło:q'-chwo, is specifically tied to the story of "Salmon's Grandmother" and explains how this yellow-breasted bird comes up the river in May with the first spring run of king salmon, which also marks a difference between the spring and fall runs" (172). In connecting the story of Salmon's Grandmother with the Hupa words for salmon and mocking-bird, Baldy is commenting on the implicit relationship between the yellow-breasted chat (*Icteria virens*), the ripening of the madrone berry (which bears a likeness to salmon eggs) on which it feeds, and the seasonal genetic change from fall to spring in Chinook salmon (Baldy 2021; see also Steinberg et al. 2000). Like the W̱SÁNEC example of the Swainson's Thrush, the migratory return of the yellow-breasted chat suggests a dependent polychronism of bird with the ripening of madrone berries, a genetic change in spring run salmon, and a time to fish. All of these happen all at once, as signals to be heeded and attended to in relation with the Hupa.

As Vanessa Watts, Mohawk and Anishinaabe scholar of Indigenous studies coins, the ontologies shown here by the examples of the W̱SÁNEC and Hupa may be known as "place-thought": "the premise that land is alive and thinking and that humans and non-humans derive agency through the extensions of these thoughts" (2013, 21). This is not a simple ecological calendar or singular body clock but a way of paying attention, of capacious agency distributed in multispe-cies knots. The berries and the salmon, in the case of the W̱SÁNEC Straits Salish and the Hupa, are each on bird time.

Joseph Pitawanakwat (2022), a plant-based educator, similarly comments on the role that Anishinaabemowin bird names reflect bird movement, timing, nesting strategies, weather, and ecological function. In part, such complex rela-tion that allows place-thought is built into the language, in which bird names can contain conglomerates of actions, places, and shifting conditions. Pitawa-nakwat offers a range of examples that speak to the ways that place-thought is embedded into Anishinaabemowin names: the winter wren (*anaamisagada-weshiinh*), whose name translates to "underneath the floor" because the bird nests in trees that have tipped over; the common nighthawk (*piyyaask*), named after the time of one hears its call (dusk); the white-throated sparrow (*kakiwa-shikikishiki macitonishi*) or "weather bird," the length of whose song is associated with rain; the vulture (*wiinaange*), or "ugly bird," with a preverb in the name that implies change, as in the vulture's function of changing carrion, something ugly, into something else (Pitawanakwat 2022).

It is this turn toward thinking about time differently, indebted to Indigenous peoples and place-thought, and positioned against settler time, that I wish to posit as an alternative to the *chronos-kairos* tension that opened this discussion, and which I argue applies to the kinds of current mitigation measures currently proposed for conservation of the bobolink. Instead of *chronos* (measurable time) or *kairos* (opportune time), here I propose a consideration of *pheno* (from the Greek *phaino*, "to appear"; "to show"; "to shine"). Rather than either a moment that is either countable or right, *pheno* speaks to the moment as it appears, as it shines—to paraphrase Rose (2017), perhaps as it shimmers. It speaks to an attuned holding open to the whens of time that cannot be scheduled or broken into comprehensible units and linear trajectories but are beholden to what appears at what place-thoughts and when.

Such a view of time is one that moves against what John Muckelbauer (2016) suggests are rhetoric's "implicit paradigms" resting on Aristotelian time measures of *chronos* and *kairos*. Instead, *pheno* is resonant with Muckelbauer's call for an ecological rhetorical model in which persuasion happens between and among humans and nonhumans, a heliotropic vision of a new material rhetoric that situates persuasion as a turning toward what appears (as in plants toward the sun), what shows itself in what time, what shines. *Pheno* also captures in itself the *waiting to appear* that characterizes so much of environmental and ecological time—for a leaf to unfurl, for water to wear down rock, for an egg to hatch—that is telltale of the natural world. It speaks to the *inopportune* time. It helps capture—more than *kairos* or *chronos*—the struggle in conservation action that characterizes, as Yusoff (2012, 579) suggests, "understandings of presence and making present those that are dead or soon to be dead." It is a turn toward *pheno* that I suggest being on bird time and doing nestwork gives us, an *alliostrophic* turning otherwise toward *that which shimmers* that positions human attention, and our perceptions of time, differently. *Pheno* allows for timescales that are based on what captures the eye; what is beautiful, what happens in an ephemeral moment. Before I make that case, I turn first to a discussion of the bobolink and its rhetorical ecology, the ways that SARA has forwarded a monochronic framework for this threatened species, and how key human attunements to *pheno* may work to widen bird-person persuasion.

Bobolinks, Clock Time, and Rhetorical Ecologies

Like barn swallows and chimney swifts, bobolinks (a threatened species in Canada) live, on average, between four and five years. A migratory bird that travels one of the longest routes on record, from North America to Argentina—twelve thousand miles round trip—they are also a species of special concern in the United States. Unlike their aerial insectivore counterparts, the bobolink is a grassland bird, a passerine that might easily pass for a common blackbird (and thus has a nickname of "skunk blackbird," or in Anishinaabemowin *waab-signaak*, or "white blackbird" because of the male bird's white back and black undersides). Yet, the bobolink is a bird that is known to have twin lives, the first as a North American spring migrator with a sweet song who feeds primarily on bugs and weed seeds, and the second as a fall-arriving South American "rice bird" or "butter bird," who feeds almost primarily on rice as the bobolink makes its way to warmer climates. The second life is one that has long caused tension between humans and birds as the bobolink eats cash seed crops—as one naturalist recounts, "I can recall visiting millet farms in Oxford County, Ontario, in the late 1950s, and seeing farm hands with sawed-off shotguns firing into vast, swirling flocks of thousands of southward-bound bobolinks attracted by the field of millet grown for the pet shop industry" (MacKay 2005). The fattened fall bobolink is still known as the "butter bird" in Jamaica and some southern US states, as it has been historically hunted as a game bird and eaten as a delicacy as it passes through its migratory flight.

Yet because of the almost total decimation of tall-grass prairie (over 99 percent [NWF (National Wildlife Foundation) 2001]), the bobolink faces a threatened status primarily because of a decline in habitat and the destruction of nests and nestlings due to agricultural cutting, as well as pesticide use, habitat fragmentation, livestock overgrazing, and climate change (COSEWIC 2010; McCracken et al. 2013). Given the bobolink's preference for nesting in now-decimated tall-grass prairie, they have settled on surrogate habitat in the form of agricultural fields, a commensality predicated on human colonization through agricultural shifts and migrant labor. Unlike the barn swallow that a passerby might still be able to see in the eaves of a human-built house or barn, or the chimney swift whose telltale swoops down an evening stack might clue an urbanite into its presence, the bobolink exclusively settles in agricultural areas that are surrounded not by forests or human development, but by other agricultural areas (USDA 2010). In other words, "most of the suitable habitat for grassland birds is held in private ownership" (2). What this means for humans interested in the bobolink and its conservation is that farmers and private landowners are the primary points of contact and experts on the birds. Yet, they also face scrutiny because of the threat farming choices and machinery have on bobolinks.

The bobolink prefers to nest in forage crops—plants grown primarily for livestock to graze on—made up of at least three kinds of grass or broadleaved plant, such as timothy, clover, Kentucky bluegrass, fescue, and of course, hay. As more and more farmers turn their cash crops into monocultured soy, corn, and wheat, or alfalfa (a crop that bobolinks don't care for), habitat for the birds continues to decline. At the same time, forage crops—hay in particular—present their own challenge as a mitigator between bird and farmer. Because of increased pesticide and fertilizer use and changes in climate, hay cutting is not only carried out two weeks earlier than it was in the 1950s, but often farmers are able to get two or even three cuttings of hay in one season. While a hay growing season is between thirty-five to forty-two days, a bobolink nesting cycle is fifty-two, inclusive of ten days needed for fledglings to avoid harvesting machinery (USDA 2010, 5). While the difference sounds small, modern farming practices wipe out 94 percent of any given generation of bobolinks in a traditional harvesting season (Bollinger et al. 1990, 148; see also Fromberger 2020). This leads many conservationists to conclude that "there is an inherent conflict between agricultural management and grassland bird conservation" (USDA 2010, 2).

Certainly, there is a good reason for this interpretation of the relationship between bobolink and farmer. Bobolinks are as choosy about their habitat as chimney swifts: not only do they not care to nest in alfalfa, but they avoid heavily grazed areas and prefer grass of a certain height (from nine to twenty inches from the start of the breeding season to the end). Within those parameters, they avoid fields with either too many litter layers of grass, a too-high forb[1]-to-grass ratio or too many patches of bare ground, or too many woody shrubs and saplings (McCracken et al. 2013, 20). They are particular about the size of their habitat grounds: smaller than about twenty-five acres, the birds aren't really interested. They also prefer the centers of fields to the margins. In other words, although surrogate habitat of farm fields sounds like a generous descriptor of bobolink habitat, in fact the birds are much more particular, preferring only hayfields and grasslands of a certain size that have been regularly maintained— that is, cut or burned—in order to keep out plant litter and growth of dense and woody brush (23). Like Robin Kimmerer's (2013) observations of sweetgrass or Anna Tsing's (2015) accounts of matsutake mushrooms, bobolinks thrive in areas of farmed disturbance, not simple fields that are left fallow for years on end.

One of the most useful human mitigations for the bobolink is a time-based one. It times the cycle of bird and hay, mandating an early first hay cut in order to allow a sixty-five-day gap before the second cut (in order to allow "14 days for regrowth, 42 days for a nesting cycle, and 9 days" for nestlings to learn how to fly [Strong and Perlut, n.d.]). Yet these mitigations are problematic for farmers.

The longer a farmer waits to harvest forage crops, the lower the protein quality of those crops. A delay in haying represents a significant decrease in the quality, and thus market value of those crops for feeding livestock also drops (USDA 2010, 4). This issue of time and timing with market mandates presents a fundamental quandary in timing: between segmenting time periods with human capital in mind (*chronos*), and acknowledging the phasal and processual paces that both bird and hay need to grow (*pheno*). This conflict was well represented by initial reactions of farmers to COSEWIC's recommendations to delay haying by popular press articles such as "Farmers Grapple with Balancing Agriculture and Protecting the Bobolink" (Riley 2012) in which one farmer queried, "Do people want to eat or not? . . . That's what it is coming down to. They're legislating farming right out of existence." Yet such coverage of the issue was not one that pitted farmers against birds but, rather, captured tensions between private landowners, government bodies, the Species at Risk Act, and time itself.

Thus, it might come as no surprise that when bobolinks' protection provisions of SARA were under consideration by the Ontario Endangered Species Act in 2011, farmers were given a three-year exemption from the policy in order to give them time to determine best management practices that might work for both the bobolink and their own livelihoods. This exemption was extended ten more years in 2015 by a government response statement (Government of Ontario). These extensions of time to implement the guidelines of SARA provincially take precedence over official SARA protections established for the bobolink in 2017. These time delays, alongside varied incentive programs for a variety of mitigations for the birds, have seemed to quell much of the initial unrest and outrage that characterized private landowners' first responses to the bobolink being listed as threatened in 2010. Yet it bears an ironic [time]stamp nonetheless: an argument about delaying haying, an adjustment of as little as 1.5 weeks in most cases, has resulted in a ten-year extension of acting on bobolink conservation. Unlike the building of a human-made structure to capture arguments about species loss for barn swallows and chimney swifts, in the case of the bobolink it is clock time through SARA and other government policy—*chronos*—that exerts the most agency in human-nonhuman persuasion. Yet the cases that you will read about below, while influenced by the bobolink being listed on SARA, are inclusive of decisions that as of this moment, have very little to do with SARA—at least until 2025. In this strange present, it is *pheno* that rules decision-making about the bobolink in the cases I next present, an opportunity to be on bird time.

The interruption of *pheno* into a discursive act of policy that tries to mandate bird, hay, and human behavior is an intervention into the kinds of present absences that are proffered by surrogate-grassland-as-hayfield habitat for a disappearing bird, and a central tenet in thinking about turning otherwise in rhetorical ecologies. Time as *pheno*—following what appears, noticing what shines—in many ways is what now enlivens any conservation effort, whether in building and monitoring an artificial structure for disappearing populations of animals or attuning oneself to the loss of human-nonhuman relations. Allowing for polychronic time, *pheno*, bird time, means thinking about 1.5 weeks as also 1.6 inches of hay growth as also 30 percent decline in protein content as also learning to fly. Attunements to bird time situate humans and nonhumans differently in relation to one another in ways that help us understand the persuasive capacity of lives lived in tandem; to, as Rose (2006) suggests, allow for the potentialities of a "future complexity of life," or what she eloquently asserts is "our potential gift to the future" (77). Perhaps the potential of *pheno* lies in turning human attention toward small repairs in nonhuman relations that are still possible. Such action may help attune us to Parreñas's (2018) four kinds of time at once in the service of greater ecological care; however, as the next three cases show, such persuasions are still bound by settler time.

The Hay Delay at Century Farm: When a Hundred Years Yields to Birds

Unlike sighting barn swallow structures at the side of the road or being given GPS coordinates for artificial chimneys by Birds Canada, when it came to "finding" bobolinks, I was at first on my own, and certainly at a loss. As the epigraph to this chapter notes, it seemed like no matter what conservation body I called or who I spoke to, monitoring programs were delayed and volunteering slowed to a standstill. Thus, it was only serendipitously as I was gathering materials for the research-creation project discussed in the conclusion of this book that I was put in touch with David Gascoigne, former president of a regional field naturalist's association, by a query to a local bird supply shop about barn swallow nesting cups. Not only did David supply those nesting cups, but he worked as a kind of birdy sponsor in the cases of both Century Farm and Sprucehaven. When I spoke to David about my interests in the bobolink, he knew exactly whom to talk to and where to go. "My friend Diane has bobolinks on her farm," he said to me. "I'm sure she would be fine if we visited."

It was in this way I found myself finally free of lockdown restrictions and driving the fifty minutes halfway to Hamilton, Ontario, near Flamborough and a few miles from the Valens Lake Conservation Area, in the heart of Treaty 3 territory. Traditional territory of the Mississaugas of the Credit First Nation, the Haudenosaunee Confederacy, and the Huron-Wendat Nation, I learn that this land is covered with a historic trail system developed by these nations that have since been turned into major transportation thoroughfares, and their sacred lakes now home to dams and golf country clubs (Tidridge 2019). To me, it looks like the middle of nowhere—at least four maze-like turns off the nearest highway separated by miles, farmhouse after field after barn as far as the eye can see. I follow David's car, and when we finally pull off onto a long dirt driveway and come to a stop, it is with some surprise that I am hailed by Diane, the farm's owner, as my daughter's mother. I am momentarily, again, as confused as barn swallows encountering a structure or swifts a fake chimney. I have only lived in my city of residence a few years, and at this point I haven't seen anyone new for at least a year. As luck would have it, Diane Hood, Century Farm owner, is also Diane, a neighbor from down the street where I live who walks faithfully past my house weekly and whom my daughter regularly chats up in my driveway. I am strangely in two places at once to be recognized as a person in this utterly strange landscape.

I explain my project to Diane and thank her for letting me observe her hayfields, then follow David on the gridlike path through calf-high hay spotted with bright yellow dandelions. As we walk, he points out tree swallows that zip across the fields and gives names to little brown birds I know I won't be able to remember. Then, flying low over a field in middle distance, he points out a black and white bird whose song is one that I've never heard—the first bobolink I've ever seen. Its song is nothing like the melodic descriptions that I've been reading about; later I hear the bobolink called the "R2D2 bird," and it is this moniker that most clearly captures the robotic *beep-boop-plink* of the male bird's call. Yet once I hear it, I can't not hear it; the field is now covered with bobolinks, most of which I cannot see, but that I hear everywhere. Pretty soon I am seeing bobolinks on the power lines over the driveway, on tall trees bordering field property lines, zig-zagging across fields, landing in small brushy scrub near the footpath, disappearing into grass, yellow heads mistaken for dandelions. They are never in one place for long, and there are so many. Seeing these bobolinks is enough to trick me, for a moment, into thinking they are abundant. Yet as Diane later tells me, she gets two to three calls a week from birder associations asking if, indeed, she does have bobolinks. This is uncommon abundance, a species presence that also stands in for the process of being lost.

I learn that Diane has bobolinks on ninety-seven-acre Century Farm primarily because she requests that the farmer who cuts her hay wait until the second week of July to do so and began making this request soon after she bought the farm from her father in 2002. She notes that this, along with her resistance to pesticide spraying, is an unpopular choice and gives me the history of Century Farm in a way that suggests that this tension between property owner and farmer has been one worth sustaining—certainly for the bobolinks involved. Century Farm gets its name because it has been in the Hood family for one hundred years, since 1892, when it was bought by Diane's great-grandfather Peter, then passed on to his son Stanley, then passed on to Stanley's son (and Diane's father), Kenneth, before finally being taken on by Diane, the second oldest of seven children. Yet the farm itself is on "hardscrabble" land, prone to drought and full of bedrock, resistant to only but the hardiest of choices. Century Farm used to have pigs, cattle, and chickens, but as Diane acknowledges, as her own father aged and the farming grew no easier, farm fields were converted into pastureland, eventually to hay alone. A moniker that hearkens to the span of one human life, it is time that has changed Century Farm into a small oasis for bobolinks among factory farms and estate severance lots with huge houses on them. And it is the past that shapes Diane's decision to keep it that way.

When I talk with Diane and her sister, Doreen, who owns a farm a few miles away and takes care of Century Farm when Diane is in the city, I ask what first interested Diane in the plight of bobolinks. She says that they have been on the farm as long as she can remember, though comments that, as far as she knows, there are only bobolinks on about three farms in the area now. She recalls that their song was one that has always stuck in her head as a bringer of the warm weather of spring. As Diane speaks, her sister interrupts to tell the story of Diane catching pneumonia as a baby, and being put in an incubator before doctors knew to cover babies' eyes. As a result, Diane had deeply reduced vision that was only realized around the age of ten. As Doreen tells it, Diane was the child who was always attuned to birdsong when her sisters and brothers were oblivious. She says she thinks that is why Diane has paid such attention to all the birds on the farm, and bobolinks in particular because their song is so very unique. Diane says she supposes that could be true but that she also remembers reading a pamphlet after taking a veterinary course on pigs about the decline of bobolinks due to the cutting of hay. Reflecting on Century Farm, she decided to implement a delayed haying to help keep the bobolinks on her property, realizing that they—and hands-off hayfields—were something special. The sisters' stories complement each other, family lore blending with conservation discourse, a double-time in trying to remember both moments and seasons and decades with what has brought us here now, listening to bobolinks overhead.

Because Diane keeps the family farm but has enjoyed a career in the city, she is technically more landowner than farmer. As a result, she gives the hay on her fields away to the farmer who cuts it—as she says of requesting a delay in haying, "If I'm giving hay away, I can wait a couple of weeks." When I ask how long she waits to cut the hay, expecting to hear the oft-cited date of July 15 in conservation literature, she surprises me with her answer. She says instead that she has learned over time by the bobolinks' song that when it fades to nothing in the fields, it is safe to cut hay. "One day they're there, the next they're gone," she says. Their song is how they show themselves, and it is this song, too, that persuades Diane into timing the cut of hay. I realize that the July 15 date that I've seen echoed in so many places is supported by the biology of bird bodies, days carefully counted from observations of birds nesting, mating, laying eggs, incubating, hatching, feeding, fledging. But it is also a date very much in accordance with settler time— a "dominant periodization scheme," as Rifkind (2017, 179) might say, that eclipses so many other possible ways of seeing, of listening, of turning.

As we wind down our conversation, talk turns to the future of Century Farm. Because Diane doesn't have children, she wonders what to do with the farm—her many nieces and nephews, starting careers and families in nearby cities, have little interest in farming life, nor could they afford to take on the costs of burgeoning land prices in the area. Of course, she could sell it outright, she muses, but the thought of watching Century Farm become another factory farm or developer's dream is not one that she relishes. Besides, she offers, neither of those choices would do much in the way of helping the refuge for bobolinks that she's created. "As my father used to say," she discloses, "you can make more money. But you can't make more land."

Diane's reflection on the end of a farming generation resonates with the ways that birds themselves measure time with their bodies, time that is captured only so much in the conservation literature or dates on the calendar. At

Century Farm, the bird's success is clear: Diane notes that she has heard them on the farm all of her life. Yet that success has clearly come at the price of a profitable, working farm, one that faces an uncertain future. To choose to be on bird time and not to conform to the pressures of market capitalism is to resist settler time in a way that is not recognized nor supported by the times we are in—it is an unfamiliar frame of reference. "I wonder what will happen to this farm," Diane says. "Who will take care of it after I'm gone?" I can tell that this is the question that sticks to our conversation and leaves it on a wistful note—it is not just the farm's fate that is precarious, it is also the bobolinks. We have no answer. Instead, as we close our conversation, she remarks confidently on what she has learned from Century Farm over time: "You have to enjoy these beautiful things for as long as you can." Our attention turns to ephemera over durée or epoch.

There is much in my experience with the bobolinks of Century Farm that resonates with *pheno*. I had anticipated in advance of my visit to Century Farm a cut-and-dried explanation of hay delaying with, perhaps, some representation of the agricultural-conservation conflict, as represented by pamphlets by the USDA. Yet what I instead received, in part experiencing the present abundance of bobolinks on Century Farm and in part reflecting on their cohabitation with generations of the Hood family, was an echo of bird time: a conversation in late spring in the fleeting moments of a short breeding season, a lesson in birdsong, a worry about bird and human futurity. It is neither calendar-based nor only experiential phenomenon that guides decision-making about haying at Century Farm. It is, instead, an ontological noticing that has emerged over human lifetimes—decisions to move from farm to pasture, from one generation to another, from an agrarian to a city-based life. The decision to delay haying on Century Farm is a decision made not by the clock but by the shimmer of the persuasion of birdsong, its presence and its absence, and the privilege of settlement. Like the salmonberry bird, it is the bobolink's song itself that predicts when the hay should be cut on Century Farm, combined with a landowner who listens and acts as a hope-practice, who honors her own attunements to the nonhumans that she has grown up with, and in so doing, has grown to love.

Such attunements to *pheno*, to what appears and shows itself, are bound by both a generational past and an unknown future. To delay haying in one season is also to situate that season in relation to all that have come before and all that will come after, beholden to the generational time of birds (whose nesting refuges have gotten smaller and smaller over the years), hay (which requires reseeding and thus human management to flourish), and damaging agricultural practices over time. The past of Century Farm is bound by one hundred years, four generations of settler humans and hundreds of generations of Indigenous ones, and at least twenty-five documented generations of birds. Its present seems to be holding at bay the pressures of the Anthropocene, acre by acre, bird by bird. Its future will be beholden, too, to what shows itself, not on the clock but in place-thought: a continued decline in bird numbers, the absence of bird-song confusing the time to harvest and making it harder to listen, the silence of a landscape, the loss of a family farm on top of the hundreds of drawn-out losses of land unfairly ceded to settlers. As I sit on a boulder at Century Farm and listen to what I now recognize as bobolinks overhead, a few weeks given to delay haying seems like so much more. It blends into the long spring of a pandemic, the haste of trying to find a vanishing bird on a strange landscape, the brief and small life of a bird soon to fly six thousand miles. It seems like the time that it will take to enjoy beautiful things for as long as I can.

When Bird Time Is Also Dog Time: Late-Cut Refuges on Handy Dog Farm

What sticks with me in leaving Century Farm is the privilege it has in suspending haying decisions no matter the cost; this is not the case for most working farms, who have to balance needs of livestock, hay prices, and keeping farms running smoothly on a day-to-day basis. Agriculture is on seasonal time, but it is also dictated by pressures of market capitalism and thus beholden to settler timetables, as its histories of labor cement. Such is the case of Handy Dog Farm, 147 acres of hayfields owned by Victoria and John Lamont in St. Agatha, Ontario, a fifteen-minute drive west from the heart of the city and only a five-minute drive away from the barn swallow structures at Ladyslipper Drive, where subdivisions slowly creep into farmland. Located on the Haldimand Tract and settled on land "sold" by Thayendanegea to Amish and Mennonites in the late 1700s, St. Agatha is still primarily farmland and still farmed by large Mennonite families. It's common to see horses and buggies on the township roads that crisscross the area; the land is both arable and suitable for pasture.

Thus, it is quite a surprise to find myself in the lushness of hip-high hay in early June alongside Victoria, who is, of all things, one of my colleagues in the English Department who also happens to breed border collies—hence the "Handy Dog" moniker of the farm's name, which is an homage to working sheepdogs. While I had once in the past been to Victoria's farm to watch sheep-dog trials, I had not otherwise put together that the farm itself might have been home to other creatures until Victoria had commented about bobolinks on social media. Following up with her, I learned that she had begun to see bobo-links on her hayfields and was trying to figure out a way to keep them safe while still meeting the mandates of her farm, set out by both a nearby farmer who harvests half of her hay for his own organic beef and lamb, and she and her partner John, who harvest the other half for their sheep. The other forty-seven acres of the farm are wetland, woodlot, and grazing pastureland. They bought the farm in 2007, and Victoria tells me that originally, most of the fields in production were alfalfa. When I ask her why she converted to hay, a less profit-able crop than alfalfa, she replies, "for the sheep." And why sheep? I inquire. "For the dogs," she says, and I realize for the first time that Handy Dog Farm emerges out of not only responsivity to market but also responsivity to the hay-sheep-dog relation. But not only that, which is of course why I am sitting quietly in a hayfield.

When I ask about bobolinks, Victoria tells me that she first started noticing them a few years ago flying over her fields, and a close friend helped her iden-tify them. This year, however, she says that it seems like there are more in her fields than ever before, though she admits that she doesn't know if it's the lush, dense hay in the fields this season or the attunement of a pandemic that has created birding as a worldwide phenomenon (Glotzer 2021). Whichever the reason, Victoria says, it is the movement of the bobolinks in the fields that has her attention: not only the males flitting about and jostling for mates, the way I had seen them at Century Farm, but the females doing nestwork among the flights of males in the dense grass. The females, which I get to see for the first time, are nondescript, robin-sized dun-colored birds, with a short, peeping song. Victoria tells me to watch not only where the females land in the grass from their posts on the tree-lined field border but where they hop to from there, as they often land near their nests but make their way over to them in short bursts to throw predators off the track. I squint at the birds in the dis-tance, the now-familiar "R2D2" sound easily recognizable, counting out five females and at least a dozen males. Yet it is nearly impossible to figure out where they are landing in a sea of yard-high grass. Are they fifty feet away? One hundred? I settle on watching a general area and try to note the amount of activity in nearby spots, giving an imprecise finger-point as to where I've seen some disappear into the dense grass.

Victoria has been watching bobolinks in her hayfields for weeks, trying to suss out where their nests are, in a race against the two-week "best cutting" window of late June. She knows that if they cut hay now, these nestlings will not survive. She tells me she has been hoping for rain, because farmers won't cut wet hay, as it increases the likelihood of mold. If we get three sunny days in a row, it is likely neither the nearby farmer who leases half the fields nor her partner John will wait to cut hay. Which is, in part, why I am here. Given that Handy Dog Farm must keep these fields in production, Victoria has settled on trying to create late-cut refuges in her fields. Because bobolinks tend to nest in the center of hayfields, it is possible to cut hay around the periphery of fields for the first cut, letting the birds fledge young before harvesting the middle of the field during the second cut in late August.

The "late-cut refuge" is one grassland bird protection recommended by conservationists (USDA 2010, 4), especially for farmers or private landowners who may have more productive land than they need to harvest, or better and poorer growing hay on different parts of their property. While Victoria doesn't fall into either of these categories and thus has had to lobby both her partner and their neighboring farmer to allow late-cut refuges on the fields, she is nonetheless adamant. We sit in the field with four-foot fluorescent orange plastic spikes. After an hour of watching where we think the birds are congregating, we place the spikes in a line in the middle of the field, one that Victoria will later wind caution tape around and tell both farmers to leave a wide berth of uncut hay around the bright yellow stripe on the landscape. My jeans grow damp at the top of my boots from the morning-wet grass as I see what we are doing as its own kind of hope-practice. This is a nestwork unlike any I have yet undertaken for this project, activity seamlessly blending in with metonymy: I observe, I listen, I walk, I hold tape and stakes, I reflect, I write. I see no nests, but there is nestwork going on all the same.

To turn to *pheno* on Handy Dog Farm is to allow for observation and hope to sit at the heart of relational time, and to let energy and motion—the building and tending to of an unseen nest, the time it takes for nestlings to fledge—be the guide of what practices to embrace, and when to act. Helping Victoria create space for a late-cut refuge was in part an act of being persuaded by the motion of bird bodies—neither she nor I had seen nests (they are often extremely difficult to find because of the denseness of the hay) but were following the guidance of bobolink bodies in motion to help create small patches of protection. This right time was not the same time as last year, nor will it be the same next year. Truthfully, neither of us could stop the cutting of the hay, driven by a two-week window and the pressures farmers face to earn a living on its sale—we are in this case, like so many others, beholden to settler time. But there is still something unique happening here, a turning differently in the face of cohabitation with nonhuman others. Bobolinks on Handy Dog Farm now contribute to its relational ecology—from hay-sheep-sheepdog to bobolink-hay-sheep-sheepdog, a recognition of the tangle of multispecies knots. There is room to be persuaded by what appears, room to change violent farming practices ever so slightly for the plight of an endangered species, room to engage hope as a practice.

There is also room here to reflect on temporality in a "late-cut" refuge for birds, as *late* takes on a relative meaning among birds, grass, farmer, sheep, and dog. It may be too late for the farmer's ideal product, but it is just in time for bobolinks to fledge, and probably good enough for most of the sheep. Perhaps "late" gets new symbolic meaning when we adjust from *chronos* to *pheno*. Instead of *late* meaning "too late for an economic good," it is instead a reminder of the *slownesses* of environmental synchrony that can allow for the relational success of grass, bird, and human to emerge. Perhaps *late* suggests a kind of time-based reciprocity that allows for all to flourish, acknowledging that, in this case, precarity is the ultimate guiding force. As Yusoff (2012, 584) notes, such an approach reconfigures what Serres (1995 [1990]) calls the "natural contract," part of which includes learning with nonhuman others. Rather than dominion over the natural world, Serres stresses a contract that privileges "admiring attention, reciprocity, contemplation, and respect" (38). Yusoff (2012) clarifies that "This *learning with* can also be part of learning to pay attention to different kinds of violence and danger that are uncovered through practice and being attentive to the impact and interference of our own practices on the lives of other subjects. It can be a way of testing and experimenting with relations, firming them up or letting them go, while being alert to the performative function of bringing the contractual into being through iterative acts" (585).

It is this acknowledgment of the violence of contemporary farming practices in the midst of still needing to engage in them that has shaped practices on Handy Dog Farm. This late-cut refuge is a material act that showcases the tension between capitalism and species precarity. It is not, yet, needing to contend with the bureaucracies of government bodies in implementing SARA as they work out how to negotiate with farmers about the birds they share land with. Instead, this is a material argument showcasing rhetorical capacity that depends far more on the coemergence of relations. It is an opening to seeing what is possible when one chooses to live in reciprocity, attuning oneself to what shows itself in (bird) time (or what one needs to squint to see)—and asks whether, in time, such action will allow for a firming up or a letting go.

As I leave Handy Dog Farm, I ask Victoria what she would like to see happen to it in the future. She says if it was totally up to her, she would take the fields out of production and reseed them with native plants. But since it isn't, she says that she hopes to experiment in the future with different kinds of hay that have different, later cutting seasons. In the meantime, she will continue to stake off areas of refuge from now on and believes that many farmers would be willing to do what she has done. "It's not much," she says, "but it's better than nothing." I think about what it means to approach growing grass in terms of birds, and sheep, and dogs, rather than only dates on a calendar. And I think again about Rose's (2006) assertion that to live is to participate "in three lives: the given, the lived and the bequeathed" (74). Rose says that to fight against man-made death is to honor the third kind of life—the life that we bequeath to others (74). Thinking about the border collies on Handy Dog Farm, I muse on the title of Rose's essay: "What If the Angel of History Were a Dog?" Perhaps the angel of history is the dog-sheep-grass-bird relation instead. I am in the middle of writing this chapter, trying to contend with all of the field notes I've collected about bobolinks in the compressed time I now have until a book deadline, when I get an email from Victoria. "I'm happy to report that there are bobolinks in the refuges we left," she writes. "Saw some fledglings this morning."

Sprucehaven: An Offset Futurity

Three miles away from Handy Dog Farm lies the 119 acres of Sprucehaven, marked off Highway 12 by a huge red barn replete with a white smiley face high up on the gambrel roof. It is in this barn where I first meet David Gascoigne, who walks me around Sprucehaven and shows me the large colony of barn swallows living in the barn, checks the bluebird houses that span the northern property line, and points out the plywood squares in the eastern woodlot indicative of the salamander monitoring program going on there. As we walk, he names each area of Sprucehaven: the huge pond near the farmhouse, the New Forest, the newly created wetland Swale, and what I've come to see, fifty-eight-acres of a big grassland field that I will watch throughout the late spring and early summer turn from gold to green. David is a steward of Sprucehaven, monitoring the goings-on of many of the critters there, as part of his work with the regional field naturalist's association and also his longstanding friendship with Sprucehaven's owners, David Westfall and Sandy and Jamie Hill.

I have come to Sprucehaven quite by accident—in service of trying to find nesting cups for barn swallows, which Sprucehaven has a few of in their barn as part of their participation in a government study that was seeking whether or not barn swallows used them in "natural" surroundings (Heagy et al. 2014). While I came to Sprucehaven for their nesting cups, I am enchanted by the rest of what I see during the tour: not only newly arrived barn swallows but tree swallows, bluebirds, vesper sparrows, savannah sparrows, eastern meadowlarks, moths, butterflies, salamanders. On the day of my first visit to Sprucehaven, we see a snapping turtle—David excitedly tells me it's the first—at the Swale, a newly made wetland just to the east of the farmhouse that used to be not much more than a dirt pit, from what I gather, but, thanks to partnering with Ducks Unlimited, is now beginning to host its first wetland creatures.

Still, it is the grassland that I am most interested in, rolling hills bordered by farm roads, a neighboring alfalfa field, and a huge cell phone tower. The field was taken out of alfalfa production only a few years ago; in 2018 it was replanted with native grasses and plants. I get the planting list from David Westfall; what has looked to me to be a sea of grass and weeds is instead sixty-six different native plants, among which are Canada blue joint, wild rye, Canada anemone, fox sedge, sand dropseed, blazing star, beard-tongue, wild bergamot, six kinds of milkweed. It is a field created for grassland birds, and it waits for them.

I learn this from sitting down with the owners of Sprucehaven, which over time has become a meeting point for all kinds of local nature enthusiasts, from educators, to scientists, to young naturalists (Lammers-Helps 2016). David (Dave) Westfall and Sandy Hill, brother and sister, together took over running Sprucehaven from their parents, who bought the property in 1977. Then, it was a working alfalfa farm on which stood a small farmhouse and pond, with a shelterbelt of spruce trees acting as a wind break on the property line, giving the farm its name. When Dave and Sandy took the property on in their own retirement, they did so as a family project, building a new house large enough for both families, enlarging the pond and installing oxygenating plants, planting over three thousand trees with the help of the local conservation authority and creating a wildlife corridor through the center of the farm—as well as putting up scores of bird and bat houses, and leaving the barn doors open for barn swallow nesting season. Much like the Boothbys of Fairnorth Farm, it is clear that both Dave and Sandy are passionate about this land, about the changes they've made to it over time, and about the relationships that they have formed with dozens of members of the community by letting others share in it.

When I ask about the newly planted grassland, they relay a story of partnering with the regional naturalist's association, of which their friendship with David Gascoigne was a key part in having them think about stewardship in new ways. While they had looked to lend stewardship over a few acres—perhaps one or two that could sponsor native plants—it wasn't until a developer had spotted an eastern meadowlark on a golf course five miles away that the owners of Sprucehaven were contacted about potentially providing an offset to that 108-acre development. The development touted itself as one that would provide the suburbs of Ladyslipper Drive with a "future employment/industrial campus" known as the West Side Employment Lands (Dillon Consulting 2021). The golf course was razed to make way for this development, but as part of a mitigative measure on SARA, was required to supply as much habitat for the eastern meadowlark as it was destroying. One of the main mitigations to such habitat destruction is in the creation of "offsets," land proffered in substitution for critical habitat being destroyed by development (much like the barn swallow structure stands in for a barn). The eastern meadowlark and the bobolink, both threatened grassland birds, have identical mitigation measures. Even though no bobolinks were sighted on the golf course, the creation of any grassland habitat would have about the same chance of attracting them as meadowlarks. Thus, the required forty-three-acre offset for the development was established at Sprucehaven, in the form of a newly planted field of native plants and grasses taken out of alfalfa production.

Of course, just as a barn swallow structure is not a barn, or an artificial chimney is not a chimney, a newly planted offset field is not an established grassland nor a conventional hayfield. As I learn from talking to conservation biologists, it takes bobolinks, on average, three years to establish themselves in a field and another five to breed, or eight years total to measure their established "success" in any one area. Yet bobolink monitoring programs on restored habitat themselves cap at five years, not long enough to measure one way or another whether bobolinks will successfully inhabit an environment. This is a complicated rhetorical ecology, dominated by money and time on behalf of the nonhuman body. It first relies on the metaphorical idea of equal substitution—that one site of grass is equal to another five miles away. It also assumes that in such a trade, land can be bought and sold on a human schedule. For developers, this is the

time it takes to break down buildings and country clubs, rezone land to com-
mercial uses, get city permits, and build more buildings. For conservation biologists and government programming, this is not even enough time for birds to
scout and decide to settle: five calendar years.

If one might learn anything from nestwork, it is how wrong these assumptions are, how choosy small aerial nonhuman beings are about where they might
live, fly to, find one another, raise and fledge young. Development offsets are
merely a way of doing business by the capital clock, of ticking a conservation
box in order to be able to move forward in time. They do not take into account
the preferences of birds, how long it takes grass to grow, the generational time of
seeking out familiar landscapes of those who have come before you. One might
frame them as a stopgap measure, but even that is incorrect. They are not getting us from here to there; they are simply removing the burden of conservation
and placing it elsewhere.

And those elsewheres have their own stories, as private landowners like Dave
and Sandy suggest. Although they were happy to take the oddly shaped and
topographically difficult acreage out of production, their farmer neighbor was
not, thinking it both a waste of land and a messy endeavor. Besides, they assert
when we talk together about the offset field itself, "the timing was absolutely
wrong." They talk about the time that fields take to grow, and the fact that the
golf course was destroyed long before any of the seeds could even take root in
their field. In the meantime—the time we are in now—they say, the birds five
miles away had nowhere to go. "In a couple years, the field will be fabulous,"
Sandy intimates. The spaces and nows of an offset are not quite lining up, not
quite place-thought—they bump up against the wrong scale, against settler
time, over and over. They suggest seconds at the expense of years, years at the
cost of considerations of trade and human history. The wrong time, the wrong
place in trying to persuade nonhuman others. Yet with us in this strange present, in which we are surrounded by a field of grass that has yet to host any bobolinks—or eastern meadowlarks, for that matter—is the overhang of the future,
a time when birds will come if we can wait long enough. At Sprucehaven, it is
pheno strung out over an indefinite period, plant-animal-ecology cycles out of
tune despite the persuasive potential such flora might have in calling birds to
attendance, to settlement. And I can't help but think that the choices made about
Sprucehaven are also those that come from thinking about invisible and unknow-
able futures; it was upon retirement from work that the Westfalls and Hills
were able to make many of the changes that the farm has seen in recent years.

Dave talks not only about the grassland field but about the trees they have planted, in part to combat the loss of many of the property's ash trees due to the emerald ash-borer beetle. "We're not going to be around another forty years," Dave says.

During our conversation, there is this hint of things done now for an unknown later, a recognition of the finitude of human life and also of ongoing nonhuman generations. Sprucehaven's owners recognize that many of these plans for the future they may not see out to an imagined fruition, but they also have seen the ways that Sprucehaven's naturalizing activities have invested the community around them. As we talk, they reel off lists of names of folks—from scientists, to beekeepers, to monitors of their Motus radio telemetry tower to track migratory birds, to citizen bat watchers, to creators of moth and butterfly atlases—all of whom they have gotten to know because of their choices to both renaturalize the landscape and to open their property up to others rather than to revel in its privacy. When they talk about the land, they agree that Sprucehaven has brought people together in ways that that they never could have imagined, and those are all predicated on the nonhuman others that occupy Sprucehaven with the Westfalls and Hills. Their collective choices are hope-practices predicated on an imagined better future, even if they may not be around to see it. "We pay it forward," Dave says.

Throughout the spring and early summer, when I am visiting Century and Handy Dog farms and experiencing the thrill of seeing bobolinks for the first time, then recognizing their sounds as they form indelible imprints in my mind, I think about the grassland field at Sprucehaven. I wonder if it will have any success, and when it might come, whether SARA species will be compelled by the arguments of the little bluestem, the yarrow, the fox sedge, the boneset.

I think about the costs of paying things forward, where that must locate you in the here and now and relative to the past, and who has the resources to make that debit. It is the middle of June when I get an email from David Gascoigne, who monitors the goings-on at Sprucehaven multiple days a week. "I am sure you will be pleased to know," he writes, "we saw our first Bobolink at Sprucehaven last week. We always thought that Eastern Meadowlarks would arrive before Bobolinks but that has turned out not to be the case." While I know now that the presence of one bobolink does not mean a negation of its absence, nor does it mean that the offset has been successful, the flyby is a whisper of a promised future, a glimmer of *pheno*, of bird and field coemerging. To think about the plight of the bobolink in the context of a conservation offset is also to think of that single bird as one with, as Rose (2006) suggests, "a multispecies history— it came into being through its own forebears and through others. Each individual is both itself in the present, and the history of its forebears and mutualists" (136). The one bobolink at Sprucehaven is now past, present, and future— starting the clock anew, a reset of perhaps eight more years of well-managed grasslands to see the first nests emerge—on bird time.

Limits to Turning Otherwise: Settler Time

The cases of Century Farm, Handy Dog Farm, and Sprucehaven all suggest alternative temporal orientations to clock time: the embodied and generational time of Century Farm, the relational dog-bird time of Handy Dog Farm, the reciprocal time of Sprucehaven. As Mark Rifkind (2017) suggests, "being temporally oriented suggests that one's experiences, sensations, and possibilities for action are shaped by the existing inclinations, itineraries, and networks in which one is immersed, turning toward some things and away from others" (2). Such attunement suggests "ways of inhabiting time that shape how the past moves toward the present and future" (2). In illustrating the different ways that humans attune themselves differently to time through their being-with bobolinks (or their absences) and drawing on the concept of *pheno* to offer up a different kind of temporal orientation, I hope to have complicated rhetorical-ecological models that situate *kairos* as a primary circulating force in considering nonhuman agencies and their places of persuasion. In so doing, it is my aim to open up conversations about affective and imaginative potentials such a reframing might offer to rhetorical ecologies.

Yet as the framing to this chapter suggests, and the three cases of bobolinks I've discussed bear out, the stories of these sites also tell us something else. Even those most attuned to different temporal orientations are limited by the logos of market capitalism, the legacies of settler colonialism and private land ownership, and the privileges of whiteness. Each of the farm cases represented here is a settler story, and the decisions made in each case point to the links between conservation action and privilege: in the case of Century Farm and Sprucehaven, the privilege of retirement and the space and time to make choices that do not impact one's economic livelihood; in the case of Handy Dog Farm, the privilege to negotiate farming practices on private land. These cases all depend on the privatization of land and the specter of land-as-future-capital, whether in imagining land passed on to another human generation, dog-eared for more human development, or "gifted" in perpetuity through conservancy. Settler time stops bird time in its tracks.

Even as those who are closest to precarious nonhuman others help us see the possibilities in different temporal orientations—listening for birdsong, watching motion in fields of hay, waiting for grass to grow—they are still bound up in a system that simultaneously stymies such possibility. While those who live in proximity to precarious species are those best positioned to listen closely to them (and to teach us all how to do better ourselves), it is hard to say definitively if the listening is created by that proximity or by the leisure time and space to pay attention. Such attention is cultivated, then, not only by attunement but also by the free market, by land as capital as opposed to relation, and by a belief of entitled settlement—that if land is "yours," you get to make decisions about it and all the creatures who live there. In these ways, even as *pheno* shines different possibilities for how we might be persuaded by nonhuman others, we are all still on settler time, a time that dissociates land from its treaties with first peoples, asserts its economic value, and thus must comply with what Rifkind terms "dominant periodization schemes" (180). One might think of this dominant schema within something as simple as the recurring tax year, and the government mandate that to enjoy the tax break of the label of a "working farm," the land itself must net at least $7,000 in a calendar year. Admittedly, then, there is no escaping this framework for land and *chronos* as a dominating force on all of us on settler time.

I close with this limitation because it is central to thinking about the ways that power circulates in conservation action and decision-making. It is not only the tension between development action and conservation action that dominates the persuasive capacities of humans and nonhumans in these specific entanglements. Settler time, and its attendant interruption of a variety of vibrant relational temporalities, underscores the contemporary damaging limits of the Anthropocene in which we are all living, under which we all suffer unequally, and under which hope-practices cease to flourish. This matters all the more as the people whose ways of knowing—Indigenous people—are becoming increasingly central to thinking through conservation action while their tribal and treaty rights continue to fray (see Pinchin 2021; Parsons and Taylor

2021). In these precarious spaces, I acknowledge that it is not enough to be on bird time, or to tell ghost stories of hauntings by disappearing creatures. Nest-work is not enough. But I would like to think that it is a start, as is fashioning different, creative spaces to help us think through this strange present and its attendant entanglements between *zoe* and *bios*. What this might look like I take up next.

Conclusions for Irreconcilability | Making Attention

As I write this final chapter, I have lived through two years of paying attention to birds differently, of seeking out the relationship between their disappearances and time and human infrastructure, of pondering whether or not these relationships are ones filled with care or filled with hubris. These two years have also been those of the first mass pandemic since 1918 and have led to a sweeping uptick of birdwatching as people of the Global North try to find entertainment from being forced into lockdown. I vacillate in my reading between Jenny Odell's How to Do Nothing *and Thom van Dooren's* Flight Ways: Life and Loss at the Edge of Extinction. *Somewhere in the middle I settle on Christopher Cokinos's* Hope Is a Thing with Feathers. *As I read the stories of the Carolina parakeet* (Conuropsis carolinensis), *the ivory-billed woodpecker* (Campephilus principalis), *the heath hen* (Tympanuchus cupido cupido), *the passenger pigeon* (Ectopistes migratorius), *the Labrador duck* (Camptorhynchus labradorius), *and the great auk* (Pinguinus impennis), *I wonder if, in my lifetime, we will add* Hirundo rustica, Chaetura pelagica, *and* Dolichonyx oryzivorus *to the list of those no longer with us. I think about the ways that paying attention to birds' disappearing has changed the way that I pay attention to the land around me, has allowed me to think differently about occupation, settlement, and land management. In this final long hot summer, wildfires rage across the country and millions of sea animals wash up dead along shores because of soaring temperatures, a testament to the IPCC's most recent report on climate change. Across Canada and the United States, ground-penetrating radar uncovers thousands of unmarked graves of Indigenous children at the sites of residential schools. I think about these two years as lost to bird time, lost to the effects of bird-induced delusion, Hirondelusia, its paces dictated by feathers and disease and generational loss and plights for sovereignty over the meaning of home. I think about the ways that I am and will always be on settler time. How much time has it taken to learn bird preferences, to know intimately their songs and hold their nests in my hands, to mourn, to fall in love? It has taken my lifetime, and two springs, and countless generations. I wonder whether this book is a practice of hope or despair. I wonder if, all this time, I have been writing extinction stories.*

I end this book with a turn to making and a turn to care—a turning toward relationships—on rhetorical-ecological landscapes. Perhaps such turns represent, for some, a simple telos of the rhetorical enterprise: observe, analyze, do. Yet as posthuman projects, making and care not only extend the idea of an imagined end goal but also help humans come to terms with their relations with nonhuman others, be they biotic or abiotic, in this complicated present moment. Human activities of making and care encourage engagement with the unknown potentials of species decline and engagement with the agency of nonhumans to respond to human intervention that do not always depend on nonhuman presence. They also mimic the rhetorical capacities of nonhumans by joining the material and discursive together while attentive to *pheno*, what appears. As final pieces of nestwork, making and care extend possibilities and allow for unknowns in moving toward change and ethical accountability, allow for a stocktaking, even as humans continue to wreak havoc on ecological systems. They bring nonhuman presences nearer so that we may be touched by their absences. They are hope-practices in a time of little hope, a way to mourn and to stay with our collective troubles as we navigate losses of the past, loss in the present, and loss in the future. They are also part of the posthuman project, a way to map the space between analysis and critique in ways that reach beyond the page, toward speculative contact filled with the risk of disappointment.

They are also ways to hone ecological attunement. Throughout this book, I have engaged—and I hope readers have—not only with the barn swallow, the chimney swift, and the bobolink but also with each of their ecological milieus. Not only does each species have its own patterns of flight and family, responsiveness to environment and weather, choosiness of habitat, interaction with infrastructure, and expertise of terrain, but each is also tangled up with human ways of being. Human destruction of habitat, human politics of land ownership and stewardship, human privileging of capital over the lives of nonhuman others, and Eurowestern bifurcations of relational whole-being into dualisms each exert pressures on the livelihoods of these nonhuman creatures. To ask what rhetorical ecology is at work with each of these specific creatures is to invoke not only their natural worlds and chosen landscapes but their material relations with humans—power to shape human policy and discursive legislative acts, to help frame better and worse human decision-making over time, to guide human dwellings and development decisions, to bear human violence, and to reflect the ways that privileged humans treat those with less power, privilege, and agency.

These relations are mimicked by human interconnections with these birds: their longstanding codwelling in and among urban buildings and agricultural fields, their disregard as nuisance or pest and thus insubstantial, their tie with human stories. The barn swallow is tied to myths of eloquence, while the chimney swift is known as the "thunderbird" because of the sounds they make in buildings (Moore 1946). The bobolink and its song characterize the pastoral poetry of Emily Dickinson and William Cullen Bryant (Freedberg 2018). These intimate entanglements of humans, nonhumans, and things, together, represent what one must attune oneself to when considering ecological matters for precarious species, admitting both the ways that "humans infect nature," in Jane Bennett's (2010) terms, as well as "nonhumanity infect[ing] culture" (115).

Joseph Pitawanakwat (2022) suggests that one way we might better concern ourselves with these entanglements is through knowledge of the interconnections of plants and animals, landscapes, and ecosystems by familiarizing ourselves with Indigenous linguistic names that better make these links. Pitawanakwat's areas of expertise are in health sciences and plant medicine, but as he noted in his dealings with plants, they required developing expertise with fauna and landscape to better understand—plants could not be separated out from their relation with other living things. For example, the Anishinaabemowin name for wild bergamot (*Monarda fistulosa*), is "elk medicine." Where you find the elk medicine, you are likely to find the elk, and vice versa. Because Anishinaabemowin bird names so often invoke landscapes and plant relationships, Pitawanakwat (2022) suggests that this traditional ecological knowledge has the potential to close the "bottleneck" in data collection around species at risk—for example, the king rail (*Rallus elegans*) is known in Anishinaabemowin as *manoominikeshiinh*, the "bird who harvests wild rice," drawing attention to its habitat as a marsh bird as well as its diet. Pitawanakwat offers an exemplar for how Western conservationists might listen more closely to Anishinaabemowin linguistic knowledge. Such knowledge might help them more quickly monitor the presence of disappearing species by following Indigenous phenological clues to hone in on particular ecosystems that might contain them. Pitawanakwat offers up one option for how we might contend with naturecultural absences.

Yet even such attunement shows clearly the imbalance between humans and nonhumans in that these entanglements cannot escape the fact that humans are the ones setting most of the guidelines for engagement, no matter how vital the agentic capacities of our nonhuman kin. Still, as humans move closer to and are more widely affected by ecological catastrophe, we might think more, engage more, care more about the other as ourselves because increasingly, the distance between the plight of nonhuman others in the face of environmental crisis is being closed as our own. Thus, a turn in this final chapter from stories of precarity to both making and care are ways to both map and engage ways forward for precarious species, to, as Parreñas (2018) has it, recognize "mutual but unequal vulnerability in an era of annihilation" (177).

Too, these rhetorical ecologies tell stories that humans—primarily Eurowestern humans—tell stories with. While each case of precarity has differing details, we might see that together, the barn swallow, chimney swift, and bobolink chronicle particular accounts of human-nonhuman relations. An examination, not just of the stories we tell about individual bird species—narratives—but about the stories we reproduce about those species losses—the stories those narratives tell—offers the posthuman project a rhetorical sensibility that allows for closer exploration of the communicative potentials between humans and nonhumans in the face of ecological crisis. The first story that is told in the relation between humans and species at risk here is one that defines the parameters of precarity—who and what counts as "in decline" or "at risk" on a species-reduced landscape. Precarity is yoked to legislated action, inclusive of both guidelines for development and behavioral changes, as well as guidelines for punishment for noncompliance. Such action is entangled in layers of bureaucracy—documents, committees, petitions, timelines, monitoring programs, adjudication—as well as layers of development capital—offsets, subdivisions, bridges, mitigation structures. It is also infused with power: not only does it privilege human agency in defining precarity, but it also privileges a settler system that frames land as something that can be owned, thus also privileging land owners over both sovereign nations and long-dwelling nonhuman inhabitants. In linking precarity with bureaucracy and capital, the story that is told is one that also stories the Anthropocene, in which the *longue durée* supports the epoch, in which the quest for never-ending growth is supported with conservation action that is caught up in settler time with few options to free itself. As nonhuman others decline, they story human definitions of precarity. Or as Helen Macdonald (2016) eloquently states in *H is for Hawk*, "the rarer they get, the fewer meanings animals can have. Eventually rarity is all they are made of" (181).

The second story that we are telling stories of precarity with is one that privileges the metaphor: the story that accepts substitution, similarity, and surrogacy as viable options for contending with species decline. For all three species considered here, surrogacy is the starting place. For the barn swallows in chapter 1 and the chimney swifts in chapter 2, logging of old-growth forests and the commensurate use of those materials were what first drew those species to inhabit human-built structures as surrogate habitat for caves and trees. For the bobolinks in chapter 3, inhabiting hayfields exists as a surrogate habitat for the decimation of 99 percent of tall-grass prairie in North America. Here, there is no "going back" to some predetermined, "natural" time of precontact in which these species might somehow function in a way that is not entangled with human beings. Thus, similarity has become the overarching story of these species' adaptability: they have been able to avoid extinction because of their willingness to inhabit similar spaces to those no longer available: barns, chimneys, farm fields. Yet as humans move toward ever-more encompassing development and mass production—of space, of monocrop agriculture—the similarity that these nonhumans rely on has become interrupted. There are fewer barns and more steel agricultural buildings. There are capped chimneys and buildings that no longer need the same kinds of heating systems. There are corn fields where hayfields used to be. The storied human response, then, has become one of an addressivity of nonhumans by substitution: a barn swallow structure for a barn as seen in chapter 1, an artificial chimney for a historic chimney stack as represented in chapter 2, a late-cut patch of hayfield for tall-grass prairie as discussed in chapter 3. Yet each of these dependencies on similarity is one that closes off possibilities for difference, for letting the Other be as other.

Perhaps to their credit, it is when nonhumans are forced to contend with human preferences for similarity that they most exhibit their own rhetorical capacities. Like de Castro's (2004) conception of "controlled equivocation" between cultures, the relationship between nonhumans and humans in these cases of precarity that depend on substitution reveal their alterity and our own fundamental misunderstanding. Nonhumans may admire the prospects of these substitutions. They may engage with them. They may refuse. They may find neighboring spaces. They may disappear. Throughout these entanglements, even when "misunderstandings are transformed into understandings," in de Castro's words, "such understandings persist in not being the same" (12). While the nonhumans may turn otherwise, engage the *alloiostrophic*, they do so in such a way that also shows humans the boundaries and limits of our own human imaginations and reveal again the Other as other. To that end, even these failed infrastructures stand as their own kind of nestwork, opening up possibilities for staying with relations that are shifting, precarious, or only partially visible.

The third story that these cases reveal to us is one of human failure in the face of nonhuman difference. In each case, there a story of a singular, misplaced hope: if we build it, they will come. Failure is told through SARA, through buildings, through structures, through materials, and through landscapes. Because this misplaced hope operates within capitalist narratives of progress at all costs, however, it obviates the more fundamental need for change to business-as-usual. In the face of unchecked development in which an artificial structure or a reseeded field is expected to entice choosy and particular nonhuman species with delicate and evolved sensibilities about where they want to live, breed, and die, this hope is the cruelest of optimisms. And it is an optimism propagated by contemporary media that, for example, highlights swallow structures alongside a highway (CBC 2016), or features an artificial chimney as an ecofriendly feature in a newly built school (Sheikh 2019), or exhibits the arguments about hay delaying as only between farmers and government agencies (Riley 2012). This is a dystopic future predicated on an optimistic now. Despite such public optimism, humans with a stake in substitutive habitat—field biologists, engineers, developers—know that no fake structure or tiny field will actually stop species decline. This is a failure both hidden and known. Such failure becomes an acceptable partner of substitution—both humans and nonhumans know mitigations are not good enough. Yet without public acknowledgment and human accountability of such failure, possibility for other options that might better act on species decline is closed off—for new ways of thinking and relating, for alternate stories, for resistance to development- and market-driven ways of navigating cohabitation with nonhuman others on earth.

The final story that the stories of the precarity of these three species tell is one of the pressures of settler time and the ways that current decision-making around precarity, which relies on similarity and substitution, sits in resistance to temporal orientations. As Rifkind (2017) reminds us, to be temporally oriented—that is, attuned to timeways that might offer resistance to a unitization and capitalization of being—means that "possibilities for action are shaped by the existing inclinations, itineraries, and networks in which one is immersed" (2). While nonexpert individuals may attempt small acts of resistance and attunement to *pheno*, as witnessed in chapter 2 by the Boothbys of Fairnorth Farm and chapter 3 by the owners of Sprucehaven, Century Farm, and Handy Dog

Farm, such acts are still bound by settler time. Experts know the inclinations and itineraries of nonhuman others that tell weightier stories of loss over time—thousands of pages of reports on aerial insectivore and passerine biology, as well as environmental impact assessments attest to that. Yet the mandated building of substitutive habitat miles away from where migrating swallows remember and return, simply because the land might be purchased cheaply; the choice of material chimney-tower blueprint and the fiction that one can import a surrogate habitat from place to place; the erection of slapstick structures or seeded fields in a breeding season and the expectation that a bird would take any interest after being displaced or violently dislocated—these actions show a resistance to a temporal orientation that would allow for a responsivity and holistic sense of relation and tempo between human and nonhuman, subject and object, animal and thing. These are misunderstandings not even trying to imagine themselves otherwise.

These stories—of precarity, substitution, failure, and denial of temporal orientation—matter. They matter because they are the stories that each swallow encountering a structure instead of a barn, each swift ignoring an artificial chimney tower, each displaced bobolink are telling with their bodies, over and over, generation after generation. They matter because they are offerings for turning otherwise: for thinking differently about conservation, about nonhuman capacity, about ecological relations, about hope-practices, about the time of the Anthropocene. Thus, my final turn to both making and care here, I hope, offers some potential to answer back to the stories that we are currently telling, to open up opportunity for truth-telling in the face of deep loss. I consider making and care ways to bear loss—ways to hold it close, ways to articulate the connection between loss and story by speaking them through other things and relations, ways to make the work of words visible in things that cross species boundaries. Instead of cruel optimism, they are moves toward an affirmative ethics, hope-practices, moves toward joy. As Braidotti (2017) notes, such joy is not synonymous with personal and psychologized affect, or "feeling good," but instead, affirmation and joy are "geometrical sets of relations. Joy or affirmation is the mode of relation that increases your ability to relate to the world. That you can take in more of the world, more difference, more challenges. More. It is an ethology. It is a question of energy and forces. The opposite of joy, which is sadness, is whatever shuts you down, makes you afraid of taking in more." In this present moment where extinction stories are the most available stories to tell, it is crucial that humans create modes of relation that increase, rather than decrease, our ability to take in more difference and more challenge, to open ourselves up to the world. Attunement to alternate linguistic forms that describe more comprehensive relations than those captured by English or Latin, as through Anishinaabemowin, as Joseph Pitawanakwat (2022) notes, is one such mode. Joy through this lens is an opportunity to examine our limits, rather than blithely ignore them. It is critical that we move beyond personal sorrow and scenes of fantasy that shut down the capacity for relation and survivance, and instead toward thinking and being that open us toward irreconcilability: hope *and* despair, growth *and* extinction, violence *and* love, *zoe* and *bios*. Thus, in this final chapter, I offer up two such joyful moves that return readers to the beginnings, to barn swallows. These moves of making and care offer up relation with nonhuman others as a culmination of the research, writing, and analytic moves of nestwork, as ways of turning otherwise with precarious species. I close with speculations of other promising extensions of such care for rhetorical-ecological being.

Research Creation and Making: *Hirondelusia*

In some ways, the guidelines for mitigations put forward by SARA represent humans'"best"—most convenient, most proximal—attempts at guessing nonhuman needs under a settler system already designed for failure. A chimney, structure, or field does not tackle larger problems of human development, pollution, impact on climate, or destruction of insect ecosystems that contribute meaningfully to problems of aerial insectivore and grassland bird precarity. While SARA speaks to its main audiences—developers and capital stakeholders—in a way that presents a problem-solution format (*if you build it, they will come*), the 105-page document and attendant processes of defining levels of species precarity through oversight committees and reports is not one that apportions spaces that actually allow for considerations of species loss. Throughout my fieldwork I was so often met with human puzzlement in the face of SARA mitigations—*What is this thing for?*—that it seemed that the larger question—*What are we losing?*—had been overlooked. Mitigation structures seem ripe for echoing Randall's (2009) findings that we prefer to ignore loss, projecting it into the future. I needed other ways to make loss real and present.

Too, I knew when I began writing this book that its messages about rhetorical ecologies, nonhuman capacity, and species decline—the ways that humans and nonhumans communicate with and through objects in a time of ecological crisis—were likely not going to be taken up in a Malcolm Gladwell–esque way by readers of the *New York Times* bestseller lists, though certainly such arguments might be well received by those working in rhetorical, posthuman, and ecological studies. Nor would its critical message be necessarily well received by those doing their very best to make headway in difficult conversations poised between issues of conservation and development. In these ways, the discursive materials that circulate and determine precarity and the stories humans tell about it, whether in government documents or academic treatises, are not those that really allow for public uptake and considerations of those stories. Nor are they accessible spaces that account for the ontological and material dimensions of loss: losses of being, losses of relations. Missing from both kinds of texts are those "moments of rupture" (Head 2016, 77) for public audiences that emerge out of the disjuncture of human growth at the cost of nonhuman others that might then prompt different kinds of public action and reflection. While humans continue to grapple with Anthropocenic pressures of our own making, we simultaneously have no real way *in* to public rituals that might create the space for human truth-telling about species loss, bearing its attendant anxiety, and increasing human capacity for taking in—and caring for—more of the world.

Thus, part of what I knew nestwork must do was to move toward other ways of making meaning through making some*thing*, something that might encourage public audiences to reflect more concretely on the question *What are we losing?* In part, such a response was one borne out of the frustration that comes with watching human-nonhuman miscommunication when the stakes for humans may be the loss of capital but the stakes for nonhumans others are the losses of lifeways. After reading government mandates and traveling across and getting to know this land that I have settled on through its first peoples and its nonhuman inhabitants; after reading popular press documents celebrating human ingenuity in the face of species loss; after sitting for hours in tall grass or dun scrub or mud puddles, waiting for a glimpse of a flash of feathers; after talking with those individual humans who live in the closest proximity to swallows, swifts, and bobolinks, I wanted a way to move outward with this research that did not just recreate business-as-usual. I wanted to reflect my own love and loss for these creatures I had come to know that did not simply rest on a taxonomic recognition and let their absence speak through objects. I wanted to more fully allow for anyone touched by those objects to be touched by what presences and absences they are near, bringing into closer view the crisis of species loss, and open up the capacity for such individuals and communities to become differently knowing subjects. I wanted to turn otherwise, and to do so with attentive care to what had already come before. For me, doing the research that informed this book, traveling across the land with my body, being touched by birds in their presences and their absences, situated a practical knowledge about species decline that would have been otherwise impossible. It seemed imperative to share this knowledge in a different way.

It is this inflection of mētis that Owen Chapman and Kim Sawchuk (2012) reflect on as the impetus for research-creation projects, or what are also known as arts-based research in the United States. While often associated with new media or multimodal projects, research-creation projects encompass the processes of both "traditional" research activities that are citation and text-based, as well as arts-based making that seeks to respond to a clearly established problem emerging from that research (10). As I documented the *alloiostrophic* "problem" of the erection of barn swallow structures in various locations, the bigger question of *What are we losing?* was made central to my inquiry, yet the answer wasn't one that these structures, speaking as they did to barn swallows at the sides of highways, could answer. Instead, I saw the possibilities of letting a structure speak to humans about barn swallow decline as one potential possibility for making a different kind of attention when it came to thinking about and grieving precarious species. *Hirondelusia* was born.

Working with a collaborator of critical design and new media, Marcel O'Gorman, as well as Christopher Rogers, a research assistant to the project, I conceptualized *Hirondelusia* as a making-based response to the question of what we lose when we lose one more species, and how we might tell the truth of human failure to mitigate species loss through the design of a mitigation structure itself (see figs. 10 and 11). While following the basic design specifications of the Ministry of Natural Resources and Forestry, the aim of *Hirondelusia* was to create a barn swallow structure that spoke to humans instead of swallows: not only to answer *what is this thing for*, but to also allow a place for both a realization of and a reflection on species loss. As such, its design was critical in that the impetus of the project was not only creation but also critique (see Malpass 2017).

Chapman and Sawchuk (2012, 15–21) note that arts-based research projects like this establish four differing articulations of research and creation: (1) research-for-creation, which involves gathering materials, collaborators, data, observation, and traditional research practices together to prepare to make a particular project; (2) research-from-creation, a phase of iterative design and testing that involves the participation of others; (3) creative presentations of research, which packages traditional academic research in evocative and creative ways; and (4) creation-as-research, in which the process of the making itself feeds back in to the theoretical premises that undergird its making, in a kind of "Mobius strip" (Loveless quoted in Chapman and Sawchuck 2012, 20) of theory and practice. The creation of *Hirondelusia*, and the life that it continues to have beyond the life of this book, has engaged with all of these articulations in a way that speaks not only to the alterity of the barn swallow but also to the slowed-down temporality of research in its material circumstances. By considering the work of writing and reading as fundamentally part of the circuit of creation-as-research, nestwork presents a rhetorically attuned version of research creation that emphasizes the role of the discursive, which may be often overlooked by designers and artists who advocate for arts-based research methods.

Hirondelusia (Rogers 2021; see also Pender 2021) is a four-by-eight-foot barn swallow structure designed for human beings, and borne from the kinds of research-for-creation activities that I've written about throughout this book: conversations with bird experts; in-depth reads of government acts and subdivision plans; calls and conversations with planners, farmers, citizen-scientists, and property owners; hours spent observing, notetaking, and sketching monuments to species loss; miles traveled over the province of Ontario; time spent reading, researching, and writing about birds and extinction (see figs. 10 and 11). *Hirondelusia* was first exhibited as part of an urban art festival and later was moved to a local charitable land trust where it spent six months as an educational feature for humans before being retrofitted to suit barn swallows in a permanent location on the land trust's property. In working with Marcel O'Gorman, an expert on critical design and media theory, it became clear to me that I wasn't and couldn't erect a modified barn swallow structure without critical making and design, a process that not only highlights the creation of an object-to-think-with as an overt form of material critique but also emphasizes the processual and collaborative nature of designing-with: with barn swallows, with farmers, with biologists. In the planning process of *Hirondelusia*, we engaged in research-from-creation, meeting with a program scientist from the land trust, a farmer, a citizen-scientist, and a research assistant with a background in journalism to help inform the design of the structure itself. We wanted *Hirondelusia* to serve not only as an object and as an argument but also potentially as an improved, more appealing (to swallows) thing-in-the-world. From these meetings, we gathered from participants material ideas (using old barn board donated from a local barn rather than the plywood common to OMNRF structures), design ideas (making creative openings in the boards' slats that would appeal to both humans

Fig. 10 | *Hirondelusia* exterior. Photo: Christopher Rogers.

Fig. 11 | *Hirondelusia* interior. Photo: Christopher Rogers.

and birds, such as stars and stained glass windows), and research ideas (allowing for participant surveys for those engaging with the structure via QR code that gauged their level of familiarity with the barn swallow as a species at risk).

The design and building processes of *Hirondelusia* were a kind of *making attention* (O'Gorman 2021). Positioned opposite of paying attention, which "implies a financial transaction that reflects our current attention economy, *making attention* describes a more deliberate and productive act" (78). Not only was the process of critical design a way of making attention for those of us engaged in the process, but it also helped us create *Hirondelusia* as a way to think through, more slowly and carefully, momentarily and ephemerally, the questions that come with the creation of a mitigation structure: Who is it really for? Who does it appeal to? Who will use it? Who will refuse it? In creating *Hirondelusia* first as a human-based art object-to-think-with, we called upon public audiences interacting with the structure to examine it through their sensorium. We chose aesthetically pleasing materials found in bourgeoisie condominiums (antique tin tiles, reclaimed barn board, vintage stained-glass windows). We framed eight cultural iconographic images of swallows,[1] from those appearing on ancient Greek vases to cigarette boxes to contemporary Cree artists. We mounted nesting cups from Sprucehaven no longer in use by swallows but filled with the construction of prior years' mud nests. Finally, we invited humans in to the structure by sound, wiring a motion sensor into the tin ceiling that would play a classical piano piece (Jef Martens's *Hirondelle*, or "Swallow") until it sensed movement, at which point it would play an audio recording of barn swallows recorded at Townsend Road. In these ways, we invited humans into a beautiful space where they could behold cultural relations with barn swallows, engage in a fantasy of presence—an icon, a chirp, a nest—all the while being made aware that the structure itself was instead filled with their absence. In these ways, all the nestwork that I had been doing from the spaces and places of the prior two years of this project were bound together in one temporal moment, in one material-discursive thing. After reading and listening to so many structures during the course of this project, *Hirondelusia* offered a chance to compose another, different kind of story.

The making of *Hirondelusia* and the decisions to move from research to creation, from text to media, were those that both engaged creative presentations of research and encouraged creation-as-research in ways filled with care. Touching barn boards, changing out daily speaker batteries, seeing a twelve-foot structure in the middle of a busy urban intersection rather than the side of a rural highway, observing the way swallows from years past put every mouthful of mud into a nesting cup, then carefully lined that cup with grass and feathers, brought me closer to articulating here these ideas about why making is a central part of care-full rhetorical-ecological work. Too, *Hirondelusia* brought a life beyond the academic to considerations of species precarity, which simply cannot remain on the page.

Hirondelusia spent two months on an urban corner, inclusive of a multimedia virtual tour that explained that barn swallow structures are, by and large, a human failure (see *CAFKA* 2.1 2021, for a link to an educational video that provides a brief overview of the goals and outcome of the project). In that time, I was asked by passersby of *Hirondelusia* if barn swallows actually lived in it, or if they would find it. Some were fooled into thinking there were birds already in the structure by virtue of hearing their song upon approach. I listened to many people talk about when they were young and lived on or near a farm and would see barn swallows every day, and then their pause before admitting that they don't see them anymore. I heard people say that they had always wondered what the structures were on the sides of roads. I heard people remark that they thought that what they were walking to from afar was a tiny house. I watched people set up picnics, write, and blow bubbles underneath *Hirondelusia*. A woman who had been through the structure emailed me, asking if I wanted to be part of a bird-friendly city initiative. Every person who experienced *Hirondelusia* was persuaded to visit it by its looming presence, and upon engaging it momentarily was faced with the confusing problem of swallows' differential presence— swallows were here but not-here. In this disjuncture, public audiences were given an opportunity to think about what it is we are losing when we substitute structures for relations, what it means to face human failure in the face of species decline, and how humans cope with species absence when their presence is, and has been, so compelling and so tied with our own.

Despite what *Hirondelusia* offered to those who made and engaged with it, it bears consideration that making, in and of itself, is not *the* answer of how we might and should respond to rhetorical-ecological problems. In fact, unless making contains a critical component that establishes its being as part of the rhetorical ecology in which it intervenes, making can risk reproducing narrow, anthropocentric, gendered, and technocultural assumptions about who and what should be made, as well as contribute problematically to various kinds of environmental waste (see Foote and Verhoeven, 2019; Riley Mukavetz and Powell, 2022). Beyond simply being made of reclaimed materials, *Hirondelusia* also was built with the intention of materially entering the circulation of swallow-human-environment as a way of speaking *between*, at each hyphenated break: swallow and human, human and human, swallow and environment, human and environment. It was built as an effort to speak to the aesthetic shift of *bir'yun*, to move from static building to dynamic object-to-think-with, from dullness to shimmer.

After *Hirondelusia*'s stint as an urban art installation, it became part of educational programming at RARE Charitable Reserve, a regional land trust. As part of that programming, Marcel and I gave an interdisciplinary public talk about barn swallows and species precarity. We were joined by Murray Burgess, a wildlife biologist conducting research on barn swallow nestlings, and Mara Silver, founder of Swallow Conservation, a nonprofit organization seeking to protect swallows in the North American Northeast. When the next spring frost has passed, we will move *Hirondelusia* again, this time stripped of sound and image, affixed to taller posts that we will bury deep in the ground, and inclusive of predator guards to imagine swallows-to-be safely tucked in its rafters. There it will sit, long past the time you have put this book away. It may again fail. We will wait to see if they come.

Acts of Care: Ray Lammens and Spearit Farms

Readers may recall my impromptu meeting of chimney swift nestlings after visiting the Fairnorth Farm in chapter 2, where I first met Ray Lammens, owner of Spearit Farms. Spearit Farms has been in the Lammens family since 1955, and though the signs outside claim it propagates asparagus and Belgian endive, whenever I talk with Ray it seems like there is a new crop to be tended: soybeans, corn, pumpkins. It is not only that Ray hosts a family of chimney swift nestlings in his barn that makes his work of special note here, as I conclude this book with reflections on nestwork, on making and on care. The other two outbuildings of Spearit Farm are just as noteworthy. There are two additional steel barns on the property, the first an equipment machinery shed longer than it is wide, with a roll-up garage door that Ray leaves open all year because cliff swallows have taken up residence in the corrugated ceiling entry. The other outbuilding that Ray walks me through is a huge steel airplane-hangar-like barn that seems like an endless space, inclusive of a large lower central loading area with a conveyor belt for produce, multiple tractors, a lofted

Fig. 12 | Ray Lammens's tarped barn. Photo: Marcel O'Gorman.

ceiling with wooden trusses, and smaller enclosed office-like rooms for the working business of the farm.

When I first encounter this large barn, I can't figure out why the interior ceiling is draped in what looks to be canvas or thick plastic. Ray explains to me as I look up that he has had a custom-made seventy-foot by fifty-foot tarp created for the ceiling of his barn because there are thirty to forty nesting swallow pairs that inhabit the barn in any given year, and because, he says, "they've been here for at least fourteen or fifteen years and I didn't feel like it was right to move them." Because this major barn is where Spearit Farms processes and packs its produce, however, it had to pass food safety inspections, something swallow guano would prohibit. So rather than exterminate the birds, Ray settled on tarping the barn, leaving the trussed roofline the property of the barn swallows, and doing his work in the space below (see fig. 12). Examining the ceiling, it is clear to see the care by which the tarp was installed. Pieced together from large industrial tarps that have had rivets punched into all sides and laced together like a large quilt, the tarp, reminiscent of circus-tent draping, separates the loft space (which Ray leaves open with a small access door to the outside) from the barn below. As I navigate the space, I hear a loud *whirring* sound. "Oh, that's a fan," Ray says. He explains that he has set up a temperature-controlled fan for the swallows so they don't get too hot, which turns on at 26°C/79°F, and has dug a shallow three-by-fifteen-foot pond out back with a pump so that they have mud with which to build throughout their breeding and nesting season.

Considering that many farmers believe barn swallows to be messy pests, I am astounded as I come to understand that this man has *tarped a 3,500-square foot space, dug a waterway, and created a temperature-controlled attic*, all so that he can live harmoniously with barn swallows. Like the Boothbys of Fairnorth Farm, his actions speak clearly to me of a care and of a different ability to stay with the trouble than government-mandated structures, as a creative intervention that helps stay with human stories of loss and precarity without substitution or temporal denial. Lammens, to the extent that any human on this landscape can, has rejected surrogacy as a mode of relation. Instead, he has enacted care. Yet this conception of care, I would argue, is one that Fisher and Tronto (1990, 40) define as "a species activity," rather than a simple individual act of caretaking or caregiving in human social worlds. It speaks to me of Serres's (1995 [1990] 38) natural contract, an ability to sit in relation with swallows that allows for "admiring attention, reciprocity, contemplation, and respect" by cultivating care-full and ethical spaces to live-with nonhuman others' presence.

Both care thinking and care ethics come out of a feminist tradition of the ethics of care that depend upon conditions of mutuality and interdependence (Tronto 1993), and this tradition has been extended by ecofeminist thinking, which moves outward from human relations of care to extensions of care to nonhuman others (see Plumwood 1993; Mallory 2009; De la Bellacasa 2017). As those who write about ethics of care note, such ethics emerge out of the awareness of power imbalances and inequalities that lay at the basis of questions of care, as well as spatial relationships that separate out who and what may be cared for and cared about at any given time, or at any given distance (see Massey 2004). They extend care out from the human and into the ecological, noting that practicing care "enable[s] the conditions in which we can live well (or as well as possible) individually and together" (Barnes 2012, 5).

Ray Lammens's demonstrations of care articulate one version of what it might look like to try to live well with nonhuman others in a spirit of mutuality. Lammens is well aware of the OMNRF guides to construct barn swallow structures and isn't surprised at all that they don't work. He talks to me about how he thinks that the birds are social animals, how they probably don't like small structures out in the country, how they need to be close to water and people, how they need to have openings, like windows, that are high up near the peaks of buildings, how the timing of appealing to where they might like to be before the nesting season is so key. He tells me that his grandfather is the person who first got him interested in barn swallows, as he had a farm five miles away from Spearit Farms when Lammens was young. "He told me how good they were for the environment as well as their beauty," Lammens writes me. He continues, "I remember my dad firing a worker and telling [him] to get off the farm for trying to shoot barn swallows with a BB gun."

Lammens not only admires the barn swallows that have long held dominion over Spearit Farms. He also shows an acute knowledge of, and reflection on, the violence that characterizes human-nonhuman relations that has long caused species to decline and offers some alternative for thinking with such violence for a more care-filled present. Through his anecdotes and actions, Ray shows me that he has lived a life with barn swallows and shown temporal attunement by bearing witness to the generational parallels of swallows and humans. In doing so he has not only shown an understanding of their imminent decline and respect for their life cycles but has made choices that emerge from the space of considering mutuality and interdependence between humans and nonhumans. This is a care borne from ordinary life.

The tarping of the barn is another way to respond to barn swallow decline that stems out of the persuasive capacities that living-with nonhuman others grants, in both flying bird bodies and messages passed through human generations, through Ray's grandfather, his father, and himself. Here, three generations of farmers are clear recipients of barn swallows' munificent care for their crops in the form of pest control, each bird eating nearly nine hundred insects a day off of their crops for over sixty-six years. It sits in stark relief—in both scale and thinking—from Ministry recommendations to create artificial habitat as the response to species decline. Rather than substitution, the tarped barn is about relationships: the relation between swallows' diet of insect pests beneficial for farming, the relation of barn swallows to human buildings and human industry, and the relation of generations of men to generations of birds. As the past speaks through him, Lammens demonstrates what interspecies care might look like, a kind of "care thinking" (Barnes 2012, 12) and care ethics (Lawson 2007, 2) that both moves away from expected demonstration of relation between swallows and farmers, and toward, as Lawson advocates, "the construction of new forms of relationships, institutions, and action that enhance mutuality and well-being" (1). It is a joyful option for *living with* precarious species' presence and their inevitable absence in a strange present, allowing humans and swallows to take in more of the world. Yet it is not a naïve joy, nor a cruel optimism: Ray and I both know that Spearit Farms will not change the fact that barn swallows are a species in decline. Yet somehow this kind of care resists the stuckness of empty hope based in some imagined future, instead offering a small promise of what it might look like to *think with* violence (see Yusoff 2012) for a more peaceable loss-in-process during a strange present. Such thinking and doing are practices of care, and practices of hope that reclaim a space for reciprocity, for dignity, for the giving of a gift, for an interweaving of bird and human time.

Ecological Care: What Matters?

In emphasizing making and care as ways to attune ourselves to ecological thinking, I also have drawn attention to the persuasive power of objects and places to, as McGreavy et al. (2018) note, "demonstrate a rhetoricity that exceed[s] the symbolic work of human agents" (19). There are "enveloping ecologies of human and nonhuman forces" (21) at work in each of these stories of making and care, research creation and living-with, negotiation of nonhuman absence and presence. Yet each is a settler story and would not be fully told without a recognition of the privilege at work: to have the time, space, money, tools, and contacts with which to make *Hirondelusia*; to have generational wealth and property that allows for the modifications of outbuildings for swallows. There has been privilege at every step of the way. Yet each chapter of *Nestwork* has also tried to cultivate a critical relation to this privilege by acknowledging how it has worked in the specific places of nonhuman and infrastructural encounter, to see such landscapes as also contemporary Indigenous spaces, as spaces of treaty rights with long histories—and presents—of violence and settlement.

It is the rhetoricity of place, in particular, that cannot be ignored when considering the rhetorical-ecological alongside the posthuman and new material, especially as we consider the role of unique landscapes in shaping decision-making about nonhumans over time and the concomitant delinking of peoples from land (and thus culture from nature). Put simply, extinction cannot be disentangled from colonialism (see Parreñas 2018). The colonial enterprise has propagated Enlightenment thinking that doubles down on both hierarchy and the universal man as the exceptional measure and determiner of all things. Such an enterprise is richly embedded in conversations about new materialism and ecological care, as the colonial capitalist narrative as a way of life—progress, commodity and consumption, and settlement at all costs—ignores a rich history and contemporary attunement of Indigenous peoples who consistently remind Eurowestern voices what their science is only beginning to wrestle with: water has memory (Awume et al. 2020); plants can see (Wohlleben 2021; Kimmerer 2013); birds can use fire (Nicholas 2018). If new material and posthuman scholars wish to do the work of ecological care, I argue that much of that work is also the work of reconciliation with Indigenous and Black people, and that much of the work of the care for ecologies, global and local, rest on care for the realities of colonial legacy—dispossession of land, for example, or the enslavement of Black bodies to agriculturalize land, or the overuse of resources by primarily white settlement (see Wells, in press). Without an embeddedness in these truths, and work toward restoring Indigenous sovereignty, it is nearly impossible to unpack the entanglements between humans and nonhuman ecologies.

To that end, a wrangling of any rhetorical-ecological problem must attend itself to human power differentials in place and space that continue to wrongly propagate ecological expectations and realities that bandy between euphoria and apocalypse while they story the Anthropocene on a scale of linear time. Critical making and practices of care will only ever go so far as policy decisions are shaped, which is why an awareness of their limits—and the limits of current "best management practices" by humans for nonhuman species—is key to thinking through human responsivity to ecological crises and possibilities for reconciling the irreconcilable. These are situations of unequal risk, even as they involve mutual vulnerability, to use Parreñas's (2018) terms. As Philip Catney and Timothy Doyle (2011) note of "green (post) politics of the future," postmaterialist approaches that often conflate all people into one ignore colonialist realities—not only of settler-Indigenous relations in the global North but also, as they maintain, in the "colonialist realities of the Global South, where people wrestle with massive environmental debts incurred upon them by centuries of exploitation by the North (the past and the present), rather than trading in sustainable environmental footprints (the present and future)" (176). A new materialist rhetoric for precarious species is an anticolonial one.

Perhaps if rhetorical and posthuman scholars examine our own relation to our specific, local, and peculiar places of ecological change, we might also examine the "circuits of power and privilege that connect our daily lives to those who are constructed as distant from us," as geographer Victoria Lawson (2007, 7) notes of the responsibilities of care ethics. Whether distanced by systems of exploitation, racialization, and privilege, disproportionate suffering from impacts of climate crises, or continents that independently determine definitions of species precarity, researchers would do well to shrink such distances by noting their entanglements and patterns across global divides and work to listen more closely both to where they diverge and where they creatively live-with. Such a grounded ethic might frame where scholars choose to turn toward or to turn otherwise and is echoed by McGreavy et al.'s (2018) claims for ecological care, in which the authors suggest that in order to embrace change in "ontological, affirmative, and hybrid terms," we "experiment[t] with how to protect, and occupy, and matter" (22).

To do this work, I argue, we must all amplify those currently doing this labor on the front lines, Black and Indigenous allies whose fights for treaty rights and racial justice are also those fights for water, for land, for equity, for nonhumans, and for home. We might see, for example, the connections between Indigenous people, land, and nonhumans to be the places and place-thoughts that are the most available for conservation action and rhetorical examination. Such work is embodied by the return of twenty-one bison in 2021 to the Poundmaker Cree nation after a 150-year absence caused by being "hunted to near-extinction by white settlers" (Mamers 2021), or the reintroduction of the California condor (extinct in the wild but bred in captivity) into Northern California after a concerted twenty-year effort by the Yurok people (DeFranco 2022). Actions such as these recognize "the possibility of creation in the future, of making life in scarred landscapes," of "hold[ing] together a world of relations" (Mamers 2021). These actions open worlds, give rise to stories that we can honor, showcase a joy that sits outside of white supremacy and ecological exploitation.

Speculative Turning, Speculative Futures (Now): A Call for Nestwork

When I try to tell people about this book, it sounds like I am describing fiction: a world that houses fake chimneys and artificial nesting kiosks, a world that mistakes a hayfield for a tall-grass prairie, all in service of communicating with nonhumans. Although I've only analyzed the ecologies that surround three species at risk and their attendant human-made infrastructures, other stranger-than-fiction facts could easily be added to our Anthropocenic present: the creation of artificial islands for nesting habitat for the common tern, the royal tern, and the black skimmer due to rising sea levels (Audubon 2021), for example, or concrete "reef balls" that stand in as artificial reef for fish and algae species in oceans from Alaska to the Caribbean to Nova Scotia (Smith 2019; Hylkema et al. 2020; Reynolds, Bishop, and Powers 2007). Facing a future (now) in crisis, humans are finding new ways to imagine what it might mean to engage in infrastructural conservation action or "ecological engineering," even as we recognize that doing so is an act predicated in a present in which humans already have failed.

Because, as Joanne Nucho (2017) reminds us, "failed infrastructure is failed politics." The disappearance of species at risk is not only an environmental crisis; it is also a human failure to stay with the trouble in ways that meaningfully engage with governing systems that protect our most vulnerable. Of course, it is possible, as barn swallows prospect and settle in a few human-built mitigation structures, or Texan chimney swifts find homes in fake chimneys, that there is some reason to believe that infrastructural mitigations at least hold steady as hope-practices in the world. Yet forwarding them as human "best management practices" is a misnomer, and embracing them wholeheartedly by ignoring their shortcomings as a matter of making good policy only retells our stories of precarity, substitution, failure, and denial of temporality with a gilded tongue. We must do better.

As I have been arguing throughout this book as I examine these practices— and the attendant practices of settler time—what they reveal, in many ways, are human limitations to stay with the troubles they have created. Yet in the time that it has taken me to write this book, small acts of survivance in the face of these limitations have emerged: in June 2021, barn swallows were officially redesignated by COSEWIC from "threatened" to a species of "special concern," in part because of their abundance in the province of Saskatchewan (Davidson 2021). During that same time in late June, developers in Caledonia, Ontario, at 1492 Land Back Lane sent letters to all homebuyers in the McKenzie Road subdivision development explaining that, "having exhausted their legal options and with no prospect of the occupation ending, the company was scrapping the planned subdivision and cancelling all purchase agreements" (Antonacci 2021). These two happenings, both explored in chapter 1, are not related, except when they are. Nestwork privileges this kind of relational thinking, an attentive engagement that sees clearly how disparate realms are close, how barn swallows and fights for sovereignty are thoroughly entangled.

While the infrastructural and time-based mitigations I've examined here are not fundamentally bad ideas, they also do not represent what such options might look like if generated with higher degrees of care and a sense of building relations with nonhuman others, of allowing nonhuman others more capacity for agency in human decision-making. What if mitigations were built with more attention to mētis? What if ecological care was reconceived speculatively and new materially as rhetorical capacity, or, as De la Bellacasa (2017) maintains, "as a generalized condition that circulates through the stuff and substance of the world, as agencies without which nothing that has any relation to humans would live well" (122)? What if every infrastructural mitigation was attended, not only with a review of environmental assessments and government reports—traditional notions of research—but also with a firm conviction that *being through there* matters? In order to move beyond substitution and into speculative realms that embrace a turn otherwise, as Dunne and Raby (2013) encourage in *Speculative Everything*, we must also look at the probable, plausible, possible, and preferable (2) when it comes to thinking through circulations of ecological care with nonhuman others—including, as De la Bellacasa (2017) reminds us, the possibility that nonhumans might care back. We might build bigger and more careful conservation worlds by acknowledging the possibility that the strange present in which we are already living carries with it a particular kind of past that has long been with us, and a futurity that may also live in and through us and our nonhuman kin. We might allow, in thinking about what is probable, plausible, and preferable, to think with nonhuman others and ask again, *Who is human here, who is human now?* We might engage in nestwork ourselves. Only by thinking beyond cruel optimism—our attachment to a healed, whole world and its creatures—and allowing for hope as a practice that emerges out of relation might we be able to honor the alterity that shows itself at every turn of human and nonhuman thinking. "It matters what stories we tell other stories with," as Haraway says (2016, 12), and now that we know our stories of precarious species, we can work to tell others.

I'm not sure what this might look like where you are. As I've documented this project, possibilities for other kinds of being-with the nonhuman creatures I've written about here seem all around: a move to uncap a large chimney in a nearby urban center and the letter-writing campaign that attends it; possibilities for gathering together all of the people I have met during this project to advocate for getting "Bird Friendly City" designation (see Nature Canada 2021); being a public ally for Indigenous-led ecological initiatives, such as those sponsored through the Conservation through Reconciliation Partnership, learning Anishi-naabemowin names for animal species; planning for more public spaces of ritu-alized mourning for nonhuman others. In getting to know bobolinks, chimney swifts, and barn swallows, in caring for them and being with their presences and absences, the stories they tell have grown far more complex, and my own curios-ity and sense of loss—about these species, about other species who may be defined as precarious—has blossomed. I see nestwork not only as birds' work, or my work, or posthuman work. Instead, I see it in every push for joyful material-rhetorical intervention, every small yearning by our species and our nonhuman kin for relational world-building, for eco-*oikos*, for home.

Notes

Introduction

1. This project received ethics approval through the University of Waterloo's Research Ethics Office, #40630 and #43228.

2. Both the barn swallow and bobolink were listed as threatened in those years but were not afforded legal protection by SARA until 2017.

Chapter 1

1. The Red List is a shortened form of the International Union for Conservation of Nature's (IUCN) Red List of Threatened Species, the guiding document on species decline in the UK.

2. Both "other-than-human" and "more than human" are phrases long associated with the work of Alfred Irving Hallowell (1960) and David Abrams (1996).

3. It should be noted that the Crown acquired these lands—nearly one million acres—from the Mississauga people for the amount of £1,180 and later claimed that they had misjudged the size of the valley. The Mississauga then ceded two million more acres to the Crown in the Between the Lakes Treaty (Treaty 3). The misinterpretation of Treaty 3 has resulted in a variety of historic and contemporary legal land claim disputes.

4. Because I am not Anishinaabeg, I do not retell Pinesi's story here, although it has been published and is otherwise commonly available.

Chapter 3

1. A forb is an herbaceous, nonwoody flowering plant that is not a grass.

Conclusions for Irreconcilability

1. Images used in *Hirondelusia* can be found at https://hirondelusia.wordpress.com/hirondelusia-artwork/.

Bibliography

Abrams, David. 1996. *The Spell of the Sensuous: Perception and Language in a More-than-Human World.* New York: Random House.

Aguilera, Jasmine. 2019. "The Trump Administration's Changes to the Endangered Species Act Risks Pushing More Species to Extinction." *Time,* August 14, 2019. https://time.com/5651168/trump-endangered-species-act.

Ahmed, Sara. 2010. "Happy Objects." In *The Affect Theory Reader,* edited by Melissa Gregg and Gregory J. Seigworth, 29–51. Durham: Duke University Press.

ALUS Canada. 2021. "Vision." ALUS Canada. https://alus.ca/home/about-us/what-is-alus/vision.

Anderson, Ben. 2006. "Becoming and Being Hopeful: Towards a Theory of Affect." *Environment and Planning D: Society and Space* 24 (5): 733–52.

Antonacci, J. P. 2021. "What's Next at Land Back Lane?" *Brantford Expositor.* https://www.brantfordexpositor.ca/news/local-news/whats-next-at-land-back-lane.

APTN News. 2020. "Conflict in Caledonia: A Time Line of the Grand River Land Dispute." APTN National News. October 15, 2020. https://www.aptnnews.ca/national-news/conflict-in-caledonia-a-timeline-of-the-grand-river-land-dispute.

Archer, Ryan. 2016. *Dashwood Road Bridge Replacement Species at Risk Habitat Assessment.* Natural Resources Solutions, Inc.

Arola, Kristin, and Thomas Rickert. 2022. "The Ancestors We Claim: Conversations Toward a Future New Materialism Across Boundaries." Forum: Rhetorical New Materialisms, *Rhetoric Society Quarterly* 52 (2): 190–98.

Audubon. 2021. "Nesting Platform Initiative Launched for Endangered Birds in Maryland Coastal Bays. Audubon Maryland-DC. https://md.audubon.org/news/nesting-platform-initiative-launched-endangered-birds-maryland-coastal-bays.

Awume, Obadah, Robert Patrick, and Warrick Baijius. 2020. "Indigenous Perspectives on Water Security in Saskatchewan, Canada." *Water* 12 (3): 1–14.

Baldy, Cutcha Risling. 2021. "Why We Fish: Decolonizing Salmon Rhetorics." In *Native American Rhetorics,* edited by Lawrence Gross, 165–94. Albuquerque: University of New Mexico Press.

Barad, Karen. 2003. "Posthumanist Performativity: Toward an Understanding of How Matter Comes to Matter." *Signs* 28 (3): 801–31.

———. 2007. *Meeting the Universe Halfway: Quantum Physics and the Entanglement of Matter and Meaning.* Durham: Duke University Press.

———. 2010. "Quantum Entanglements and Hauntological Relations of Inheritance: Dis/Continuities, SpaceTime Enfoldings, and Justice-to-Come." *Derrida Today* 3 (2): 240–68.

———. 2017. "No Small Matter: Mushroom Clouds, Ecologies of Nothingness, and Strange Topologies of Spacetimemattering." In *Arts of Living on a Damaged Planet,* edited by Anna Tsing et al., G103–G120. Minneapolis: University of Minnesota Press.

Barnes, Marian. 2012. *Care in Everyday Life: An Ethic of Care in Practice.* Bristol: Policy Press.

Barnett, Joshua Trey. 2022. *Mourning in the Anthropocene: Ecological Grief and Earthly Coexistence.* East Lansing: Michigan State University Press.

Barnett, Scot, and Casey Boyle, eds. 2016. *Rhetoric, Through Everyday Things*. Tuscaloosa: University of Alabama Press.

Bastian, Michelle. 2012. "Fatally Confused: Telling the Time in the Midst of Ecological Crises. *Environmental Philosophy* 9 (1): 23–48.

———. 2017. "Encountering Leatherbacks in Multispecies Knots of Time." In *Extinction Studies: Stories of Time, Death and Generations*, edited by Thom van Dooren, Deborah Bird Rose, and Matthew Chrulew, 149–86. New York: Columbia University Press.

BECO (Bird Ecology and Conservation Ontario). 2015. "Barn Swallows and Social Cues." Bird Ecology and Conservation Ontario. https://www.beco-birds.org/portfolio-item /barn-swallows-and-social-cues.

Bell, Mark, and Su Rynard. 2021. "Cheep Accommodation in Downtown Toronto." Songbird SOS. http://songbirdsos.com/cheep-accomodation-in-downtown-toronto.

Bennett, Jane. 2010. *Vibrant Matter: A Political Ecology of Things*. Durham: Duke University Press.

Berlant, Lauren. 2011. *Cruel Optimism*. Durham: Duke University Press.

Bird Studies Canada. 2012. *Ontario Swiftwatch 2012 Summary Report*. Bird Studies Canada.

Bishop, Lynn. 2018. "Wild at Heart." ALUS. https://alus.ca/alus_news_and_events/wild -at-heart-2/.

Blair, Carole. 1999. "Contemporary U.S. Memorial Sites as Exemplars of Rhetoric's Materiality." In *Rhetorical Bodies*, edited by Jack Selzer and Sharon Crowley, 16–57. Madison: University of Wisconsin Press.

———. 2001. "Reflections on Criticism and Bodies: Parables from Public Places." *Western Journal of Communication* 65 (3): 271–94.

Bollinger, E. K., et al. 1990. "Effects of Hay-Cropping on Eastern Populations of the Bobolink." *Wildlife Society Bulletin* 18 (2): 142–50.

Booher, Amanda K., and Julie Jung, eds. 2018. *Feminist Rhetorical Science Studies: Human Bodies, Posthumanist Worlds*. Carbondale: Southern Illinois University Press.

Bowker, Geoffrey. 2004. "Time, Money and Biodiversity." In *Global Assemblages: Technology, Politics, and Ethics as Anthropological Problems*, edited by Aihwa Ong, and Stephen J. Collier, 107–23. Hoboken: Wiley.

Bowman, R. I. 1952. "Chimney Swift Banding at Kinston, Ontario, from 1928 to 1947." *Canadian Field Naturalist* 66 (6): 151–64.

Braidotti, Rosi. 2006. *Transpositions: On Nomadic Ethics*. Cambridge: Polity Press.

———. 2011. *Nomadic Theory: The Portable Rosi Braidotti*. New York: Columbia University Press.

———. 2013. *The Posthuman*. Cambridge: Polity.

———. 2016. "The Critical Posthumanities, or Is Medianatures to Naturecultures as Zoe Is to Bios?" *Cultural Politics* 12 (3): 380–90.

———. 2017. "On Affirmative Ethics." Keynote lecture at the Nederlandse Filosofie Olympiade, January 20, 2017. https://rosibraidotti.com/2019/11/21/on-affirmative-ethics.

———. 2019. "A Theoretical Framework for the Critical Posthumanities." *Theory, Culture, and Society* 36 (6): 31–61.

Brown, M. B., and C. R. Brown. 2019. "Barn Swallow (*Hirundo rustica*), Version 2.0." In *The Birds of North America*, edited by P. G. Rodewald. Ithaca: Cornell Lab of Ornithology. https://doi.org/10.2173/bna.barswa.02.

Buchanan, Brett. 2008. *Onto-Ethologies: The Animal Environments of Uexküll, Heidegger, Merleau-Ponty, and Deleuze*. New York: SUNY Press.

Bumelis, Kaelin. 2021. "Question About Successes of Artificial Swift Towers in Ontario." Personal communication.

Butler, Judith. 1993. *Bodies That Matter: On the Discursive Limits of "Sex."* New York: Routledge.

———. 2004. *Precarious Life: The Powers of Mourning and Violence.* London: Verso.

CAFKA 2.1: Critical Media Lab, Hirondelusia, Educational Virtual Tour. July 2, 2021. https://www.youtube.com/watch?v=FB-U7ujTCI8.

Campomizzi, Andrew J., Zoe M. LeBrun-Southcott, and Kristyn Richardson. 2019. "Conspecific Cues Encourage Barn Swallow (*Hirundo rustica erythrogaster*) Prospecting, but Not Nesting, at New Nesting Structures." *Canadian Field Naturalist* 133 (3): 235–45.

Carolinian Canada. 2012. "The Boothbys: Naturalizing the Farm." Landowner Leaders, Carolinian Canada Archives. https://caroliniancanada.ca/landowner-leaders/boothby.

Catney, Philip, and Timothy Doyle. 2011. "The Welfare of Now and the Green (Post) Politics of the Future." *Critical Social Policy* 31 (2): 174–93.

CBC News. 2016. "Barn Swallows Have a New Place to Live Along Highway 401." Canadian Broadcasting Company. May 4, 2016. https://www.cbc.ca/news/canada/windsor/barn-swallows-habitats-highway-1.3566966.

Cedillo, Christina V. 2022. "Smoke and Mirrors: Re-creating Material Relation(ship)s Through Mexica Story." In *Decolonial Conversations in Posthuman and New Material Rhetorics*, edited by Jennifer Clary-Lemon and David Grant, 92–114. Columbus: Ohio State University Press.

Chapman, Owen, and Kim Sawchuck. 2012. "Research-Creation: Intervention, Analysis, and 'Family Resemblances.'" *Canadian Journal of Communication* 37 (1): 5–26.

Chen, Sibo. 2021. "'Blockadia' Helped Cancel the Keystone XL Pipeline—And Could Change Mainstream Environmentalism." *The Conversation,* March 10, 2021. https://theconversation.com/blockadia-helped-cancel-the-keystone-xl-pipeline-and-could-change-mainstream-environmentalism-155276.

Clary-Lemon, Jennifer. 2019a. "Gifts, Ancestors, and Relations: Notes Toward an Indigenous New Materialism." *enculturation.* https://enculturation.net/gifts_ancestors_and_relations.

———. 2019b. *Planting the Anthropocene: Rhetorics of Natureculture.* Logan: Utah State University Press.

———. 2020. "Examining Material Rhetorics of Species at Risk: Infrastructural Mitigations as Non-Human Arguments." *enculturation.* https://enculturation.net/material_rhetorics_species_at_risk.

Clary-Lemon, Jennifer, and David M. Grant, eds. 2022. *Decolonial Conversations in Posthuman and New Material Rhetorics.* Columbus: Ohio State University Press.

Cocker, Mark, and Richard Mabey. 2005. *Birds Brittanica.* London: Chatto & Windus.

Cokinos, Christopher. 2009. *Hope Is the Thing with Feathers: A Personal Chronicle of Vanished Birds.* New York: TarcherPerigee.

Columbo, Gianfranco. 2003. "*Hirundo Rustica.*" *Monaco Nature Encyclopedia.* https://www.monaconatureencyclopedia.com/hirundo-rustica/?lang=en.

Connors, Stompin' Tom. 1989. *A Proud Canadian.* EMI Music Canada—80010 2 7, compact disc.

Conservation Through Reconciliation Partnership. 2021. https://conservation-reconciliation.ca.

Cooper, Marilyn M. 2019. *The Animal Who Writes: A Posthumanist Composition.* Pittsburgh: University of Pittsburgh Press.

Cornell University. 2019. "All About Birds." The Cornell Lab of Ornithology. https://www.allaboutbirds.org.

COSEWIC, Committee on the Status of Endangered Wildlife in Canada. 2007. *COSEWIC Assessment and Status Report on the Chimney Swift* Chaetura pelagica *in Canada*. Committee on the Status of Endangered Wildlife in Canada.

———. 2010. *COSEWIC Assessment and Status Report on the Bobolink* Dolichonyx oryzivorus *in Canada*. Committee on the Status of Endangered Wildlife in Canada.

———. 2011. *COSEWIC Assessment and Status Report on the Barn Swallow* Hirundo rustica *in Canada*. Committee on the Status of Endangered Wildlife in Canada.

———. 2018. *Chimney Swift* (Chaetura pelagica)*: COSEWIC Assessment and Status Report 2018*. Committee on the Status of Endangered Wildlife in Canada.

Cox, Amelia Robin. 2018. *Population Decline in an Avian Aerial Insectivore* (Tachycineta bicolor) *Linked to Climate Change*. Master's thesis, Queen's University. https://qspace.library.queensu.ca/bitstream/handle/1974/24866/Cox_Amelia_R_201709_MSC.pdf.

Cryer, Daniel A. 2018. "Withdrawal Without Retreat: Responsible Conservation in a Doomed Age." *Rhetoric Society Quarterly* 48 (5): 459–78.

Cunsolo, Ashlee, and Karen Landman. 2017. *Mourning Nature: Hope at the Heart of Ecological Loss and Grief*. Montreal: McGill-Queens University Press.

Davidson, Pete. 2021. "Status of Five Bird Species Assessed by COSEWIC in May." Birds Canada. https://www.birdscanada.org/status-of-five-bird-species-assessed-by-cosewic-in-may.

Davis, Diane. 2014. "Autozoography: Notes Toward a Rhetoricity of the Living." *Philosophy and Rhetoric* 47 (4): 533–53.

———. 2017. "Rhetoricity at the End of the World." *Philosophy and Rhetoric* 50 (4): 431–51.

De Castro, Eduardo Viveiros. 2004. "Perspectival Anthropology and the Method of Controlled Equivocation." *Tipití: Journal of the Society for the Anthropology of Lowland South America* 2 (1): 3–22.

DeFranco, Elyse. 2022. "Absent for More than a Century, California Condors Soar Above the Redwoods Again." *Audubon Magazine*. May 17, 2022. https://www.audubon.org/news/absent-more-century-california-condors-soar-above-redwoods-again.

De la Bellacasa, María Puig. 2017. *Matters of Care: Speculative Ethics in More than Human Worlds*. Minneapolis: University of Minnesota Press.

Deleuze, Gilles, and Felix Guattari. 1994. *What Is Philosophy?* New York: Columbia University Press.

Demarée, Gaston R., and This Rutishauser. 2011. "From 'Periodical Observations' to 'Anthochronology' and 'Phenology'—The Scientific Debate Between Adolphe Quetelet and Charles Morren on the Origin of the Word 'Phenology.'" *International Journal of Biometeorology* 55:753–61.

Despret, Vinciane. 2022. *Living as a Bird*. Cambridge: Polity.

Diaz, Sandra, et al. 2019. "Summary for Policymakers of the Global Assessment Report on Biodiversity and Ecosystem Services of the Intergovernmental Science-Policy Platform on Biodiversity and Ecosystem Services, Advanced Unedited Version." Report of the United Nations IPBS. https://www.ipbes.net/system/tdf/spm_global_unedited_advance.pdf.

Dickinson, Greg, and Giorgia Aiello. 2016. "Being Through There Matters: Materiality, Bodies, and Movement in Urban Communications Research." *International Journal of Communication* 10:1294–308.

Dickinson, Greg, Carole Blair, and Brian L. Ott, eds. 2010. *Places of Public Memory: The Rhetoric of Museums and Memorials*. Tuscaloosa: University of Alabama Press.

Dillon Consulting. 2021. *West Side Employment Lands Urban Design Guidelines, January 2021*. Prepared for the City of Waterloo. https://www.waterloo.ca/en/government /resources/Documents/Development-charges-and-guidelines/West-Side -Employment-Lands-Design-Guidelines.pdf.

Dubinski, Kate. 2019. "Researchers Hoping Small Purple Martin Birds Can Offer up Big Answers." CBC News. July 14, 2019. https://www.cbc.ca/news/canada/london /ontario-purple-martins-radio-transmitters-1.5209970.

Dunne, Anthony, and Fiona Raby. 2013. *Speculative Everything: Design, Fiction, and Social Dreaming*. Cambridge: MIT Press.

Dunsworth, Edward Ira. 2019. "The Transnational Making of Ontario Tobacco Labour, 1925–1990." PhD diss., Department of History, University of Toronto.

Durand, Stéphan. 2022. "A Poetic of Attention." Afterword to *Living as a Bird*, by Vinciane Despret, 167–69. Cambridge: Polity.

Edbauer, Jenny. 2005. "Unframing Models of Public Distribution: From Rhetorical Situation to Rhetorical Ecologies." *Rhetoric Society Quarterly* 35 (4): 5–24.

Ehrenfeld, Dan. 2020 "'Sharing a World with Others': Rhetoric's Ecological Turn and the Transformation of the Networked Public Sphere." *Rhetoric Society Quarterly* 50 (5): 305–20.

Environment Canada. 2019. "Species at Risk Fall into These Four Categories." Government of Canada. https://www.canada.ca/content/dam/eccc/migration/sara/d5cefc12-e936 -4fdd-94be-6d56846739ab/poster_0408-eng.pdf.

Finity, Lean, and Joseph J. Nocera. 2012. "Vocal and Visual Conspecific Cues Influence the Behavior of Chimney Swifts at Provisioned Habitat." *The Condor* 114 (2): 323–28.

Fisher, Bernice, and Joan C. Tronto. 1990. "Toward a Feminist Theory of Care." In *Circles of Care: Work and Identity in Women's Lives*, edited by Emily K. Abel and Margaret K. Nelson, 35–62. State University of New York Press.

Fitzgerald, Trina M., et al. 2014. "Loss of Nesting Sites Is Not a Primary Factor Limiting Northern Chimney Swift Populations." *Population Ecology* 56:507–12.

Foote, Gareth, and Eva Verhoeven. 2019. "Tactics for a More-Than-Human Maker Culture." In *The Critical Makers Reader: (Un) Learning Technology*, edited by Loes Bogers and Letizia Chiappini, 72–85. Amsterdam: Institute of Network Cultures.

Freedberg, William. 2018. "Two Poems for Bobolinks: Dickinson and Bryant." Mass Audubon. https://www.blogs.massaudubon.org/distractiondisplays/two-poems-for-bobolinks -dickinson-and-bryant.

Freeman, Elizabeth. 2010. *Time Binds: Queer Temporalities, Queer Histories*. Durham: Duke University Press.

Fromberger, Monica A., et al. 2020. "Factors Affecting Bobolink Nest Survival Across Grassland Types." *Avian Conservation and Ecology* 15 (2): 1–17.

Gamblin, Ronald. N.d. "Land Back! What Do We Mean?" 4Rs Youth Movement. https:// 4rsyouth.ca/land-back-what-do-we-mean.

Gan, Elaine, et al. 2017. "Introduction: Haunted Landscapes of the Anthropocene." In *Arts of Living on a Damaged Planet*, edited by Anna Tsing et al., G1–G14. Minneapolis: University of Minnesota Press.

Geernaert, Barbara. 2019. "Understanding Wrongs and Seeking Justice for First Nations." *Guelph Today*, November 19, 2019. https://www.guelphtoday.com/rooted/under standing-wrongs-and-seeking-justice-for-first-nations-1854804.

Glenn, Cheryl, and Martin Carcasson. 2008. "Rhetoric as Pedagogy." In *The SAGE Handbook of Rhetorical Studies*, edited by Andrea Lunsford et al., 285–92. London: SAGE.

Glotzer, Paige. 2021. "Pandemic Birding as Positive Change." *Visualizing Climate and Loss*. Harvard University, Joint Center for History and Economics. https://histecon.fas .harvard.edu/climate-loss/birding/index.html.

Gottschalk Druschke, Caroline. 2019. "A Trophic Future for Rhetorical Ecologies." *enculturation*. http://enculturation.net/a-trophic-future.

Gottschalk Druschke, Caroline, and Bridie McGreavy. 2016. "Why Rhetoric Matters for Ecology." *Frontiers in Ecology and the Environment* 14 (1): 46–52.

Government of Canada. 2011. "Species Profile: Barn Swallow." Species at Risk Public Registry, November 29. https://species-registry.canada.ca/index-en.html#/species /1147-790.

———. 2019. "Description of Residence for Barn Swallow (*Hirundo Rustica*) in Canada." Species at Risk Public Registry (Residence Descriptions) https://species-registry. canada.ca/index-en.html#/documents/3522.

———. 2020. Species at Risk Public Registry. Ottawa: Government of Canada. https://www .canada.ca/en/environment-climate-change/services/species-risk-public-registry .html.

———. 2021. The Species at Risk Act. Ottawa: Government of Canada. https://laws.justice .gc.ca/eng/acts/S-15.3.

Government of Ontario. 2015. *Bobolink and Eastern Meadowlark Government Response Statement*. Government of Ontario. https://www.ontario.ca/page/bobolink-and-eastern -meadowlark-government-response-statement.

———. 2021. "Map of Ontario Treaties and Reserves." Government of Ontario. https://www .ontario.ca/page/map-ontario-treaties-and-reserves#t7.

Graham, Frank, Jr. 2011. "High Hopes." Audubon Society. https://www.audubon.org/maga zine/july-august-2011/high-hopes.

Graves, Gary R. 2004. "Avian Commensals in Colonial America: When did *Chaetura pelagica* Become the Chimney Swift?" *Archives of Natural History* 31 (2): 300–307.

Greer, Kirsten. 2010. "Chimney Swifts Return to Queen's University." Network in Canadian History and Environment. April 9, 2010. https://niche-canada.org/2010/04/09 /chimney-swifts-return-to-queens-university.

Gries, Laurie. 2020. "New Materialist Ontobiography: A Critical-Creative Approach for Coping and Caring in the Chthulucene." *College English* 82 (3): 301–25.

Gries, Laurie, et al. 2022. "Rhetorical New Materialisms (RNM)." *Rhetoric Society Quarterly* 52 (2): 137–202.

Gross, Lawrence, ed. 2021. *Native American Rhetorics*. Albuquerque: University of New Mexico Press.

Grosz, Elizabeth. 2004. *The Nick of Time: Politics, Evolution, and the Untimely*. Durham: Duke University Press.

Halberstam, Jack. 2005. *In a Queer Time and Place: Transgender Bodies, Subcultural Lives*. New York: New York University Press.

Hallmann, Caspar, et al. 2017. "More than 75 Percent Decline over 27 Years in Total Flying Insect Biomass in Protected Areas." *PLoS ONE* 12 (10): 1–21.

Hallowell, Alfred Irving. 1960. "Ojibwa Ontology, Behavior, and World View." In *Culture in History: Essays in Honor of Paul Radin*, edited by S. Diamond, 19–52. New York: Columbia University Press.

Haraway, Donna. 2016. *Staying with the Trouble: Making Kin in the Chthulucene*. Durham: Duke University Press.

Harris, Richard, and Doris Forrester. 2003. "The Suburban Origins of Redlining: A Canadian Case Study, 1935–54." *Urban Studies* 40 (13): 2661–86.

Hayden, Dolores. 2003. *Building Suburbia: Green Fields and Urban Growth, 1820–2000*. New York: Pantheon Books.

Hayles, N. Katherine. 2012. *How We Think: Digital Media and Contemporary Technogenesis*. Chicago: University of Chicago Press.

Head, Leslie. 2016. *Hope and Grief in the Anthropocene: Re-Conceptualizing Human-Nature Relations*. London: Routledge.

Heagy, A., D. Badzinski, D. Bradley, M. Falconer, J. McCracken, R. A. Reid, and K. Richardson. 2014. *Draft Recovery Strategy for the Barn Swallow* (Hirundo rustica) *in Ontario*. Ontario Recovery Strategy Series. Peterborough, Ontario: Prepared for the Ontario Ministry of Natural Resources.

Hiebert, Megan. 2020. *Habitat Preservation and Creation Techniques for Chimney Swifts: Overview of Approaches and Feasibility*. Ontario Species at Risk Stewardship Program, Birds Canada.

Hinchliffe, Steve. 2008. "Reconstituting Nature Conservation: Towards a Careful Political Ecology." *Geoforum* 39:88–97.

Hines, Richard E., Troy J. Bader, and Richard R. Graves. 2013. "Chimney Swifts (*Chaetura pelagica*) Nest in Tree Cavities in Arkansas." *Southeastern Naturalist* 12 (4): N18–N20.

Hodder, Ian. 2012. *Entangled: An Archaeology of the Relationships Between Humans and Things*. Hoboken: John Wiley & Sons.

Hokuwhitu, Brendan, et al. 2021. *Routledge Handbook of Critical Indigenous Studies*. London: Routledge.

Holmes, Joan, and Associates. 2015. *Aboriginal Title Claim to Water Within the Traditional Lands of the Mississaugas of the New Credit*. http://mncfn.ca/wp-content/uploads/2017/02/MNC-Aboriginal-Title-Report.pdf.

Hylkema, Alwin, et al. 2020. "Fish Assemblages of Three Common Artificial Reef Designs During Early Colonization." *Ecological Engineering* 157:1–9.

IEER (Institute for Energy and Environmental Research). 2012. "Uranium: Its Uses and Hazards." IEER. https://ieer.org/resource/factsheets/uranium-its-uses-and-hazards.

Ingold, Timothy. 2013. *Making: Anthropology, Archaeology, Art, and Architecture*. London: Routledge.

———. 2000. *The Perception of the Environment: Essays in Livelihood, Dwelling, and Skill*. London: Routledge.

Iovino, Serenella, and Serpil Opperman, eds. 2014. *Material Ecocriticism*. Indianapolis: Indiana University Press.

IPCC (Intergovernmental Panel on Climate Change). 2021. AR6 Synthesis Report: Climate Change 2022. https://www.ipcc.ch/report/sixth-assessment-report-cycle.

The IUCN Red List of Threatened Species. 2022. https://www.iucnredlist.org.

Jackson, Zakiyyah Iman. 2015. "Outer Worlds: The Persistence of Race in Movement 'Beyond the Human.'" *GLQ* 21 (2–3): 215–18.

Jensen, Tim. 2019. *Ecologies of Guilt in Environmental Rhetorics*. London: Palgrave.

Johnson, Ron. 2017. "Tobacco Country Gets a Makeover." *Globe and Mail*, October 11, 2017. https://www.theglobeandmail.com/life/travel/norfolk-countys-rise-from-the-ashes-as-a-new-hub-ofagritourism/article36526751.

Kafer, Alison. 2013. *Feminist, Queer, Crip*. Indianapolis: Indiana University Press.

Kennedy, George A. 1992. "A Hoot in the Dark: The Evolution of General Rhetoric." *Philosophy and Rhetoric* 25 (1): 1–21.

Killingsworth, M. Jimmie, and Jaqueline S. Palmer. 2012. *Ecospeak: Rhetoric and Environmental Politics in America*. Carbondale: Southern Illinois University Press.

Kimmerer, Robin. 2013. *Braiding Sweetgrass: Indigenous Wisdom, Scientific Knowledge, and the Teachings of Plants*. Minneapolis: Milkweed Press.

King, Tiffany Lethabo. 2017. "Humans Involved: Lurking in the Lines of Posthumanist Flight." *Critical Ethnic Studies* 3 (1): 257–337.

Klein, Naomi. 2014. *This Changes Everything: Capitalism vs. The Climate*. New York: Simon and Schuster.

Kohn, Eduardo. 2013. *How Forests Think: Toward an Anthropology Beyond the Human*. Berkeley: University of California Press.

Kristeva, Julia, Alice Jardin, and Harry Blake. 1981. "Women's Time." *Signs* 7 (1): 13–35.

Krzyżanowska, Natalia. 2016. "The Discourse of Counter-Monuments: Semiotics of Material Commemoration in Contemporary Urban Spaces." *Social Semiotics* 26 (5): 465–85.

Kyle, Paul D., and Georgean Z. Kyle. 2005. *Chimney Swifts: America's Mysterious Birds Above the Fireplace*. College Station: Texas A&M University Press.

Lammers-Helps, Helen. 2016. "SpruceHaven Is St. Agatha's Own 'Magic Kingdom.'" *Grand: Living Well in Waterloo Region*. http://www.grandmagazine.ca/sprucehaven-is-st-agathas-own-magic-kingdom.

Langlois, Annie. 2005. "Barn Swallow." *Hinterland Who's Who*. https://www.hww.ca/en/wildlife/birds/barn-swallow.html.

Lantz, Trevor C., and Nancy J. Turner. 2003. "Traditional Phenological Knowledge of Aboriginal Peoples in British Columbia. *Journal of Ethnobiology* 23 (2): 263–86.

Lawson, Victoria. 2007. "Presidential Address: Geographies of Care and Responsibility." *Annals of the Association of American Geographers* 97 (1): 1–11.

Lefebvre, Henri. 1991. *The Production of Space*. Translated by Donald Nicholson-Smith. Malden, MA: Blackwell Publishing.

Le Guin, Ursula. 1989. *Dancing at the Edge of the World*. New York: Grove Press.

Levine, Robert N. 1998. *A Geography of Time: On Tempo, Culture, and the Pace of Life*. New York: Basic Books.

Liu, Alan. 2022. "Critical Infrastructural Studies." https://cistudies.org.

Lloyd, Genevieve. 1996. *Spinoza and the "Ethics."* London: Routledge.

Lorimer, Jamie. 2007. "Nonhuman Charisma." *Environment and Planning D: Society and Space* 25 (5): 911–32.

Macdonald, Helen. 2016. *H Is for Hawk*. London: Penguin.

MacKay, Barry Kent. 2005. "Bobolink." *County Connection Magazine* 50: n.p. http://www.pinecone.on.ca/MAGAZINE/stories/Bobolink.html.

Mallory, Chaone. 2009. "Val Plumwood and Ecofeminist Political Solidarity: Standing with the Natural Other." *Ethics and the Environment* 14 (2): 3–21.

Malm, Andreas, and Alf Hornborg. 2014. "The Geology of Mankind? A Critique of the Anthropocene Narrative." *Anthropocene Review* 1:62–69.

Malpass, Matt. 2017. *Critical Design in Context*. London: Bloomsbury.

Mamers, Danielle Tashereau. 2021. "Reintroducing Bison to Indigenous Land Is a Small Act of Reconciliation." *Globe and Mail*. https://www.theglobeandmail.com/opinion/article-reintroducing-bison-to-indigenous-land-is-a-small-act-of.

Manning, Erin. n.d. "About SenseLab." Erin Manning. http://erinmovement.com/about-senselab.

Marback, Richard. 1998. "Detroit and the Closed Fist: Toward a Theory of Material Rhetoric." *Rhetoric Review* 17 (1): 74–92.

Marcel, Gabriel. 1965. *Being and Having: An Existentialist Diary*. New York: Harper and Row.

Massey, Doreen. 2004. "Geographies of Responsibility." *Geografiska Annaler* 86 (B): 5–18.

Matamura, Rangi. 2021. "Matariki and the Decolonisation of Time." In *Routledge Handbook of Critical Indigenous Studies*, edited by Brendan Hokuwhitu et al., 65–77. London: Routledge.

McCarty, John P., and David W. Winkler. 1999. "Relative Importance of Environmental Variables in Determining the Growth of Nestling Tree Swallows *Tachycineta bicolor*." *Ibis* 141 (2): 286–96.

McConnell, Lorne. 2002. "NPD: Canada's First Nuclear Power Station." Canadian Nuclear Society. http://www.cns-snc.ca/media/history/npd/2002_NPD_Lorne_McConnell.htm.

McCracken, J. D., et al. 2013. *Recovery Strategy for the Bobolink* (Dolichonyx oryzivorus) *and Eastern Meadowlark* (Sturnella magna) *in Ontario*. Ontario Recovery Strategy Series. Peterborough: Ontario Ministry of Natural Resources.

McFarlane, Colin. 2011. *Learning the City: Knowledge and Translocal Assemblage*. Oxford: Blackwell.

McGreavy, Bridie, et al., eds. 2018. *Tracing Rhetoric and Material Life: Ecological Approaches*. London: Palgrave.

McLeod, Susanna. 2019. "Land 'as Far as a Man Can Travel in A Day.'" *Kingston Whig Standard*. December 3, 2019. https://www.thewhig.com/opinion/columnists/land-as-far-as-a-man-can-travel-in-a-day.

Milman, Oliver. 2022. "Back From the Dead? Elusive Ivory-Billed Woodpecker Not Extinct, Researchers Say." *The Guardian*, April 13, 2022. https://www.theguardian.com/environment/2022/apr/13/ivory-bill-woodpecker-not-extinct-researchers-say.

Minche-de Leon, Mark. 2020. "Race and the Limitations of 'the Human.'" In *After the Human: Culture, Theory, and Criticism in the Twenty-First Century*, edited by Sherryl Vint, 206–19. Cambridge: Cambridge University Press.

Mississaugas of the Credit First Nation. N.d. "Title Claim to Water Within Traditional Lands of MCFN." http://mncfn.ca/about-mncfn/title-claim-to-water-within-traditional-lands-of-mncfn.

Moore, A. D. 1946. "Chimney Swift 'Thunder.'" *The Auk* 63 (1): 70–72.

Morris, Viveca. 2020. "COVID-19 Shows That What We're Doing to Animals Is Killing Us, Too." *Los Angeles Times*, April 2, 2020. https://www.latimes.com/opinion/story/2020-04-02/coronavirus-pandemics-animals-habitat-ecology.

Morton, Timothy. 2011. "Here Comes Everything: The Promise of Object-Oriented Ontology." *Qui Parle* 19 (2): 163–90.

Muckelbauer, John. 2016. "Implicit Paradigms of Rhetoric: Aristotelian, Cultural, and Heliotropic." In *Rhetoric, Through Everyday Things*, edited by Scot Barnet and Casey Boyle, 212–25. Tuscaloosa: University of Alabama Press.

Nature Canada. 2021. "Bird Friendly City: A Certification Program." https://naturecanada.ca/defend-nature/how-you-help-us-take-action/bfc.

Nebel, Silke, et al. 2010. "Declines of Aerial Insectivores in North America Follow a Geographic Gradient." *Avian Conservation and Ecology—Écologie et conservation des oiseaux* 5 (2): n.p.

Nicholas, George. 2018. "It's Taken Thousands of Years, but Western Science Is Finally Catching Up to Traditional Knowledge." *The Conversation*. https://theconversation.com/its-taken-thousands-of-years-but-western-science-is-finally-catching-up-to-traditional-knowledge-90291.

Nocera, Joe, et al. 2012. "Historical Pesticide Applications Coincided with an Altered Diet of Aerially Foraging Insectivorous Chimney Swifts." *Proceedings of the Royal Society B* 279 (1740): 1–7.

Nucho, Joanne Randa. 2017. "Failed Infrastructure Is Failed Politics." *Public Books*. https://
www.publicbooks.org/failed-infrastructure-failed-politics.

NWF (National Wildlife Foundation). 2001. *The American Prairie: Going, Going Gone? A
Status Report on the American Prairie*. Rocky Mountain Natural Resource Center.

Ockwell, David, Lorraine Whitmarsh, and Saffron O'Neill. 2009. "Reorienting Climate Change
Communication for Effective Mitigation." *Science Communication* 30 (3): 305–27.

O'Gorman, Marcel. 2021. *Making Media Theory: Thinking Critically with Technology*. New York:
Bloomsbury.

OMNRF (Ontario Ministry of Natural Resources and Forestry). 2016. *Creating Nesting
Habitat for Barn Swallows, Best Practices Technical Note Version 1.0*. Species Conservation Policy Branch.

O:se Kenhionhata:tie. 2022. "History." O:se Kenhionhata:tie. https://www.landbackcamp
.com/history.

Parreñas, Juno Salazar. 2018. *Decolonizing Extinction: The Work of Care in Orangutan Reha-
bilitation*. Durham: Duke University Press.

Parsons, Meg, and Lara Taylor. 2021. "Why Indigenous Knowledge Should Be an Essential
Part of How We Govern the World's Oceans." *The Conversation*. https://theconversat
ion.com/why-indigenous-knowledge-should-be-an-essential-part-of-how-we
-govern-the-worlds-oceans-161649.

PEARL (Paleoecological Environmental Assessment and Research Library). N.d. "Chimney
Swift Project High-Resolution Images." PEARL. https://www.queensu.ca/pearl
/projects/Biovector/subprojects/swiftdiet/swiftphotos.php.

Pender, Terry. 2021. "CAFKA Art Exhibit Along the Iron Horse Trail Draws Attention to
Plight of Barn Swallows." *Waterloo Region Record*. June 4, 2021. https://www
.cambridgetimes.ca/news-story/10408950-cafka-art-exhibit-along-the-iron-horse
-trail-draws-attention-to-plight-of-barn-swallows.

Peters, John Durham. 2015. *The Marvelous Clouds: Toward a Philosophy of Elemental Media*.
Chicago: University of Chicago Press.

Phelps, Louise Wetherbee. 2014. "The Historical Formation of Academic Identities: Rhetoric
and Composition, Discourse and Writing." *Canadian Journal for Studies in Discourse
and Writing/Rédactologie* 25 (1): 3–25.

Pimm, Stuart L., et al. 1995. "The Future of Biodiversity." *Science* 269 (5,222): 347–50.

Pinchin, Karen. 2021. "How Indigenous Memories Can Help Save Species from Extinction." *Vox*. https://www.vox.com/22524908/indigenous-knowledge-memories-saving
-species-fish-crab.

Pinesi, Kagige (John), and William Jones. 1919. "The Woman Who Married a Beaver." In
Ojibwa Texts, edited by Truman Michelson, 251–57. Leyden: E. J. Brill.

Pitawanakwat, Joseph. 2022. "An Evening with Joe Pitawanakwat." Webinar hosted by Bird
Friendly London. March 25, 2022. https://www.youtube.com/watch?v=LvGIwG
w6gYo.

Pittendrigh, Colin S. 1981. "Circadian Systems: Entrainment." In *Biological Rhythms*, edited by
Jürgen Aschoff, 95–124. New York: Plenum Press.

Plumwood, Val. 1993. *Feminism and the Mastery of Nature*. London: Routledge.

———. 2002. *Environmental Culture: The Ecological Crisis of Reason*. London: Routledge.

Praxis Research Associates. 2018. "The History of the Mississaugas of the New Credit First
Nation." Mississaugas of the Credit First Nation. https://www.oakvillehistory.org
/uploads/2/8/5/1/28516379/the-history-of-mncfn-final.pdf.

Propen, Amy. 2018. *Visualizing Posthuman Conservation in the Anthropocene*. Columbus: Ohio
State University Press.

Rai, Candace, and Caroline Gottschalk Druschke. 2018. *Field Rhetoric: Ethnography, Ecology, and Engagement in the Places of Persuasion.* Tuscaloosa: University of Alabama Press.

Ramírez, A. I. 2022. "Perpetual (In)Securities: (Re) Birthing Border Imperialism as Understood Through Facultades Serpentinas. In *Decolonial Conversations in Posthuman and New Material Rhetorics,* edited by Jennifer Clary-Lemon and David Grant, 115–45. Columbus: Ohio State University Press.

Randall, Rosemary. 2009. "Loss and Climate Change: The Cost of Parallel Narratives." *Ecopsychology* 1 (3): 118–29.

Ravenscroft, Alison. 2018. "Strange Weather: Indigenous Materialisms, New Materialism, and Colonialism." *Cambridge Journal of Postcolonial Literary Theory* 5 (3): 353–70.

Reid, Geneviève, and Renee Sieber. 2016. "Comparing Geospatial Ontologies with Indigenous Conceptualizations of Time." In *UC Berkeley International Conference on GIScience Short Paper Proceedings,* 248–51. Berkeley: University of California.

Reid, Geneviève, Renee Sieber, and Sammy Blackned. 2020. "Visions of Time in Geospatial Ontologies from Indigenous Peoples: A Case Study with the Eastern Cree in Northern Quebec." *International Journal of Geographical Information Science* 34 (12): 2335–60.

Reynolds, Brad, Mary Ann Bishop, and Sean Powers. 2007. "Artificial Reefs as Restoration Tools for Alaska's Coastal Waters." Excerpt from a presentation at the Alaska Marine Science Symposium, Anchorage, AK. http://www.handsontheland.org /cacs/images/stories/attachments/Whittierd-Artificial-Reef-Research-PowerPoint .pdf (site discontinued).

Rickert, Thomas. 2013. *Ambient Rhetoric: The Attunements of Rhetorical Being.* Pittsburgh: University of Pittsburgh Press.

———. 2020. "Preliminary Steps Towards a General Rhetoric: Existence, Thrivation, Transformation." In *The Routledge Handbook of Comparative World Rhetorics: Studies in History, Application, and Teaching of Rhetoric Beyond Traditional Greco-Roman Contexts,* edited by Keith Lloyd, 414–21. London: Routledge.

Rifkind, Mark. 2017. *Beyond Settler Time: Temporal Sovereignty and Indigenous Self-Determination.* Durham: Duke University Press.

Riley, Mary. 2012. "Farmers Struggle with Balancing Agriculture and Protecting the Bobolink." *Peterborough This Week.* https://www.mykawartha.com/news-story/3699000 -farmers-grapple-with-balancing-agriculture-and-protecting-the-bobolink.

Riley Mukavetz, Andrea, and Malea Powell. 2022. "Becoming Relations: Braiding an Indigenous Manifesto." In *Decolonial Conversations in Posthuman and New Material Rhetorics,* edited by Jennifer Clary-Lemon and David Grant, 192–211. Columbus: Ohio State University Press.

Ritchie, Hannah, and Max Roser. 2021. "Biodiversity." Ourworldindata. https://ourworldin data.org/biodiversity.

Rivers, Nathaniel A. 2015. "Deep Ambivalence and Wild Objects: Toward a Strange Environmental Rhetoric." *Rhetoric Society Quarterly* 45 (5): 420–40.

Rogers, Christopher. 2021. "Hirondelusia." https://hirondelusia.wordpress.com.

Rose, Deborah Bird. 2006. "What If the Angel of History Were a Dog?" *Cultural Studies Review* 12 (1): 67–78.

———. 2012. "Multispecies Knots of Ethical Time." *Environmental Philosophy* 9 (1): 127–40.

———. 2013. "In the Shadow of All This Death." In *Animal Death,* edited by Jay Johnston and Fiona Probyn-Rapsey, 1–20. Sydney: Sydney University Press.

———. 2017. "Shimmer: When All You Love Is Being Trashed." In *Arts of Living on a Damaged Planet,* edited by Anna Tsing et al., G51–G64. Minneapolis: University of Minnesota Press.

Rose, Deborah Bird, Thom Van Dooren, and Matthew Chrulew. 2017. "Introduction." In *Extinction Studies: Stories of Time, Death, and Generations*, edited by Deborah Bird Rose, Thom Van Dooren, and Matthew Chrulew, 1–17. New York: Columbia University Press.

Rosenberg, Kenneth V., et al. 2019. "Decline of the North American Avifauna." *Science* 366 (6,461): 120–24.

Rosenfeld, Cynthia. 2021. "Bowers of Persuasion: Toward a Posthuman Visual Rhetoric." In *Posthumanist Perspectives on Literary and Cultural Animals*, edited by Krishanu Maiti, 75–86. Cham, Switzerland: Springer.

Roy, Eleanor Ainge. 2017. "New Zealand Gives Mount Taranaki Same Legal Rights as a Person. *The Guardian*, December 22, 2017. https://www.theguardian.com/world/2017/dec/22/new-zealand-gives-mount-taranaki-same-legal-rights-as-a-person.

Ruiz, Iris D. 2021. "Critiquing the Critical: The Politics of Race and Coloniality in Rhetoric, Composition, and Writing Studies (RCWS) Research Traditions." In *Race, Rhetoric, and Research Methods*, by Alexandria L. Lockett, Iris D. Ruiz, James Chase Sanchez, and Christopher Carter, 39–79. Fort Collins: WAC Clearinghouse.

Ruiz, Iris D., and Sonia C. Arellano. 2019. "*La Cultura Nos Cura*: Reclaiming Decolonial Epistemologies Through Medicinal History and Quilting as Method." In *Rhetorics Elsewhere and Otherwise: Contested Modernities, Decolonial Visions*, edited by Romeo Carci and Damián Baca, 141–68. Urbana: National Council for Teachers of English Press.

Rupnik, Claudia. 2019. "New Course at Queen's Delves into Kingston's Treaty Land." *Queen's University Journal*. April 4, 2019. https://www.queensjournal.ca/story/2019-04-03/news/new-course-at-queens-delves-into-kingstons-treaty-land.

Ryan, John Charles. 2017. "Where Have All the Beronia Gone? A Posthumanist Model of Environmental Mourning." In *Mourning Nature: Hope at the Heart of Ecological Loss and Grief*, edited by Ashlee Cunsolo and Karen Landman, 117–43. Montreal: McGill-Queens University Press.

Sackey, Donnie, et al. 2019. "Perspectives on Cultural and Posthumanist Rhetorics." *Rhetoric Review* 38 (4): 375–401.

Saino, Nicola, et al. 2011. "Climate Warming, Ecological Mismatch at Arrival and Population Decline in Migratory Birds." *Proceedings of the Royal Society B* 278:835–42.

Samuels, Ellen. 2017. "Six Ways of Looking at Crip Time." *Disability Studies Quarterly* 37 (3): n.p. https://dsq-sds.org/article/view/5824/4684.

Sandilands, Catriona. 2017. "Losing My Place: Landscapes of Depression." In *Mourning Nature: Hope at the Heart of Ecological Loss and Grief*, edited by Ashlee Cunsolo and Karen Landman, 144–68. Montreal: McGill-Queens University Press.

Serres, Michael. 1995 [1990]. *The Natural Contract*. Translated by E. MacArthur and W. Paulson. Ann Arbor: University of Michigan Press.

Shanahan, David. 2018. "Land for Goods: The Crawford Purchases." *Anishinabek News*. November 8, 2018. http://anishinabeknews.ca/2018/11/08/land-for-goods-the-crawford-purchases.

Sheikh, Maleeha. 2019. "Demolished Chimney Rebuilt to Protect Rare Birds." *CTV News*. December 2, 2019. https://toronto.citynews.ca/video/2019/12/02/chimney-demolition-rare-birds.

Sheldon, Rebekah. 2015. "Form/Matter/Chora: Object-Oriented Ontology and Feminist New Media." In *The Nonhuman Turn*, edited by Richard Grusin, 193–222. Minneapolis: University of Minnesota Press.

Shivener, Rich, and Dustin Edwards. 2020. "The Environmental Unconscious of Digital Composing: Climate Change Rhetorics in Data Center Ecologies." *enculturation*. http://enculturation.net/environmental_unconscious.

Shomura, Chad. 2017. "Exploring the Promise of New Materialisms." *Lateral* 6 (1): 1–7.

Simpson, Leanne Betasamosake. 2021. *A Short History of the Blockade*. Edmonton: University of Alberta Press.

Sinha Chris, et al. 2011. "When Time Is Not Space: The Social and Linguistic Construction of Time Intervals and Temporal Event Relations in an Amazonian Culture." *Language and Cognition* 3 (1): 137–69.

Skafish, Peter. 2016. "The Metaphysics of Extra-Moderns: On the Decolonization of Thought—A Conversation with Eduardo Viveiros de Castro." *Common Knowledge* 22 (3): 393–414.

Smith, Emma. 2019. "Mi'kmaw Conservation Group Builds Artificial Reefs to Give Sea Life a New Home. *CBC News*. https://www.cbc.ca/news/canada/nova-scotia/reef-balls-fish-habitat-pictou-landing-first-nation-ocean-1.5343284.

Spiller, Kimberly, and Randy Dettmers. 2019. "Evidence for Multiple Drivers of Aerial Insectivore Declines in North America." *Condor Ornithological Applications* 121:1–13.

Spoel, Philippa, et al. 2008. "Public Communication of Climate Change Science: Engaging Citizens Through Apocalyptic Narrative Explanation." *Technical Communication Quarterly* 18 (1): 49–81.

Springgay, Stephanie, and Sarah E. Truman. 2017. "On the Need for Methods Beyond Proceduralism: Speculative Middles, (In)Tensions, and Response-Ability in Research." *Qualitative Inquiry* 24 (3): 1–12.

Star, Susan Leigh. 1999. "The Ethnography of Infrastructure." *American Behavioral Scientist* 43 (3): 377–91.

Steinberg, Sabra L., Jeffrey R. Dunk, and TallChief A. Comet. 2000. *In Hoopa Territory*. Hoopa, CA: Hoopa Valley Tribal Council.

Stengers, Isabelle. 2015. *In Catastrophic Times: Resisting the Coming Barbarism*. Translated by Andrew Goffey. Paris: Open Humanities Press.

Stevenson, Michael D. 2001. *Canada's Greatest Wartime Muddle: National Selective Service and the Mobilization of Human Resources During World War II*. Montreal and Kingston: McGill-Queen's University Press.

Stewart, Jessie, and Greg Dickinson. 2008. "Enunciating Locality in the Postmodern Suburb: FlatIron Crossing and the Colorado Lifestyle." *Western Journal of Communication* 72 (3): 280–307.

Stewart, John. 2015. "One Man's Struggle to Save the Chimney Swifts." Mississauga.com. https://www.mississauga.com/blogs/post/5474395-one-man-s-struggle-to-save-the-chimney-swifts.

Stormer, Nathan, and Bridie McGreavy. 2017. "Thinking Ecologically About Rhetoric's Ontology: Capacity, Vulnerability, and Resilience." *Philosophy and Rhetoric* 50 (1): 1–25.

Strang, Veronica. 2017. "Justice for All: Inconvenient Truths and Reconciliation in Human-Non-Human Relations." In *Routledge International Handbook of Environmental Anthropology*, edited by Helen Kopnina and Eleanor Shoreman-Ouimet, 259–75. London: Routledge.

Strong, Allan, and Noah Perlut. N.d. "Delay Hay Cuttings to Let Birds Successfully Fledge Young." US Department of Agriculture Natural Resource Conservation Service. https://www.nrcs.usda.gov/Internet/FSE_DOCUMENTS/nrcs143_010033.pdf (site discontinued).

Sullivan, Helen. 2022. "Extinction Obituary: Why Experts Weep for the Quiet and Beautiful Hawaiian Po'ouli." *The Guardian*, May 4, 2022. https://www.theguardian.com/environment/2022/may/04/extinction-obituary-hawaiian-poouli-bird-aoe.

Sutton, Jane S., and Mari Lee Mifsud. 2012. "Towards an Alloiostrophic Rhetoric." *Advances in the History of Rhetoric* 15:222–33.

———. 2019. *A Revolution in Tropes: Alloiostrophic Rhetoric.* Lanham: Lexington Books.

Thrift, Nigel. 1999. "Steps to an Ecology of Place." In *Human Geography Today*, edited by Doreen Massey, John Allen, and Phil Sarre, 295–323. Cambridge: Polity Press.

———. 2004. "Intensities of Felling: Towards a Spatial Politics of Affect." *Geografiska Annaler* 86 B (1): 57–78.

———. 2008. *Non-Representational Theory: Space, Politics, Affect.* London: Routledge.

Tidridge, Nathan. 2019. "Flamborough's Early Indigenous History." https://www.tidridge.com/uploads/3/8/4/1/3841927/flamboroughs_indigenous_history.pdf (site discontinued).

Todd, Zoe. 2016. "An Indigenous Feminist's Take on the Ontological Turn: 'Ontology' Is Just Another Word for Colonialism." *Journal of Historical Sociology* 29 (1): 4–22.

Tompkins, Kyla Wazana. 2016. "On the Limits and Promise of New Material Philosophy." *Lateral* 5 (1): 1–6.

Topinka, Robert J. 2012. "Resisting the Fixity of Suburban Space: The Walker as Rhetorician." *Rhetoric Society Quarterly* 42 (1): 65–84.

Towns, Armond R. 2018. "Black 'Matter' Lives." *Women's Studies in Communication* 41 (4): 349–58.

Tronto, Joan C. 1993. *Moral Boundaries: A Political Argument for an Ethic of Care.* New York: Routledge.

Tsing, Anna. 2015. *The Mushroom at the End of the World: On the Possibility of Life in Capitalist Ruins.* Princeton: Princeton University Press.

Tuck, Eve, and K. Wayne Yang. 2012. "Decolonization Is Not a Metaphor." *Decolonization: Indigeneity, Education and Society* 1 (1): 1–40.

Turner, Angela. 2006. *The Barn Swallow.* Berkhamstead: T&A. D. Poyser.

Turner, Nancy J., and Jonaki Bhattacharyya. 2016. "Salmonberry Bird and Goose Woman: Birds, Plants, and People in Indigenous Peoples' Lifeways in Northwestern North America." *Journal of Ethnobiology* 36 (4): 717–45.

USDA (US Department of Agriculture). 2010. "Management Considerations for Grassland Birds in Northeastern Hay-Lands and Pasturelands." *Wildlife Insight.* Washington, DC: Natural Resources Conservation Service.

US Fish and Wildlife Service. 1973. *The Endangered Species Act of 1973.* Washington, DC: Department of the Interior. https://www.fws.gov/endangered/esa-library/pdf/ESAall.pdf.

Van Dooren, Thom. 2014. *Flight Ways: Life and Loss at the Edge of Extinction.* New York: Columbia University Press.

Virilio, Paul. 2007. *The Original Accident.* Cambridge: Polity.

Watts, Vanessa. 2013. "Indigenous Place-Thought and Agency Amongst Humans And Non-Humans (First Woman and Sky Woman Go on a European World Tour!)." *Decolonization: Indigeneity, Education and Society* 2 (1): 20–34.

Webster, Richard. 2008. *The Encyclopedia of Superstitions.* Woodbury: Llewellyn.

Weintrobe, Sally. 2013. "The Difficult Problem of Anxiety in Thinking About Climate Change." In *Engaging with Climate Change: Psychoanalytic and Interdisciplinary Perspectives*, edited by Sally Weintrobe, 33–47. Sussex: Routledge.

Wells, Justine. In Press. "Monumentality, Ruination, and the Milieux of Memory: Lessons from W. E. B. Du Bois." *Western Journal of Communication.*

Whale, Helen, and Franklin Ginn. 2017. "In the Absence of Sparrows." In *Mourning Nature: Hope at the Heart of Ecological Loss and Grief*, edited by Ashlee Cunsolo and Karen Landman, 92–116. Montreal: McGill-Queens University Press.

Whitaker, Matthew. 2022. "Corn, Oil, and Cultivating Dissent Through 'Seeds of Resistance': A Case Study on Rhetorics of Survivance and the Protest Assemblage." In *Decolonial*

Conversations in Posthuman and New Material Rhetorics, edited by Jennifer Clary-Lemon and David Grant, 146–73. Columbus: Ohio State University Press.

White, Bruce M. 1999. "The Woman Who Married a Beaver: Trade Patterns and Gender Roles in the Ojibwa Fur Trade." *Ethnohistory* 46 (1): 109–47.

White, Hayden. 1978. *Tropics of Discourse: Essays in Cultural Criticism*. Baltimore: Johns Hopkins University Press.

White, Stephen K. 1990. "Heidegger and the Difficulties of a Postmodern Ethics and Politics." *Political Theory* 18 (1): 80–103.

Whyte, Kyle Powys. 2017. "Our Ancestors' Dystopia Now: Indigenous Conservation in the Anthropocene." In *Routledge Companion to the Environmental Humanities*, edited by Ursula Heises et al., 206–15. London: Routledge.

Wilcox, Bruce A. 1988. "Tropical Deforestation and Extinction." In *IUCN Red List of Threatened Animals*, edited by International Union for Conservation of Nature, v–x. Cambridge: The IUCN Conservation Monitoring Centre.

Wohlleben, Peter. 2021. "Plants Feel Pain and Might Even See." *Nautilus*. https://nautil.us/plants-feel-pain-and-might-even-see-238257/.

Wolfe, Carey. 2010. *What Is Posthumanism?* Minneapolis: University of Minnesota Press.

World Nuclear Association. 2020. "Storage and Disposal of Radioactive Waste." World Nuclear Association. https://www.world-nuclear.org/information-library/nuclear-fuel-cycle/nuclear-waste/storage-and-disposal-of-radioactive-waste.aspx.

Wybenga, Darin P., and Kaytee Dalton. 2018. "Mississaugas of the Credit First Nation: Past and Present." Mississaugas of the Credit First Nation. http://mncfn.ca/wp-content/uploads/2018/10/MississaugasoftheNewCreditFirstNation-PastPresentBooklets-PROOFv4-1.pdf.

Young, James. 1992. "The Counter-Monument: Memory Against Itself in Germany Today." In *Art and the Public Sphere*, edited by W. J. T. Mitchell, 49–78. Chicago: University of Chicago Press.

Yusoff, Katheryn. 2012. "Aesthetics of Loss: Biodiversity, Banal Violence and Biotic Subjects." *Transactions of the Institute of British Geographers* 37:578–92.

———. 2019. *A Billion Black Anthropocenes or None*. Minneapolis: University of Minnesota Press.

Zwicky, Jan. 2018. "A Ship from Delos." In *Learning to Die: Wisdom in the Age of Climate Crisis*, Robert Bringhurst and Jan Zwicky, part 2. Regina: University of Regina Press.

Index